The first R
Yesterday, today and
tomorrow

A selection of papers from conferences of the
United Kingdom Reading Association

edited by
Joyce M. Morris

Ward Lock Educational

146558

372.4
M 876

ISBNs
0 7062 3120 1 cased
0 7062 3121 X paperback

Set in 10 on 11 point Linotype Caledonia
Made in England
Printed by Willmer Brothers Limited, Birkenhead
for Ward Lock Educational
116 Baker Street, London W1M 2BB

Contents

Preface   5

The first R: Yesterday, today and tomorrow   7
Joyce M. Morris

THEORY AND PRACTICE
1   Early reading   24
    Vera Southgate
2   The importance of structure in beginning reading   36
    Vera Southgate
3   Teaching beginners to read: USA   50
    Josephine B. Wolfe
4   Early reading skills   53
    Geoffrey R. Roberts
5   The intermediate skills   61
    John E. Merritt
6   Reading through the grades   81
    Elizabeth Thorn
7   Utilizing the learner's experience in reading comprehension   91
    H. Alan Robinson
8   Learning to listen   100
    Robert Farrar Kinder
9   Listening skills and reading performance   104
    Mary Wootton Masland
10 Stimulus models for teaching reading   110
    Harry W. Singer

MEDIA AND MATERIALS
11 Teaching reading through the medium of i t a   121
    John Downing
12 Words in colour   134
    Joan Dean
13 What is colour story reading?   149
    J. Kenneth Jones
14 The use of television with backward readers in the Glasgow area   162
    Margaret M. Clark
15 The SRA reading laboratories: review of a programmed course
    in reading   170
    John E. Merritt

REMEDIAL READING
16 The comprehension difficulties of the deprived reader   179
    Constance M. McCullough
17 Reading difficulties and what else?   185
    A. T. Ravenette

18   Criteria for a remedial reading programme   194
     Donald Moyle
19   Backward readers – research into auditory-visual integration   200
     Asher Cashdan

RESEARCH

20   A critical appraisal of *Standards and Progress in Reading* by
     Joyce M. Morris   208
     Maurice Chazan
21   An evaluation of the research report on the British experiment
     with i t a   220
     John E. Merritt
22   Evaluation of prereading skills   236
     Shirley C. Feldmann
23   Research to improve the teaching of reading   244
     Ruth Strang

Preface

Over the last ten years, the United Kingdom Reading Association has become firmly established not only in the hearts and minds of individual members, but as a force to be reckoned with on the wider educational scene. In consequence, there is an increasing demand for UKRA publications including the proceedings of its annual study conferences.

This volume contains a selection of papers from the conference proceedings listed on page 6. It is published as the most economical way of meeting a constant stream of requests for publications which are either out-of-print or very close to being so. It also represents a method of making relevant literature available to new members in a convenient form.

Three main criteria were used in selecting the papers. Naturally, the first was that the content should be of topical or perennial interest and, hence, would require little if any up-dating or revision. The second took cognizance of the popularity of an out-of-print volume entitled *Reading Skills*, and the concomitant desirability of balancing the total content of the new volume in favour of practice rather than theory. The third criterion was that the final selection of papers should be approved by the Publications Subcommittee and the National Executive Committee of UKRA.

Regrettably, several otherwise excellent papers had to be omitted to meet these criteria and the need to produce a book speedily of reasonable size and price.

As will be seen, the selected papers are broadly grouped under four sectional headings. No particular significance should be attached to the order of presentation either in terms of interest, importance of subject matter or style of writing. Indeed, in their various ways all contribute a special quality to the whole.

The introductory paper is a revised and up-dated version of my

5

presidential address in 1966. Its basic purpose is to provide a background for the main content, especially that contributed by British authors.

Essentially, this is not a book to be read at a sitting but one to be dipped into and returned to again and again. Its content is rich, varied and wide-ranging. Bearing in mind the criteria of selection, there is something for all interests and tastes. For instance, the teacher who has had a surfeit of immediately useful information and advice (if this is possible) can turn to page 110 and get to grips with 'stimulus models for teaching reading'. Alternatively, it might be equally stimulating to turn to page 179 and learn about deprived readers in India.

The value of this collection speaks for itself and needs no further recommendation or interpretation from me. But I must express gratitude to the authors who, without exception, so promptly and generously responded to a request to include their papers in a book whose royalties will all go to UKRA. Moreover, I greatly appreciate the fact that, where necessary, they readily agreed to make suggested amendments or allowed the addition of editorial notes.

Thanks are also due to Cassell and to Chambers for granting permission to include papers from conference proceedings originally published under their respective imprints.

Joyce M. Morris
April, 1972

Sources
The papers in this selection are drawn from the following sources which are referred to by title only at the head of each paper:

DOWNING, J. A. (ed) (1966) *The First International Reading Symposium* London: Cassell

DOWNING, J. A. and BROWN, A. L. (eds) (1967) *The Second International Reading Symposium* London: Cassell

BROWN, A. L. (ed) (1966) *Reading: Current Research and Practice* Edinburgh: Chambers

DANIELS, J. C. (ed) (1970) *Reading: Problems and Perspectives* UKRA

CLARK, M. M. and MAXWELL, S. M. (eds) (1970) *Reading: Influences on Progress* UKRA

GARDNER, W. K. (ed) (1970) *Reading Skills: Theory and Practice* London: Ward Lock Educational

The first R: Yesterday, today and tomorrow

JOYCE M. MORRIS
Language arts consultant

Although an authoritative and up-to-date history of reading instruction and research in the USA was published in 1965,[1] no one, to my knowledge, has yet produced a corresponding volume for the United Kingdom. If this gap were to be filled, we should be able to gain a clearer perspective of current practices. We should also find that many recent innovations in reading are not new at all.

Within the space available I cannot attempt to fill this gap in a scholarly way. What I propose to do, therefore, is to give a kind of historical sketch of the past, bring out a few salient points about what is happening today and take a peep into the future.

YESTERDAY

Before 1870

Before 1870 only a privileged minority of children in the United Kingdom was given opportunities to learn to read either by literate parents, governesses and tutors in their homes or by teachers in fee-paying schools. Most of those who gave instruction were not specifically trained for their task; their main qualification was that they themselves could read. Conditions for learning and teaching were generally poor, and it is not suprising that some children failed to learn to read effectively. However, the mere fact that they had been provided with schooling suggested that the cause of failure lay in the children themselves, and parents turned to doctors and others outside the teaching profession for advice. Hence the seeds of the hypothesis 'word-blindness' due to congenital brain defect were planted and it was subsequently, that is, in 1896, advanced by Morgan[2] in the *British Medical Journal*.

1870–1921

When compulsory schooling was introduced in 1870 its prime purpose was to secure a minimum standard of literacy for all. Conditions for learning and teaching in early State schools were in some ways worse than those provided by upper-class parents for their children. Teachers had to cope with as many as a hundred pupils at a time, ranging in age from three to eleven and including children with severe physical and mental handicaps. Books and other materials were not only inadequate but scarce, and teachers were further harassed by the system of 'payment by results' and unsatisfactory school buildings.

In the early years the small proportion of teachers who were 'trained' spent the greater part of their time in college attending lectures and demonstrations in 'Method'. Since little was known about the reading process and individual differences at that time, there was not much, basically, to choose between the way they thought about and approached their task and that of their 'untrained' colleagues. For example, they generally conceived reading ability narrowly as the mechanical recognition of words, and used only alphabetic and phonic methods. They also began a rigid programme of formal reading instruction with new school entrants and did not consider whether the children were 'ready' for it.

Although much of the school day was spent on reading as the 'first R', it is not surprising in these circumstances that many children who left State schools in the nineteenth century never got beyond the stage of reading monosyllabic words and simple stories. However, when it came to attributing causes there was a division of opinion. As already stated, the medical and associated professions advanced the view, mainly from studies of privileged children, that some pupils were 'congenitally word-blind'. Others suggested that the irregularities of English spelling were largely to blame and cited evidence from a few experiments that a new alphabet was the answer to the problem. Children themselves were accused of being dull, inattentive and so on, and teachers began to urge the building of separate schools for the mentally and physically handicapped. Methods of teaching reading were also suspect but, in comparison with other possible causes, investigators did not focus as much attention on the qualifications of teachers and other school conditions, perhaps because deficiencies in these were self-evident.

At the beginning of the twentieth century, pioneer work in mental measurement advanced knowledge of individual differences, and the first standardized test of reading attainment by Ballard was published in 1914.[3] Experiments comparing the effectiveness of alphabetic, phonic and the recently-introduced whole-word sentence methods were also reported about the same time.

During World War I illiteracy among men and women in the Armed Forces came to light and provided a fresh impetus to ascertain the causes of reading disability and to improve reading standards in general. Social pressures, plus the recently-acquired knowledge of individual differences, were largely responsible for the Education Act of 1921, which stressed the need for local authorities to make special provision for severely handicapped children, that is, for children who could not be expected to learn to read effectively in ordinary school circumstances.

1921–1944

Soon after this Education Act was passed the comprehensive *Beacon Reading Scheme*[4] was introduced in the United Kingdom from the USA, and for the first time teachers and children could use materials embodying synthetic and analytic methods and encouraging systematic progression. Work in the schools was still impeded by cramped and dilapidated accommodation, classes of fifty pupils or more and a considerable proportion of 'unqualified' teachers. However, training college courses continued for a time to place great emphasis on reading as the first 'R', and at least gave prospective infant teachers opportunities to learn about and practise with the methods and materials then available. I stress at least as far as prospective *infant* teachers were concerned because, in the absence of facts about the reading standards of seven-year-olds, training in the teaching of reading was not generally considered essential for students who hoped to work with juniors. Moreover, the prevalent belief that this training was not very necessary is implicit in the 1931 Board of Education report[5] in so far as it stated that 'few children would not have mastered the mechanics of reading by the age of seven'.

In the late 1920s and '30s the ideas of Decroly, Dewey and Froebel, etc., began to have an increasing influence on educational practice. Student teachers were advised to consider meaning as almost the only factor in word perception, and reading as an integral, but small, part of a child's total growth. Courses in child psychology and development started to take much of the time previously allotted to studying reading methods and materials. Many experienced infant teachers continued to give systematic instruction in word-analysis skills, but, by the late 1930s, only a minority had not accepted the principles of 'progressive' education and all that it entailed for the teaching of reading.

Between the passing of the 1921 Act and the outbreak of World War II, no national reading surveys were carried out, and so we have no definite knowledge of children's reading standards and the incidence of reading disability during this period. However, investigators such as Burt and Schonell, who were concerned (though not exclusively) with reading problems gave us an idea of the situation from their local surveys and it is reasonable to conclude that there was room for much improvement. In their respective books *The*

Backward Child[6] and *Backwardness in the Basic Subjects*[7] they drew together findings from their own inquiries and those of others about the causes of reading failure and poor reading standards. Burt is against the use of the term 'congenital word-blindness' and the theory underlying this concept, and Schonell says there is 'no evidence to suggest an inborn cerebral deficiency theory of reading backwardness'. Both support the multiple causation theory of reading disability but they place more emphasis on unfavourable factors centred in the child and in the home than in the school. This is not surprising, in so far as they and other investigators usually looked first for adverse characteristics in backward readers themselves and then in their home circumstances. Finding sufficient reasons for reading difficulties in one or both areas of study, either they did not seek a further explanation in the children's schooling or limited their search to a few aspects. It must also be pointed out that, until the 1950s, investigators were rarely in a position to make detailed, systematic observations in schools over a long period.

During the early years of World War II, I trained as a teacher at one of the colleges of London University, and so I have personal experience of the kind of professional courses given at that time. In my college, prospective infant teachers were given a series of lectures in which reading methods, materials and problems were discussed within the context of child growth, and they were generally advised to use an informal, individualized, whole-word approach with incidental phonics. For students who, like myself, intended to teach children aged seven upwards, there were few lectures in which reading was discussed at all, and these focused attention mainly on the need to divide pupils into groups for oral practice and to set them exercises in reading comprehension. Reading backwardness was not treated as a specific issue but as part of the general problem of educational backwardness. Moreover, the impression created by lecturers that few children could not read after the age of seven, and that the cause of their difficulties lay outside the control of the schools, was strengthened when students read the strongly-recommended Board of Education Report[5] and Burt's *The Backward Child.*[6]

I shall never forget my first day as a qualified teacher in a large primary school in a lower-middle-class London suburb. Indeed, it was the shock of finding that my class consisted of forty nonreaders aged seven to eleven which initially determined that my professional career should be devoted mainly to the cause of literacy. The size of the problem was far greater than my college course had led me to believe. Moreover, my training had provided me with few practical suggestions about how to begin tackling it. However, by trial-and-error, with suggestions from colleagues and through my own further reading, I managed to survive the first year, although I cannot honestly say that my pupils made much progress.

Not long afterwards the 1944 Education Act was passed. This, like the Act of 1921, required LEAs to provide special schools for the educationally and physically subnormal, but it went further in requiring them to make special provision for the more seriously retarded pupils attending ordinary schools. In this further requirement there was hope that the task of teachers of backward readers would be lightened. Unfortunately, there was no immediate prospect of it being fully realized because there were few extra teachers or classrooms available to form small remedial classes. Educational psychologists to diagnose and treat the more difficult cases were also few and far between.

1944–1959

In the period of rehabilitation immediately after World War II, public concern about the reading instruction given in State schools was aroused, as it had been after World War I, by reports of illiteracy among the Armed Forces. However, concern was greater than before for three main reasons. First, in a world advancing towards universal literacy and a technological age, Britain needed a literate population to retain her place as a major power. Second, there was a determined movement in Britain towards equality of educational opportunity and the ideal of a classless society. (The election of a Labour Government was indicative of this movement.) Third, there was evidence of dissension among educationists about the prevalent reading practices in State schools. Some advocated, for example, returning to a more formal, systematic approach for children aged from five to eight with an emphasis on word-analysis skills.

Thus, reading assumed a new importance in the late 1940s, and the need to allay anxiety provided the impetus for a number of inquiries. For example, local surveys were carried out in such places as Brighton[8] and Burton-upon-Trent[9] to ascertain the reading standards of the school population and, in particular, the proportion in need of remedial provision. In 1948, the Ministry of Education conducted the first-ever national reading survey in England and Wales. Comparisons were made between the reading attainments of children who attended schools using progressive and traditional methods respectively. Relationships between children's reading standards and their home backgrounds were also explored.

Reports on some of these inquiries did not begin to appear until 1950. In that year, the Ministry published results of the 1948 survey which showed that 24% of fifteen-year-olds could be classed as 'backward' readers and a further 6% as 'semi-literate' and 'illiterate'.[10] Explanations for these results, such as 'The schools have not yet recovered from the effects of the War', naturally did little to allay anxiety, especially as they were not unreservedly accepted by the educationists who had previously criticized modern methods of teaching reading. These educationists were not satisfied that Gardner, in her report on *Long-Term Results of Infant School Methods*,[11] published the same year, had provided sufficient evidence to suggest that progressive methods were more effective than traditional methods. Accordingly, they continued their own inquiries and set in train a series of studies by other investigators into the value of an informal versus a formal approach to reading.

In 1952, the Ministry of Education carried out a second national survey but did not publish the results until 1957[12] when findings from a third survey (in 1956) could be included in the report. However, preliminary statistics from the second survey for pupils in English schools were made available to the National Foundation for Educational Research (NFER), and these indicated that progress since 1948 had not been as satisfactory as expected. For example, no significant change had occurred in the proportions of fifteen-year-olds who could be classed as 'backward' readers, 'semi-literate' and 'illiterate' respectively. Moreover, the percentage of pupils in these categories combined was the same (30%) as it had been four years before.

Clearly it was desirable in 1953 that the NFER should begin a programme of reading research and that this should differ in at least three respects from previous investigations. First, it should include a survey of the reading standards of seven-year-olds. Second, children's reading standards and progress should not be assessed only in terms of test scores but in terms of the books they could read. Third, and most important of all, priority among the variables to be studied in relation to children's reading achievement should be given to school conditions, because it is here that educationists can most readily initiate improvements and where, at that time, guidance from research was most lacking.

The Foundation's research programme began in September, 1953, and it was not until 1959 that the first report was published.[13] During the intervening years, controversy about methods of teaching infants to read reached a new level of intensity. Much of it centred on the 'phonic-word approach' created by Dr John Daniels and his colleague Hunter Diack.[14] This period was also notable for an increasing insistence among publishers that new reading schemes submitted for publication should be based on the findings of research (especially that involving British children) and not merely on the author's practical experience. Publishers also were more willing to publish materials suitable only for minority groups such as older backward readers.

1959–1966

Publication of the Foundation's first report in 1959 had unforeseen but important consequences. The report[13] contained results of the survey of seven-year-olds, previously mentioned, which showed that, by the end of the infant course, approximately 45% of the children had not mastered the mechanics of reading, and, of these, about 19% had hardly begun to learn to read at all. The report pointed to the implications of these results for the training of teachers of older children which, hitherto, had been based on the assumption that their main task would be to develop reading comprehension. The Press, however, interpreted the results as meaning that changes were necessary in teaching infants to read and, in doing so, created a favourable climate for the introduction of new ideas and the reappearance of old ones in different guises.

Sir James Pitman suggested that the low reading-attainment of many seven-year-olds disclosed by the Foundation's survey was attributable to the irregularities of English spelling and that the alphabet he had invented might be an answer to the problem. The University of London Institute of Education (in cooperation with the NFER) decided to put this old hypothesis and his new alphabet to the test, and, in 1960, the first experiment was initiated.

Gattegno also suggested that the irregularities of English spelling are largely responsible for child's reading difficulties, and he has revived the old idea that if, in primers, the letters in words are coloured to indicate their sounds, this will solve or, at least, alleviate the problem. *Words in Colour*,[15] the approach he created, was published in 1962.

In the same year, there was a revival of interest in another old hypothesis, namely, that reading disability is caused by a condition called 'word-blindness' or 'specific developmental dyslexia'. The 'Invalid Children's Aid Association' called a conference to decide whether there was sufficient evidence to show that this condition existed, and, if so, what action should be taken.[16] A motion that a 'Word Blindness Association' should be formed was opposed by teachers and educational psychologists, but was carried because parents of children with reading difficulties supported members of the medical and associated professions in their belief that the case was proved. Two years later, in 1964, the 'Word Blindness Association' established a centre in London for the study and treatment of 'specific developmental dyslexia'.

By this time I had updated my original survey of *Research Relating to Reading in England and Wales*.[17] This[18] indicated that, besides i t a and 'specific dyslexia', the main topics of investigation were: the development of vocabulary, language and reading skills *per se* and in relation to home circumstances; reading readiness; remedial treatment; reading ability in relation to intelligence, birth-month, sex, speech development, attitudes, emotional and social adjustment, home circumstances, the use of informal/formal methods of teaching, the size and composition of classes ('streamed' or 'unstreamed').

Compared with other topics, comparatively few investigations focused attention on aspects of children's schooling which, on rational grounds, might be expected to determine their reading standards and progress. Moreover, those investigations which had been concerned with these aspects concentrated mainly on the methods by which children are taught and the organization of their classes. Except for the Foundation's inquiries reported in 1966,[24] none to my knowledge had included detailed studies of the development of children's reading ability in relation to the kinds of teachers, classroom conditions and reading materials they happen to have. In short, the practice, begun in the nineteenth century, of looking everywhere else for the causes of reading difficulties but the place under our noses still continued to a large extent.

Nevertheless, the period was marked by a number of events which were to have important consequences in the British reading field. Briefly, these include:

1961: Formation of the United Kingdom Council of the International Reading Association. This was subsequently given a charter as a national affiliate and renamed the United Kingdom Reading Association or UKRA for short.

1962: Establishment of a British affiliate of the American National Council for the Teaching of English. Like the UKRA the aims of NATE include the improvement of reading at all levels.

1962: Establishment of the Association for Programmed Learning which, naturally, has encouraged the development of reading machines and programmed reading materials generally.

1963: Reconstitution of the Central Advisory Council for Education with the object of reporting (among other things) on reading standards, methods, media and materials as well as suggesting ways of solving literacy problems.

1964: Establishment of the Schools Council, and the initiation of a ten-year programme of research and development in the field of English. This included a much-needed inquiry into the teaching of English as a second language to immigrant school children in the United Kingdom who, at that time, numbered over 100,000.

1964: Formation of an experimental television unit by the British Broadcasting Corporation to 'pioneer' programmes designed to motivate backward pupils to learn to read and to give them reading practice.

It should also be pointed out that, by 1966, a number of people working independently of organizations had contributed to improving reading standards in so far as they had published fresh and, on the whole, more appropriate tools for learning and teaching. For instance, most materials placed greater emphasis than before on systematic progression and word analysis skills. There were now available basal schemes and library books founded on research into the speaking, reading and writing vocabulary of British children. There was also Stott's *Programmed Reading Kit*[19], the Rank *Reading Master*[20], the Moxon *Method*[21] and, in general, far more materials suitable in content and style for older, backward readers.

Thus, six years ago, a review of publications and events might have suggested that the battle to give reading the priority it merits had already been won. Whereas, in fact, much greater attention and funds were still being devoted to research and development in the fields of primary school French, science and mathematics as well as secondary school reorganization. Moreover, within the reading field itself, comparatively little, concentrated effort was being made to remove major, long-standing impediments to progress which could be attributed to inadequate recognition of the following truths:

1 Effective reading involves the acquisition of a wide range of skills throughout a child's school career and beyond.
2 Since reading is a developmental process, every teacher has to be a teacher of reading and must be trained accordingly.
3 Those who train teachers must not only have successful, practical experience but 'specialist' knowledge of the reading field.
4 Newly-qualified teachers need to attend inservice courses and to be given 'expert' advice in school.
5 If a choice has to be made, children with adverse home circumstances and personal attributes should be given the better teachers and school conditions generally.

Obviously, there was little hope of radically changing the situation simply by talking and writing about it though, like other UKRA members, I seized every opportunity to 'preach the gospel of the first R'. In August, 1966, at the First World Congress on Reading in Paris I also reiterated a suggestion I had initially put forward in 1959, namely that one of the best ways of achieving our reading goals would be to establish reading (or 'language arts') centres in the United Kingdom. Undoubtedly, because of the importance of the Congress, the inclusion of this idea in my paper[22] was a good move. For, subsequently, several influential educationists who had hitherto been lukewarm towards the idea now actively supported it. At last they had accepted that such centres could perform the three vital functions of (a) training reading specialists for work in schools, clinics, colleges and institutes of education; (b) conducting and co-ordinating research; and (c) providing an information and advisory service.

Joyce M. Morris

1966–1971
The First World Congress marked the beginning of a most exciting period in the history of British reading. This was because the research projects, events and other developments of the previous seven years began to produce results.

In December, 1966, the Department of Education and Science started the ball rolling by publishing findings of a national reading survey conducted in 1964. The report[23] began by stating, 'Since the end of the war there has been a remarkable improvement in standards of reading. In 1964 boys and girls aged 11 reached on the average the standard of pupils 17 months older in 1948. . . . There has been a corresponding advance among boys and girls aged 15.'

Admittedly, the statistics indicated that some progress had been made, but it was not sufficient to warrant the adjective 'remarkable'. In any case, as reviewers were quick to point out, the 1948 test scores were naturally depressed because the testees had suffered wartime conditions of schooling.

A few days later the NFER published the final report on the Kent inquiries which had covered a span of ten years. As a critical appraisal of *Standards and Progress in Reading*[24] is given on pages 204–219, there is no need to say more than that its disclosures dispelled any feelings of complacency which might have been engendered by results of the 1964 national survey and the Plowden Report[25] which followed early in 1967.

Because the Plowden Report was prepared by the Central Advisory Council for Education what it has to say about reading may be regarded as the 'official view' and as such a very influential one. Accordingly, I made it the focal point of my paper[26] at the Second World Congress on Reading held in Copenhagen in 1968. My conclusion then was that although the Plowden path to progress was paved with excellent recommendations, with few exceptions, their implementation required enormous financial resources unlikely to be forthcoming in the current economic situation. In the circumstances, therefore, I recommended one road to progress which would not cost any extra money to follow. This is to give top priority to the teaching of reading when preservice and inservice courses for teachers are planned.

Besides teacher-training, to which I shall be returning later, there were other subjects of heated debate during this period. Understandably, in 1967, publication of the first definitive report[27] on the British experiment with i t a provoked widespread discussion. But perhaps even greater attention was focused on the new medium when, two years later, an independent evaluation of i t a carried out for the Schools Council was published[28].

Both reports are too complex and detailed for adequate discussion of their findings here, and in any case, Dr Downing, author of the definitive report has summarized the it a position on pages 121–133. It is also interesting to note that on pages 149–161 Kenneth Jones brings us up to date with regard to research with his own system *Colour Story Reading*. In other words, he expands on the results he first published in 1967,[29] and concludes once again that experimentation has proved CSR to be more effective than it a.

By 1971, two more colour codes had entered the arena of competition for teachers' attention. One of them is incorporated in a scheme for beginning readers,[30] and the other in a programmed course for older backward pupils.[31]

Aids to helping children recognize and recall phoneme-grapheme correspondence in English are to be welcomed provided, of course, they are designed by authors with a sound knowledge of linguistics. This, as I recently pointed out elsewhere,[32] is not always the case not only with regard to such aids but to classroom materials generally. Not surprisingly, therefore, the new materials which have attracted most attention come from a 'linguistics stable', that is, the Department of General Linguistics, University College, London. Called *Breakthrough to Literacy*, the materials are a Schools Council project, and are accompanied by a Teacher's Manual[33] which is virtually a textbook on initial literacy.

Another kind of breakthrough took place during this period. This was the establishment of the first-ever Centre for the Teaching of Reading at the University of Reading. Then followed the setting up of different types of reading centres by (and in) colleges of education and by local education authorities, perhaps the most notable of the latter being London's Centre for Language in Primary Education.

Linked with the development of the 'centre' idea came the provision of inservice courses of a more advanced nature than hitherto, and the recent award by Liverpool University of the first-ever Diploma in the Teaching of Reading.

In the space available, it is not possible to mention all the research reports published during the last five years which, by highlighting the need for the above innovations in provision, undoubtedly helped to bring them about. But, one of the last to appear in 1971 should be mentioned because of the implications of its findings for beginning reading instruction now and in the future. This is *The Roots of Reading*,[34] the last report on the London reading inquiries conducted by the NFER. Its final conclusion is that 'early attention to phonic analysis, a systematic teaching approach and a well organized staff are ingredients for success in the teaching of reading'.

TODAY

This year (1972) began with a feeling of expectancy in educational circles. Three government-sponsored reports on highly controver-

Joyce M. Morris

sial subjects were due to be published in the Spring term. At the time of writing, they have all been reviewed, much debated on television and elsewhere with repercussions of various kinds which will doubtless continue for some years to come.

The first report *Teacher Education and Training*[35] was prepared by a Committee of Inquiry under the Chairmanship of Lord James of Rusholme. As its title implies, the report is not specifically concerned with reading though, naturally, reading and the related language arts are discussed within its pages because of their central place in the educational process. Moreover, for this same reason, the proposals of the James' Committee obviously have implications for the teaching of reading and could, if implemented, affect future reading standards.

Perhaps I should point out that evidence on various aspects of the teaching of reading had been made available to the James' Committee before the full inquiry began. As one who supplied a little of it,[36] I was pleased to note the following statement on page 7 of the report:

> Teachers in the primary schools—and those in secondary schools who are faced with illiteracy or semi-literacy in their pupils—will need to continue to improve their understanding and competence in the language arts , i.e., language development and the teaching of reading and writing. Although this deeper understanding, however much emphasized in initial training cannot be fully acquired without prolonged experience, suitable inservice training, rooted in the experience teachers have already had, could be a powerful aid.

Not unexpectedly, response to the James' Report has been mixed, but one recommendation associated with the above statement and others in similar vein relating to different aspects of the curriculum, has been universally acclaimed. This emphasizes, 'There must be adequate opportunities for the continued education and training of all teachers, at intervals throughout their careers'.

Now a brief word about the concise second report *Child with Specific Reading Difficulties*.[37] In this case, the title is particularly significant in that it was chosen as a 'more usefully descriptive term' than 'dyslexia'.

The Advisory Committee on Handicapped Children which prepared the report came to the conclusion that 'specific developmental dyslexia' was still as much a hypothesis as it was in 1896 when Dr Morgan described a case of 'congenital word blindness'.[2] In other words, a clinical entity with a specific underlying cause and specific symptoms had not so far been identified. Accordingly, the report suggests that the small group of children with specific reading difficulties should be considered as part of the wider problem of reading

18

backwardness of all kinds. Furthermore, one of the nine recommendations listed is that such children, like other backward readers, should normally be given skilled remedial treatment in their ordinary schools.

Naturally, this report has aroused strong feelings especially among parents of children assessed as 'dyslexic', for it dampens their hopes of obtaining special treatment for their children within the State educational system. However, if the report's recommendations are followed, eventually all children with reading problems will receive appropriate help. Meanwhile, limited resources will not be deployed in assisting only those whose parents are sufficiently interested in their educational progress to press for special treatment.

The third report published by the NFER in March, 1972 and called *The Trend of Reading Standards*[38] has caused widespread concern among parents, teachers and, indeed, all who care about children's educational welfare. This is because results of a national survey of reading comprehension undertaken in 1970–71, at the request of the government, indicate that standards today are no better than they were a decade ago.

Apparently, the postwar improvement in reading standards has ceased, and there is no hard experimental evidence to explain why. The authors of the report suggest that the juxtaposition of their survey findings and the recently reported low proportion of primary teachers with training in the teaching of reading might have provided an explanation. But, they point out this NFER survey did not have the consideration of such a plausible explanation as one of its terms of reference.

Understandably, the Secretary of State for Education and Science requires an explanation for the survey findings. And, at this year's conference of the National Union of Teachers Mrs Thatcher announced her intention of setting up yet another Committee of Inquiry into the Teaching of Reading.

In the circumstances, it is not surprising that comparatively little attention has been paid to the fact that this year two, new, basal reading schemes have already been published at least in part. The first, called *Dominoes*[39] has coloured photographs to illustrate the materials for stages one and two. It is the work of Dorothy Glynn, a leading figure in the 'child-centred curriculum' movement and, hence, it is interesting to see how she tackles the questions of phonic analysis and systematic progression especially in the light of recent research findings on these issues.[34] Likewise of interest is the second scheme *Sparks*[40] in that it has been devised by four experienced members of the teaching profession who are also well-known for their support of 'progressive' educational principles and practices.

Thus, today there is no shortage of materials for reading instruction, though there are still improvements required and gaps to be filled especially in the provision for immigrant pupils and slow learners. There is also a steadily increasing output by the BBC of televised reading series both for backward readers (*Look and Read* Series), and for infants (*Words and Pictures* Series). For example, whereas in 1964 I helped to devise four pioneer programmes, this year I am working with the production team on 30 programmes to be filmed in colour.

TOMORROW

As we look to the future, there will almost certainly be further developments in the use of television to help children with reading and related language skills. This potent medium will also be used more and more to increase the knowledge of their teachers as in the case of the foundation reading course of the Open University beginning in 1973.

Already there are rumours that, in the next few years, classroom materials will be more soundly based on linguistic knowledge than they have generally been hitherto. Indeed, a basal scheme of this kind is scheduled for publication just in time for the Ninth Annual Study Conference of UKRA.

As for the conference itself, the theme is 'The Teaching of Reading and Related Skills', thereby emphasizing the prime importance of the teacher and the need to consider reading in the total context of language arts and their uses. It is, of course, significant that the final session is to be devoted to taking a 'new look at teacher-training' in the light of the conference. Our Association must continue to lead the way towards reinstating reading as the 'first R' in the training of *all* teachers, and be prepared to give wise counsel when it comes to the detailed planning of their courses.

Doubtless, advice of this nature will be urgently sought when results of the recently-announced reading inquiry are available. For, there is already a great deal of research evidence and first-hand experience to suggest that the Committee of Inquiry must surely find serious inadequacies in the training of reading teachers.

However, it would be foolhardy to make further predictions about the outcome of this inquiry. Much depends on the composition of the Committee, its terms of reference, duration and the financial resources available for its conduct.

Nevertheless, there is no harm in hoping the Committee will recommend that future national surveys of reading standards should be based on a better appraisal of the levels and kinds of reading ability required to function adequately as a member of society in this technological age. Surely, it is not too much to ask that we stop using limited, out-dated tests to measure such a complex ability as reading, and cease to measure progress in terms of whether scores on these tests have gone up or down since 1948. The subject is of such vital importance to us all that the government should not be afraid to require schools to adminster a battery of well-designed tests and make other appropriate assessments every four years, starting the whole process of surveying on this new footing as soon as possible.

Lest some readers fear this is but a fond hope, perhaps it would be as well to recall that, only a few years ago, reading centres, university diplomas in the teaching of reading and so on seemed like pipe-dreams. But, all have come to pass thanks, to a large extent to the strivings of UKRA members. Therefore, let us make every effort to increase membership so that, with a larger army of reading enthusiasts, we can fight an even better fight and, eventually win the cause of 'The first R: Yesterday, today and tomorrow'.

References

1 SMITH, N. B. (1965) *American Reading Instruction* Newark, Delaware: International Reading Association
2 MORGAN, P. (1896) A case of congenital word blindness *British Medical Journal* 7 November
3 BALLARD, P. B. (1914) *A Standardized Reading Scale* London: University of London Press
4 THE BEACON READERS (1922) *Original Approach* London: Ginn
5 BOARD OF EDUCATION (1931, reprinted 1952) *Report of the Consultative Committee on the Primary School* London: HMSO
6 BURT, C. (1937, 5th edition, 1961) *The Backward Child* London: University of London Press
7 SCHONELL, F. J. (1942, ninth impression 1962) *Backwardness in the Basic Subjects* Edinburgh: Oliver and Boyd
8 HAMMOND, D. (1948) Attainment in reading: a Brighton research *Times Educational Supplement* 14 August
9 BIRCH, L. B. (1949) The remedial treatment of reading disability *Educational Review*
10 MINISTRY OF EDUCATION (1950) *Reading Ability: Some Suggestions for Helping the Backward* London: HMSO
11 GARDNER, D. E. M. (1950) *Long-Term Results of Infant School Methods* London: Methuen
12 MINISTRY OF EDUCATION (1957) *Standards of Reading, 1948 to 1956* London: HMSO
13 MORRIS, J. M. (1959) *Reading in the Primary School* London: Newnes
14 DANIELS, J. C., and DIACK, H. (1954) *The Royal Road Readers* London: Chatto & Windus
15 GATTEGNO, C. (1962). *Words in Colour* Reading, Berks.: Educational Explorers Ltd

Joyce M. Morris

16 FRANKLIN, A. W. (ed) (1962) *Word Blindness or Specific Developmental Dyslexia* London: Pitman Medical

17 MORRIS, J. M. (1960) *Report on Research Relating to Reading in England and Wales 1946–60* (Prepared for the Hamburg Conference, 1960: mimeo)

18 MORRIS, J. M. (1965) *Report on Research Relating to Reading in England and Wales 1960–64* (Prepared for the Plowden Committee: mimeo)

19 STOTT, D. H. (1962) *Programmed Reading Kit* Glasgow: W. & R. Holmes Ltd

20 RANK READING MASTER London: Rank Audio Visual Ltd

21 MOXON, C. A. V. (1962) *A Remedial Reading Method* London: Methuen

22 MORRIS, J. M. (1966) The scope of reading in the United Kingdom in: *Reading Instruction: An International Forum* Proceedings of the First World Congress on Reading, Newark, Delaware: International Reading Association

23 DEPARTMENT OF EDUCATION AND SCIENCE (1966) *Progress in Reading* London: HMSO

24 MORRIS, J. M. (1966) *Standards and Progress in Reading* Slough, Bucks: National Foundation for Educational Research in England and Wales

25 CENTRAL ADVISORY COUNCIL FOR EDUCATION (1967) *Children and Their Primary Schools* (Plowden Report) London: HMSO

26 MORRIS, J. M. (1969) Beginning Reading in England in: *Reading: A Human Right and a Human Problem* Proceedings of the Second World Congress on Reading, Newark, Delaware: International Reading Association

27 DOWNING, J. (ed) (1967) *The i t a Symposium Research* Report on the British Experiment with i t a Slough, Bucks: National Foundation for Educational Research in England and Wales

28 WARBURTON, F. W. and SOUTHGATE, VERA (1969) *i t a an independent evaluation* The report of a study carried out for the Schools Council Edinburgh and London: W. & R. Chambers and John Murray

29 JONES, J. K. (1967) *Research Report on Colour Story Reading* London: Nelson

30 BLEASDALE, E. and W. (1969) *Reading by Rainbow* Horwich, Lancs: Moor Platt Press

31 MOSELEY, D. (1970) *English Colour Code Programmed Reading Course* London: NSMHC Centre for Learning Disabilities

32 MORRIS, J. M. (1972) From speech to print and back again in: *Literacy at All Levels* Proceedings of the Eighth Annual Study Conference of the United Kingdom Reading Association Manchester 1971 London: Ward Lock Educational

33 MACKAY, D., THOMPSON, B. and SCHAUB, P. (1970) *Breakthrough to Literacy: Teacher's Manual* The theory and practice of teaching initial reading and writing London: Longman

34 CANE, B. and SMITHERS, J. (1971) *The Roots of Reading* A study of 12 infant schools in deprived areas Slough, Bucks: National Foundation for Educational Research in England and Wales

35 DEPARTMENT OF EDUCATION AND SCIENCE (1972) *Teacher Education and Training* London: HMSO

36 MORRIS, J. M. (1970) *Teacher Training: Teaching of Reading* Minutes of Evidence taken before the Select Committee on Education and Science (Sub-Committee B) London: HMSO

37 DEPARTMENT OF EDUCATION AND SCIENCE (1972) *Children with Specific Reading Difficulties* London: HMSO

38 START, K. B. and WELLS, B. K. (1972) *The Trend of Reading Standards* Slough, Bucks: National Foundation for Educational Research in England and Wales

39 GLYNN, D. (1972) *Dominoes* Edinburgh: Oliver & Boyd

40 FISHER, R. M., HYNDS, M., JOHNS, A. M., McKENZIE, M. G. (1972) *Sparks* London: Blackie

THEORY AND PRACTICE

1 Early reading

VERA SOUTHGATE

Lecturer in curriculum studies,
School of Education, University of Manchester

Paper presented at Third Annual Conference of UKRA Cambridge
1966, first published in *Reading: Current research and practice*

I have collected here a number of points which are often made both
for and against early reading. These I have tried to systematize and
enumerate under two main headings: first, the arguments which are
usually brought forward against early reading, and, secondly, points
which I think could well be made in reply to these arguments against
early reading. The presentation of these opposing points of view will
afford me the opportunity to list my own conclusions on this subject.
Thus my contribution, rather than being in the form of a piece of
prose, represents a collection of points presented within a particular
framework.

Arguments against early reading

Arguments against 'early reading', whatever that may be taken to
mean, may be divided into two main categories. The first category
represents the belief that children cannot learn to read at an early
age because the task is too difficult for them. The second group of
arguments against early reading concludes that even if children could,
they shouldn't.

Children cannot
The most common arguments brought forward by people who state
that children cannot learn to read at a very early age may be summarized as follows:

1 Children are not ready to begin to read until they have a mental
   age of 6½.
2 Young children are not able to make fine visual discriminations.
3 Young children are not able to make fine auditory discriminations.
4 When some children first attend school their speech is not sufficiently fluent for them to be ready to begin to read.

5 In short, the task of learning to read is too difficult for many children when they first start school.

6 Because the task is too difficult for young children, attempts to teach them to read at an early age must necessarily result in pressure being placed on them.

7 If young children are 'pushed' into reading and made to work, they may be unhappy.

8 Because the task is too difficult many children will fail.

Even if children can—they should not

The arguments of those who believe that, even if children are able to learn to read at an early age, they should not be encouraged to do so, usually run along the following lines:

1 Time devoted to the teaching of reading is time snatched from more important activities; for example, play, creative activities and exploration of the environment.

2 If we left the teaching of reading until later (7 or some other specified age), it would come naturally and more easily.

3 Even if children are taught to read at an earlier age, they will be no further forward at 11 (or some other specified age).

4 Attempts should not be made to teach children to read earlier because many of them will fail.

The failing child

The thought of the failing child is inherent in both the foregoing main lines of argument. On all sides there emerges a real concern about children who are expected to learn to read, whom teachers try to teach to read, who nevertheless fail to learn to read and who may thus develop adverse attitudes to reading. This sort of argument, put forward by both sets of opponents of early reading, is the one which merits our most serious consideration.

Points in reply to the arguments against early reading

Children can

1 There is no doubt about it that many children can, and do, begin to read at a very early age. A mass of evidence is accumulating on this score and it is important to notice that this evidence does not relate merely to bright children. A few examples of such evidence may be cited:

(a) Diack (1963) gives details of some children as young as two years being able to recognize letters and words.

(b) Lynn (1963) lists a number of children with chronological ages of less than 3 and mental ages of less than 3½, successfully identifying whole words.

(*c*) Dorothy Glynn (1964) in her book, *Teach Your Child to Read,* although in no way advocating that parents should 'push' their children into early reading, does show mothers '... some of the ways in which you can, without forcing his pace, help your child to be busy about reading, even before he goes to school. ...'

(*d*) Some parents now report that their pre-school children are learning to read, using the early books of *Key Words Reading Scheme* (Murray, 1964).

(*e*) Downing (1963), Harrison (1964), Southgate (1963) and others have given examples of many 4-year-olds learning to read with ita.

(*f*) Glenn Doman, who worked with a team of specialists on brain-injured children in the U.S.A., says, 'When the team had seen many brain-injured children read, and read well, at 3 years of age and younger, it became obvious that something was wrong with what was happening to normal children'. He further states that 'Tiny children *want* to learn to read, *can* learn to read, *are* learning to read and *should* learn to read'.

(*g*) Omar K. Moore describes children aged between 2½ years and 6 years, in the U.S.A., learning to read and write by means of an electric 'talking' typewriter. Not all these children are what he describes as 'ultra-rapid learners'; some, in fact, are 'ultra-slow learners'.

2 The concept of a mental age of 6½ being the 'minimum for probable success' in reading, as put forward by Morphett and Washburne in 1931, while being helpful in drawing attention to some of the problems of slower children, has, because of the manner in which it was taken up by later writers, done untold harm to the cause of reading. The results have been that some teachers and other educators have assumed that no one should begin to do anything about reading until children are 6½ years of age and that, even then, half the age-group are not sufficiently mature to begin reading. Sanderson (1963), Lynn (1963) and Downing (1963), provide an interesting re-examination of the idea. The growth of this concept of the importance of a mental age of 6½ has tended to encourage the idea that reading readiness is a stage to be waited for and not something for which training programmes can be planned. In fact, for many years infants teachers have, with success, been helping many children to read, although their mental ages were less than 6½ years.

3 The belief that young children cannot make fine visual discriminations is rapidly being exploded. Diack and Lynn both give examples of children from 2–5 years being able to do so, after a little practice. Some recent research of my own showed that many children less than 5-years-old, who had not begun to read, could make fine visual discriminations between words of similar appearance. For example, one child of 4 years was able to discriminate between the

words 'boot' and 'boat' (although he could not read these words), by the fact that one 'had an extra stick—there', as he said, pointing to the letter 'a' in 'boat'. Furthermore, in this research, the investigators, who were making every effort not to teach, all reported on the enormous increase in the children's ability to make fine visual discriminations during the course of three or four short experimental sessions.

4 Exactly the same can be said about young children's ability to make fine auditory discrimination. To be able to do so is not merely an aspect of normal maturation. It can be helped immensely by graded practice, in the form of various games, as many infant teachers have already discovered.

5 I would agree with those who state that, at the stage when they enter school, some children's speech is so inadequate that it would be inappropriate for them to try to learn to read. Nevertheless, while a certain fluency in speech is desirable before reading begins, one should not forget that reading readiness training is a great aid to an improvement in the spoken language. Furthermore, reading instruction and reading practice can increase the child's vocabulary, not merely of the words which he understands but also of those he uses in both written and spoken expression.

6 To those who believe that the task of learning to read is a complicated one which is too difficult for many children at the stage when they first start school, one must suggest that it is a mistake to assume that *all* ways of learning to read are too difficult. It has always been accepted that exceptionally able teachers were able to use methods which greatly simplified the learning process for the child. This is now being carried further by those interested in programmed learning. The use of various systems of simplified spelling has, in the past and more recently in the case of ita, been shown to make the process easier. Modern teaching aids including tape-recorders, typewriters (electric and otherwise), television, films and various teaching machines may all contribute to a simplification of the process of learning to read. And all such simplifications will tend to make earlier reading possible.

7 With those who oppose early reading on the grounds that children may be asked to work and that this will be bad for them and make them unhappy, I have no patience whatsoever. Why should we assume that an interesting task is hard work which young children will wish to avoid and that to ask them to do it will cause them suffering? Most young children do not differentiate between work and play. They love to 'work hard' at something in which they are interested and with which they can achieve a measure of success. Most of the authors mentioned earlier tell of young children's joy, pride and satisfaction in early reading.

Vera Southgate

Children should
I am inclined to think that the majority of the arguments put forward
by those who say that even if children can begin to read earlier, they
should not do so, are nonsense. I believe that if children want to
learn to read, if they are interested in doing so and if they can do so,
we should not discourage them. I listed four of the usual arguments
put forward by opponents of early reading. I shall make a brief
reply to the first three of these arguments and add a number of
further reasons why I think children should learn to read as early
as possible. (The fourth argument of opponents of early reading,
regarding failing children, will be dealt with separately later.)

1 Some educationists hold that the time devoted by young children
to learning to read is time that would be better devoted to other
pursuits. I heartily disagree with this line of thought, for two reasons.

(*a*) Surely language, in its spoken, written and printed forms, is just
as much part of the child's environment as water, clay, paint, paste
and paper. I am at a loss to understand why we should be expected
to commend children's explorations of these aspects of their environment, but not their interest in, and exploration of, printed and written words and letters which form an equally important and interesting aspect of their environment. Why is it so horrifying to some
teachers if we encourage a child when he shows signs of being
interested in words? The child who can differentiate and identify
different makes of cars, trains, aeroplanes or flowers is applauded
by all of us. We say that he is showing initiative and we must encourage him to explore this interesting world around him. Yet clearly
some people think it more valuable for the young child to delve into
archaeology, ornithology or any other field of study, than that of the
printed word.

(*b*) Secondly, those who deplore time spent on early reading rarely
pause to consider the shortness of the actual time which would be
devoted to it. Most of the teaching and learning in the early stages is
incidental; speaking, as well as writing and reading a few words go
on alongside, and are intermingled with, all the other activities of
the infant classroom. Specific instruction, if indeed it takes place at
all, is unlikely to last for more than a few minutes. Practice in
recognizing sentences, words or letters is usually in the form of
games and I am afraid that I am not convinced that it is more
profitable, or indeed more enjoyable, for young children to indulge
in games and activities concerned with, say, number concepts than
in similar activities concerned with words or letters.

2 The second argument produced by the opponents of early reading
is that reading will come naturally if it is left until later—but they
do not often say how much later. This I believe to be a fallacy, and

those who have dealt with non-readers in junior schools and in secondary modern schools will, I am certain, support me in this. Learning to read is not a feature of physical maturation, as for example, walking, which occurs naturally in nearly all children. It is a complex skill and most children need a good deal of help and guidance if they are to acquire it. Certainly some of our brighter children learn very easily, almost without apparent help. With other children, however, it might never come naturally. Some children might never want to read. They might never be motivated to begin unless someone inspired them to do so or got them started. They would never know that they would enjoy it until they had commenced, in the same way as a child does not know how much pleasure he will gain from eating certain foods until some adult has encouraged him to try them.

3 The third argument against early reading generally takes the line that there is no point in children learning to read at an early age, as they will be no better readers anyway by the time they reach, for example, the age of 10 or 11. Two points may be made in reply to this argument.

(a) Even if children who learn to read at an early age are not any further advanced in their reading ability at 11, this does not represent a valid reason for decrying early reading. Such an argument assumes that each stage of development in the child is only important because of what it leads to. Clearly the end product in education is important, but I should like to think that each stage on the way to the end product is also of value for its own sake. Accordingly I would suggest that, if reading at 5 or earlier gives the child pleasure and satisfaction, widens his horizons, enriches his environment or produces any other benefits, this is a fact which merits great value being attached to it, even if early reading is not followed by better performance at a later age.

(b) If children who learn to read at, say, 5 are no further advanced in reading ability at 11, than if they had commenced two years later, it may well be because we, as teachers, have not yet learned to help children to develop and utilize this skill to the full. There is a tendency for teachers in junior classes to assume that if children are reading fluently at the level represented by a reading age of 7 or 8, that instruction in the skill of reading is completed and that all the child requires is practice, mainly in silent reading. If children begin to learn to read earlier, as I am certain they will, we must be prepared to devote more time to perfecting children's study skills in reading, as well as training them to utilize the skill to the utmost extent.

The following points are some of the additional reasons why I believe that children should be encouraged to learn to read as soon as they can happily do so:

4 Many children *want* to learn to read and write. We are all familiar with the old story of the child who came home disappointed after his first day at school because he had not learned to read. Most children want to imitate grown-ups in all sorts of ways. If a child wants to garden or use woodwork tools, we offer him every assistance. We are amused and pleased by his efforts to imitate daddy. We provide him with real tools and real wood. The same is true of the little girl who wishes to cook. We do not say to her nowadays, 'Cooking is too hard for you; when you are a bigger girl you'll be able to learn'. Some modern infants schools not only provide woodwork benches and tools but also cooking stoves so that young children can enjoy baking real cakes. Yet if the child wants to read real books or write real words, there are some educationists who throw up their hands in horror because the 5-year-old is too young to read! I feel that, however young the child, if he desires to explore this aspect of his environment, if he wishes to imitate adults by reading and writing, then it is the duty of the adults concerned to devise the simplest possible means for initiating him into this skill.

5 As well as most children themselves wanting to learn to read, most parents also want their children to read. This is partly because it is the one tangible measure that parents have of their children's progress in schools. When parents visit infant schools on open days, this is the question they most often ask teachers. I am not suggesting that teachers should always react to pressure from parents in this way. Yet there is a case for appreciating that many parents whose children are unable to read by the age of 7 feel worried about it. Such anxiety can easily rub off on the children and create an atmosphere unfavourable to learning. Early reading can help to avoid this detrimental aspect of the situation, although I am aware that there could be dangers in parents endeavouring to bring pressure on teachers regarding children who are unable to read at an early age.

6 One great advantage of early reading and writing is that it provides children with an additional means of self-expression. One only needs to read some of the examples of infants' free writing in *The Excitement of Writing*, edited by Clegg (1964), to appreciate this point. Many publications referring to the use of ita have also given delightful examples of young children expressing themselves in writing. One recent example I came across springs to mind. I visited a school in a very poor area, on a day of pouring rain, in June. The area surrounding the school held very little of beauty but there were a few flowering cherry trees in blossom in some of the gardens. A rather pathetic-looking little boy, just under 6, had written something

like this in his diary. (The original was in ita and was not punctu-
ated.)

It is raining today and I am sad. We cannot go out to play because
it is raining so hard. But I guess the blossoms like the rain. They
are so lovely that I could just kiss them.

This piece of prose, which starts off by relating facts and how they
affect the child personally, then goes on to reveal a marvellous
experience of æsthetic appreciation. The boy was not very intelligent
and rather inarticulate. If he had not acquired some fluency in reading and writing by this stage, it could well have been that this
particular experience of appreciation of beauty would never have
found expression.

7 Early reading and writing not only gives children an additional
mode of expression but it also provides them with a further means
of communication. If they can read books, then the authors can
communicate directly with the children. If children can read hand-
written notes and letters, distant relatives and friends can communicate directly with them, as can the adults and children nearby. Once
they can write, there is no barrier to the child communicating in this
way with whomever he wishes, in any part of the world. I saw an
amusing instance of this aspect of communicating recently. As the
5-year-olds were leaving an infants school, it was noticed that Kevin
was clutching a large folded piece of drawing paper. The headmistress asked him what it was and Kevin replied that it was a note
for his mummy. As it did not look like the sort of letter his teacher
would have sent to a parent, the headmistress asked if she could
look at it. Inside was a message from Kevin's friend, John, to Kevin's
mother. It read: 'Please tell your Kevin to stop fighting or you will
put him to bed.' (The spelling has been corrected.) John had not
told Kevin what was in the note and Kevin, being rather dull, had
not asked! One may deplore or be amused by the tale-telling aspect
of this incident, but one must accept that this young child was, in
order to fulfil a need which he felt, utilizing a newly-acquired means
of communication with an adult.

8 The foregoing story leads easily to the next advantage of early
reading and writing. Children who have made a beginning in reading and writing are thereby given independence and an aid to
the development of initiative. John, when he wrote his note, demonstrated both these qualities. Teachers do not need me to give them
further examples of how children who have achieved even a simple
level of these two skills soon begin to depend less on the teacher
and more on themselves.

9 The next point is related to the probable staffing position in infant
schools in the foreseeable future. It seems highly likely that large

classes and changing staffs are going to be with us for a considerable number of years. The hardships experienced by both children and teachers in these difficult circumstances can be mitigated somewhat by children's independence when they have mastered even the initial stages of the skills of reading and writing.

10 Finally, the growing trend in primary education is towards heuristic methods. While it is true that discovery methods can be, and are being, utilized in many different ways by children who cannot read and write, yet it must be accepted that the inability to employ either skill will necessarily prove a limiting factor. The child who can read and write, and is consequently able to consult books on the subjects which currently interest him, will be able to progress much further with discovery methods on individual lines, than the child who must rely only on the evidence of his own senses supplemented by verbal enquiries to his teacher.

Need children fail?
Both the people who say that children cannot learn to read and those who say that even if children can, they should not, are concerned with the thought that early reading will increase the proportion of reading failures. Equally concerned about this problem are those of us, who, in certain circumstances, are not opposed to early reading. I am certain that we all ask ourselves if children need to fail or, even more important, if they need feel that they have failed. It is unnecessary to labour this point. Having accepted that we all agree that children should not be placed in situations in which there is a likelihood of their feeling failures, I can go on to make a few points which occur to me:

1 When a child feels that he has failed to learn to read, his feelings are more often related to what he thinks parents and teachers expect of him than to his own expectations. Consequently both parents and teachers must be on their guard against setting aims and standards which the child may not be able to reach.

2 The climate of expectation in a school is extremely important. For example, a school which gives very high priority to teach children to read may, in fact, teach more children to read than a school which has more broadly based aims. Yet it is possible that this very strong emphasis on reading may cause the few children who fail to learn, to feel much greater failures than do the non-readers in the second school.

3 I am not certain that delaying the beginning of reading will necessarily either avert or reduce the problem of children failing. It is not easy to draw comparisons of reading results between different countries in which children begin school at different ages. However,

there does not appear to be a smaller percentage of retardation in the USA or in some European countries where children start school later, than in Great Britain. In fact there is some evidence to the contrary, for example:

(a) Doman (1965) suggests that the later we leave reading, the more difficult it becomes, but he does not give any concrete evidence about this;'
(b) Taylor's (1950) experiments suggest that early teaching of reading increases performance;
(c) Anderson's (1964) study, comparing American, Scottish and English children has similar results.

4 As Teachers, I think we must accept that, at whatever age children begin to learn to read and whatever means we use to help them, not all children will be successful or not all will be equally successful. This will be true even when we are much more skilled than we are at present in preparing for and assessing reading readiness, in simplifying the task, in utilizing motivation, in diagnosing difficulties and in all the many other factors which contribute to our ability to help children to learn to read. If we accept that not all children will be equally successful, then it is important that the children themselves should accept differences in reading skills as coming within the normal range of differences. Most young children accept that some of them are tall and some short, that some are better at painting than others, and some are good at kicking a ball while others are not so good. We need to create an atmosphere in which differences in reading ability are no more emotionally toned than differences in hair colouring.

5 The feeling of failure in children can be substantially reduced by a release of tension and anxiety about reading in both teachers and parents. Teachers need truly to accept a wide range of individual differences in children and hence a wide range of different beginning ages. I feel that at present we pay lip-service to individual differences in children, while at the same time a fairly common classroom procedure is to try to make a beginning with reading with all children aged about 5½ years.

6 Differences between children's performances are less noticeable in the informal classroom than the formal one. Similarly, reading abilities are not so easily comparable within classes comprising children of different ages, as for instance in a vertically grouped class or a class in a small rural school, as in classes in which children are all the same age. Within a mixed age-group a child is much less likely to realize that he is a late starter or a slow learner and consequently unlikely to feel himself a failure.

7 It is less likely that children, and their parents, will be so conscious

of failure if children within a class are using a wide variety of reading books rather than adhering closely to one basic reading scheme.

8 While accepting that not all children will be ready to begin to read at the same time, nevertheless I consider it fatal just to wait for reading readiness to appear as if by magic. There is much that we can do to help children to be ready for reading. We need to be more highly qualified ourselves in the skills of reading. Then we will:

(a) do more planning about encouraging children's interests in books and reading and writing;
(b) do more programming in the form of early visual and auditory discrimination practices;
(c) and arrange for much more spoken communication.

By these means we shall ensure that the process of working towards reading readiness will be a dynamic programme for the slower child, which will satisy him, as well as carry him forward to the point at which he is ready for a more formal reading programme.

9 When a child has actually begun to read, we need to be specialists who can give him specific guidance and instruction which will help him to avoid or overcome the 'sticking points'. Such skilled help would go a long way beyond merely 'hearing him read' and prompting him as he fails.

10 We need to be always willing to explore new ways of simplifying the task, as simplification must necessarily result in fewer failures. However successful we feel we have been in teaching children to read in certain ways, we should still look with open minds at further ideas which might help some, although not necessarily all, children to read more easily.

Conclusions

1 We need to accept a far greater range of ages for beginning reading than we do at present. This implies that many children should begin earlier, as well as that some should start much later.

2 Many young children can and do begin to read very happily. I have long suspected that we seriously underestimate children. In the right situations many more may enjoy reading at an early age than at present.

3 There is every reason why children who can begin early should do so. Their own enjoyment and pride, the extension of their interests, the growth of their independence and initiative and the fact that they will have another medium of communication, all support this view. Conditions in present-day schools, as well as modern

heuristic methods reinforce the conclusion that we should encourage children to read and write as soon as they are able to do so.

4 We should accept that a few children may not be ready to begin formal reading even by the time they leave the infants school. We need to be able to recognize such children at an early age so that we may arrange for them a developmental programme of pre-reading experiences which will form a firm basis for later reading, while at the same time providing them with the satisfaction of perceiving their own progress.

5 We need to be continually aiming to simplify the task of learning to read and write. New media, in the form of simplified alphabets, colour codes or other ideas, new teaching methods, as well as new reading materials and teaching aids should all be explored.

References

ANDERSON, I. H. (1964) Comparison of the reading and spelling achievement and quality of handwriting of groups of English, Scottish and American children *Co-operative Research Project 1903* University of Michigan

CLEGG, A. B. (ed) (1964) *The Excitement of Writing* London: Chatto & Windus

DIACK, H. (1963) *Reading and The Psychology of Perception* Nottingham: Ray Palmer

DOMAN, G. (1965) *Teach your Baby to Read* London: Jonathan Cape

DOWNING, J. A. (1963) Is a mental age of six essential for reading readiness? *Educational Research* VI, 1

GLYNN, D. (1964) *Teach Your Child to Read* London: Pearson

HARRISON, M. (1964) *Instant Reading: The Story of the Initial Teaching Alphabet* London: Pitman

LYNN, R. (1963) Reading readiness and the perceptual abilities of young children *Educational Research* VI, 1

MOORE, O. K. (1963) *Autotelic Responsive Environments and Exceptional Children* Connecticut: Responsive Environments Foundation

MORPHETT, M. V. and WASHBURNE, C. (1931) When should children begin to learn to read? *Elementary School Journal* 31

MURRAY, W. (1964) *Key Words Reading Scheme* Loughborough: Wills & Hepworth

SANDERSON, A. E. (1963) The idea of reading readiness: a reexamination *Educational Research*, VI, 1

SOUTHGATE, V. (1963) Augmented roman alphabet experiment: an outsider's report *Educational Review* 16, 1

TAYLOR, C. D. (1950) The effect of training on reading readiness in Scottish Council for Research in Education *Studies in Reading*, Vol. 2, 63–80 London: University of London Press

2 The importance of structure in beginning reading

VERA SOUTHGATE
Lecturer in curriculum studies,
School of Education, University of Manchester

Paper presented at Sixth Annual Conference of UKRA Nottingham
1969, first published in *Reading skills: Theory and practice*

Reading in progressive infant classes

In primary education in Britain today the most noticeable trend is
towards what are usually termed 'progressive' schools or classes. The
keynotes of such schools are fluidity and informality in the grouping
of children and in timetabling, freedom of movement, individual choice
of activities and discovery methods of learning. In view of what
follows in the remainder of this paper, I should like to stress from
the outset that I approve of this development in primary education,
with its emphasis on the child himself and how he may learn rather
than on the teacher's instruction. Indeed, it would be difficult not to
appreciate the opportunities which such schools provide for highly
motivated and purposeful learning, for individual progress, for the
development of independence, responsibility and attitudes of
enquiry, for the encouragement of creativity and for social interaction.

On the other hand, I am seriously concerned by the fact that the
movement towards child centred learning in progressive schools is
frequently accompanied by a decline in the belief of the importance
of young children learning to read. The Plowden Report (1967), for
example, very clearly reflects this attitude. In this 500 page report,
covering all aspects of primary education, only five pages deal specifically with reading, and of these only one relates to 'Teaching children
to read'. This is certainly a far cry from the time when the work of
the primary school was centred on the 'three rs'. While one would
not wish to advocate a return to such concentration on 'three r' work,
I fear that we are in danger of going too far in the opposite direction. I still consider that one of the main functions of primary education should be the inculcation of literacy. Accordingly, we should
guard against any tendency to believe that it is less important for

36

young children to learn to read and write than it is for them to learn about mathematics and science or for them to have opportunities to express themselves, to create and to discover.

The current deprecation of the importance of learning to read is accompanied by a swing in emphasis from teaching to learning. Progressive teachers try to avoid the use of the phrase 'teaching children to read' and replace it with 'providing an environment in which children will be encouraged to learn to read'. A wide variety of books, which the teacher reads to the children and which they freely handle, reading apparatus, paper and pencils all form important parts of this environment. These teachers believe that in such a situation children will soon want to learn to read and, with a little encouragement and guidance, will succeed in doing so.

Both the older approach to reading tuition, that of systematically planned instruction and the newer theory of incidental learning, contain inherent dangers. When teachers pin their faith on instruction, the grave danger is that they may assume that what has been taught has also been learned. One has only to observe either class or group reading instruction taking place to realize the fallacy of this assumption. The proportion of pupil time devoted to features of the environment other than the teacher or the task, and likewise the proportion of the teacher's time devoted to attempts to focus children's attention on her instruction, increases rapidly as the lesson proceeds.

In contrast, when the emphasis is on learning, the main danger is that the teacher will assume that in a stimulating environment, with freedom to explore and experiment, all children will eventually want to learn to read and will be able to do so without specific instruction. Brighter pupils or those from homes in which literacy is valued frequently do so. Yet I am certain that many other children will fail to learn to read in infant classes unless a good deal of guidance and instruction is undertaken by the teacher. There are some children who would be neither 'motivated' nor 'ready' by the time that they were eight or nine or ten, if someone did not do something about it. The situation is somewhat similar to that of children learning to eat green vegetables or salads; many would never do so unless adults encouraged them to try, and fed them with small initial doses.

Furthermore, I do not see why it should be assumed that it is bad for young children to do some directed work. On the contrary, children both want and enjoy a certain amount of direct teaching and systematic practice. It would be a pity if teachers were to reach the stage when they became almost ashamed of doing some teaching. Yet this situation is in sight. I have been in infant schools where teachers apologize when one finds them actually teaching a small group of children; they hasten to assure one that this is exceptional!

Incidentally, it is interesting to note that many of the strongest supporters of the incidental learning theory are advisers, inspectors, lecturers or writers on infant education; in other words, those who do not have to cope with the aftermath, in junior classes and remedial groups, of children who have been left in infant classes to explore the reading environment. Such children have more often ignored or floundered in the reading environment than explored it purposefully.

Nevertheless, there is no doubt that the good teacher in the informal infant class does manage to ensure that each child makes progress in reading, according to his individual needs and abilities, in ways which might be described as 'incidental learning'. Close observation in such a class, however, would show the experienced teacher to be structuring the learning situation for the individual child, and particularly for the slower child. It would be seen that both individual diagnosis and planned learning were being carried out intuitively and functionally by this teacher and that individual records of children's progress were being kept. Ensuring reading progress for all children in these conditions, however, is an extraordinarily difficult task, and younger, less experienced or less able teachers are not always able to succeed.

The need for structure

I have three main reasons for believing in the need for structure in reading tuition. In the first place, written English does not constitute a regular spelling system. If the written form of our language represented a one-to-one relationship between written symbol and spoken sound we might have a reasonable basis for hoping that, by heuristic methods children could be encouraged to discover these relationships and so form generalizations. But our spelling system actually prevents children from making generalizations. For example, the child who has just begun to form a mental concept of the letter 'a' after meeting it in 'cat', 'man' and 'bag', will quickly have his theory demolished when he comes across words such as 'cake', 'father', or 'water'. Such a situation not only discourages the child from trying to discover things for himself but makes it practically impossible for him to do so. Discovery methods in the fields of mathematics and science are much more practical propositions, for here there are regular rules waiting to be discovered. Given sufficient opportunities and encouragement in the appropriate environment, which contains a wealth of carefully structured equipment, brighter children are able to explore these subjects by heuristic methods. Yet, in passing, it should be noted that certain teachers are already realizing that slower children make little progress in discovering for themselves even the unalterable laws of mathematics and science without a great deal of teacher guidance, as well as a certain amount of direct instruction.

Secondly, discovery methods of learning, to be effective, require certain basic skills of which reading is probably the most important, followed closely by the knowledge of how to use an index, simple dictionaries and reference books. While it is true that young children, even before they have started to read and write, can begin to discover, observe, experiment and compare, their progress is necessarily limited by lack of these skills. Thus, heuristic methods of learning will be greatly facilitated, and can only be fully developed, when children are able to read and write.

Thirdly, the staffing position in our primary schools today presents a picture of constantly changing members of staff. The newly trained teacher is often in schools only two or three years before she is married and leaving to have a family. Older married women return to teaching when the youngest of their children have started school, which may be after absences of fifteen years or more. There is also a floating population of temporary teachers. The older, experienced infant teacher is frequently the exception rather than the rule. This pattern of changing staffs in primary schools seems likely to continue. It has already been suggested that the informal infant class is far from easy to handle, and that mastery of the printed and written forms of our language represents a difficult task. In these circumstances continuity in reading tuition is unlikely to be achieved for individual children if learning to read is an informal, often haphazard, feature of the school environment. New members of staff will be greatly helped, and children's reading progress more easily ensured, within a planned reading programme based on a certain amount of structured reading materials.

It is not always realized that the meticulous planning of a framework for learning to read does not have to be accompanied by formalized instruction. In fact, I should go so far as to say that the reverse is true. My observations and experience in infant classes have led me to conclude that the freer the atmosphere and the more informal the working procedures the more imperative it becomes that the reading environment should be structured so as not only to encourage reading but also to forward its progress.

Structuring the reading environment

In the past ten years or so, in contrast to the growth of progressive primary schools, there has been a noticeable movement towards structured reading materials and procedures. This trend can be seen in a re-emphasis on phonics; in an awareness of the contributions of linguistics to reading tuition; in the publication of equipment such as Sullivan's *Programmed Reading* (1963) and the *Reading Laboratories* (Parker & Scannell 1963), in the introduction of new media; and in the growing interest in teaching machines and programmes for reading tuition. Teachers in progressive primary schools have usually stood aside from this stream of thought My contention is that progressive teachers, even more than relatively formal teachers, should give serious consideration to this movement towards structure. I am certain that if they would examine, adapt and incorporate into their progressive schools some of these forms of structuring, progress in reading and writing, as well as other work in the school would benefit.

In this paper I shall limit myself to a dicussion of only three of the many areas within the total reading environment which may be restructured in such a way as to facilitate the acquisition of early reading skills. The first relates to either regularizing the written code or drawing attention to the regularities within it which already exist. The second entails devising a master plan of reading tuition, with built-in diagnostic and recording devices. The third concerns the selection, organization and use of reading materials in a manner designed to further the master plan. I shall only touch on the first two points and devote the majority of my time in this paper to presenting you with samples of reading materials to illustrate the third point.

1 *Structuring the written code*

Most practising teachers of beginning reading are well aware of those difficulties caused by the irregularities of the English system of spelling which children experience when they first try to read. Our efforts to ease this burden may turn in either of two directions. We can either carefully examine the new media for beginning reading which are being advocated or we can concentrate on ways of emphasizing the regularities of the language.

One of the most noticeable innovations in beginning reading materials in recent years has been the introduction of a variety of regularized codes. We have had, among others, *i t a* (Pitman 1959), *Words in Colour* (Gattegno 1962), *Diacritical Marking System* (Fry 1967), *Colour Story Reading* (Jones 1967) and *Reading by Rainbow* (Bleasdale 1967). New media for beginning reading have been devised with the aim of regularizing, or at least simplifying, the code. The elimination of alternative pronunciations for the same printed symbol should not only simplify the process of learning to read for the child but should also make discovery methods of learning to read a more practical proposition. Yet progressive teachers who favour heuristic methods are often those who are most reluctant to experiment with new media. It would seem that they have assumed that any attempt to regularize the medium must necessarily be accompanied by a return to formal teaching procedures. Yet this need not be so.

The more regular the new medium and the more reading materials which are available in it the more feasible does the possibility of children learning to read by discovery methods become. With an absolutely regular medium and an abundance of reading materials discovering how to read would fall into the same class as discovering about mathematics and science. While none of the new media mentioned fulfils both criteria each may be found in different ways to have a certain value for heuristic methods. Reading materials printed in all three colour codes are limited in contrast to i t a with its long list of published reading materials. From the point of regularity *Words in Colour* is an absolutely regular code; i t a, as far as decoding is concerned, approaches regularity very closely; and the remaining two colour codes are better described as partial codes which will help children to pronounce many, but not all, irregular words.

Alternatively, teachers in progressive schools who do not want to employ a regularized medium for beginning reading should seriously consider the various current means of drawing attention to the regularities of our traditional spelling system. Approaches to reading such as linguistic methods do require formal teaching procedures of which such teachers would not approve. On the other hand, certain phonic approaches could fit in very well with the progressive infant teacher's aims regarding active participation and discovery by the children; for example *Programmed Reading Kit* (Stott 1962), *Fun with Phonics* (Reis 1962). Other approaches such as *Royal Road Readers* (Daniels and Diack 1957), *Sounds and Words* (Southgate and Havenhand 1959), *Step Up and Read* (Jones 1965), *Six Phonic Workbooks* (Grassam 1965) and *A Remedial Reading Method* (Moxon 1962), while they do require the teacher to adopt the role of instructor for very short periods of time, they also provide plenty of active and individual learning by children. Yet the progressive infant teacher has been inclined to ignore phonic approaches to reading, as much as new media, probably because she has associated them solely with rigid, formal teaching. She might do well to consider whether phonic schemes or colour codes, for example *Words in Colour*, which depend to a certain extent on teacher instruction in the early stages should be automatically eliminated on that count. She might then conclude that their use would be more than justified if it led, as it inevitably would, to the child becoming independent earlier. The child whose attention has been drawn to the phonic regularities of our language has been provided with a structured framework which will encourage his interest in words and their spellings, help him to discover and learn the irregularities, and generally make him an independent reader much earlier than the child who is left to discover the regularities and irregularities himself. His mastery of reading skills, by enabling him to acquire information from books, will then place him in a much more favourable position for discovery methods of learning in all subjects.

I am therefore suggesting that teachers in progressive infant

Vera Southgate

schools, who have frequently been those most strongly opposed to reading approaches which emphasize the regularities of the code and to attempts to regularize the code, should be the very ones to show the greatest interest in such developments.

2 *A master plan for reading tuition*

Efficient reading entails the mastery of many different sub-skills. This is unlikely to occur by chance, without adequate guidance and a certain amount of direct instruction. Accordingly the teacher needs to have a clear idea of her aims and a detailed plan of exactly what has to be learned and the order and progression of the small steps which will lead to the ultimate goal. In other words unless she has a master plan, children's reading progress will be extremely patchy. Such a plan will include preparatory work before formal reading tuition commences, arrangements for the acquisition of a sight vocabulary of commonly used words, the development of word attack skills, training in reading with understanding, and reading for different purposes and at different speeds. Plans for graded practice and for supplementary reading at progressively more difficult levels will form part of the plan. Such a programme must also include some form of checking what has been learned and the keeping of meticulous records. Unless a teacher knows exactly all the minute stages in learning which each child has actually mastered how can she plan for the next stage?

We are often rather scornful about the formal, detailed plans for reading instruction which exist in American, Canadian and most European schools. We might do better to look carefully at these meticulous plans of what needs to be learned and then, rather than set about *teaching* all of it, attempt so to structure the reading environment that children would be led to discover much of it for themselves.

Only a well considered master plan accompanied by accurate diagnosis and meticulous recording can lead to structuring the learning situation for continuous individual progress. The more informal the classroom situation and the more individualized the reading programme the more essential does this behind the scenes structure become.

3 *Selecting and organizing the reading materials*

The majority of infant schools today contain large collections of miscellaneous books, many of them beautifully produced and illustrated, which children are quite free to handle at any time. In such an environment there is no doubt that for many children the motivation to learn to read is strong. Yet if all or the majority of children are to learn to read I suggest that this reading environment needs structuring in two ways. First, the selection of books, charts, apparatus and all reading equipment must be the result of a careful appraisal carried out in the light of the master plan for reading tuition. Secondly, planned procedures for the use of certain of the reading materials need establishing so that freedom of choice for the child operates within a framework of graded stages.

The discussion which follows does not apply to those general books such as picture dictionaries, reference books and illustrated story books which are usually available on display shelves and book corner units in infant classrooms, corridors and entrance halls. It refers particularly to those books and pieces of equipment which have been planned to further specific stages in learning to read.

Reading books and other reading equipment need to be examined in respect of both content and the required procedures. The content should be so planned as to facilitate child learning, while the procedures for mastering the content should necessitate the child being active rather than require great efforts from the teacher in order to achieve small returns from the children. It might be suggested that five minutes' teacher guidance and instruction and fifteen minutes' pupil activity is a more appropriate proportion than if these figures are reversed.

The teacher who decides to begin reading with phonic training will find that most phonic reading schemes require quite a large amount of teacher instruction in the initial stages, although in the later stages minimal teacher guidance can lead to considerable amounts of learning in the form of pupil directed activities. If, however, phonic training is introduced after the initial stages of a look-and-say approach, it is possible to find published apparatus, games, equipment and supplementary workbooks which provide active learning situations for children.

If reading begins with a look-and-say method, the first books the child handles should be such that the teacher does not have to put each word into his mouth and repeat this procedure ad nauseam until he has learned the words by rote. If the teacher is to step down from this role of permanent prompter, illustrations, vocabulary control and sentence structure must all be planned to aid the child's independent learning. The illustrations in the books should be so simple, unambiguous and appropriate that the words printed on the page are those which will spring immediately to the child's mind. The structure underlying the build up of words from page to page should be such as to lead the child inevitably and successfully forward. A simple form of sentence structure used repetitively will be found more helpful than complicated and varied sentence structures. Many well known look-and-say reading schemes and popular supplementary series of books are deficient in these respects.

Yet look-and-say books can be so structured with simple words, phrases and stories, accompanied by illustrations which are apposite

43

that a child can 'read' his first books himself with very little teacher guidance. *What is Little?* (Melser 1960) one of the *Read It Yourself Books*, is a good example of this, with the text on successive pages reading 'A baby is little', 'A doll is little', and so on. The same is true of *Martin's Toys* (Southgate 1968), one of the series entitled *First Words*, in which the text under succeeding illustrations reads 'Martin'. 'Martin's ball', 'Martin's book', and so on. *This Is the Way I Go* (Ingleby and Taylor 1965) and Methuen's *Caption Books* (Randell 1966) are additional examples of simple introductory books, so constructed that children can read them with little help from the teacher.

At a slightly later stage, many of the well known traditional tales containing repetitive phrases, such as 'The Three Little Pigs' and 'The Little Red Hen' and 'The Grain of Wheat', do help the child to read for himself. So too do books such as the *Reading With Rhythm* books (Taylor and Ingleby 1961), *Mouse Books* (Piers 1966), *Stories for Me* (Ryder 1957) and *Springboard Readers* (Mail 1966). Most of these books also employ the helpful technique of presenting meaningful phrases as separate lines of print. They are all simple stories which by means of phrasing, rhythm and repetition are so structured that very little teacher guidance is required. The *Oxford Colour Readers* (Carver and Stowasser 1963) are a particularly good example of a reading scheme for older retarded pupils and are planned in such a way as to help the child to help himself.

The selection of equipment supposedly designed to help children to read requires particular caution, as it can frequently prove no more than a time filler. One should consider exactly what the child will be learning by playing a game or using a piece of apparatus; whether the apparatus has been designed to guide the child towards a particular discovery, to reinforce his learning or to provide him with practice in a newly acquired skill. Different cues and self-checking devices are required at different stages. For instance, if the child is being guided to recognize the initial sounds of words, by matching two pieces of card, one bearing the letter 'e' and the other the picture of an egg, a simple clue such as a background colour or a jigsaw shape might help him to do so with little chance of failure. At the same time, the teacher needs to be aware that the child is likely to use the minimum clue necessary to achieve success. If he can match a red colour to a red colour or fit a sticking out curve into an inward bending curve, he will not necessarily note that the printed symbol 'e' related to the initial sound of the word 'egg'. After some practice at this particular stage his knowledge of initial letter sounds could only be checked by removing extraneous clues from the fronts of the pieces of card and replacing them by self-checking devices on the back.

This raises the important point of the distinction between

clues and self-checking devices. Clues are clearly visible and help the child to make the correct moves. The clues themselves should be sufficiently simple for the child to understand them on his own; for example indistinguishable colours or similarly shaped jigsaw pieces which require the teacher's aid defeat their own object. Clues cannot be considered as real self-checking devices, however, because they do not necessarily indicate to the teacher whether or not the child has mastered the reading skill which the apparatus was designed to help him to learn. Clues should therefore only be used in the pre-liminary stage of learning any skill. Real self-checking devices only come into effect *after* the child has completed the operation. They should indicate that the child has mastered the relevant skill *without* extraneous clues. A teacher needs to consider very carefully before purchasing or using reading games and apparatus which lack true self-checking devices, unless she can see ways in which such devices may be added. Otherwise children will spend a few brief minutes carrying out the activity and long periods waiting for the teacher to check what they have done.

With all equipment and apparatus, as with books, the teacher needs to consider the ratio of her instruction time to the pupil's learning time. Apparatus and games which require lengthy or com-plicated instructions are rarely worthwhile, unless the technique be-ing mastered is one which can be repeatedly utilized for other learn-ing. The game of bingo or lotto, for instance, is well worth teaching as it can be played over and over again for practising different skills.

It should also be noted that many sets of apparatus for beginning reading relating to both sight words and phonically regular words concentrate almost exclusively on nouns. Yet McNally and Murray (1962) who list 200 'key' words which account for 'half to three-quarters of the running words occuring in everyday reading matter', note that only twenty-one of these are nouns. Clearly children's early reading progress will be facilitated if the sight of these 200 key words evokes automatic responses from them. In fact much of the time which children spend playing with ill designed pieces of appa-ratus, relating to nouns they are unlikely to encounter in their read-ing books, could be much more profitably spent in activities designed to aid their instant recognition of the most common, and often irregular, words in our language. This need not be done by drilled instruction. Although, as children are unlikely to discover how to read these irregular words for themselves, the teacher may need to take a leading role in group games at first to ensure superficial mastery of the words. Perfect mastery can then be completed by groups of children or individual children without the teacher's help. McNally and Murray (1962) in *Key Words To Literacy* suggest a few games for learning key words. Galt published games entitled *Key Words Self-Teaching Cards* consisting mainly of nouns, and also

45

Basic Words Lotto and *Key Words Lotto* containing a proportion of words other than nouns. Many practising teachers have also developed their own apparatus and games designed to aid children's mastery of these words. It is a pity that their ideas are not more widely publicized.

Yet the selection of appropriate reading materials is only part of the plan for structuring the reading situation towards individualized child learning. My second suggestion was that the skilful preorganization by the teacher of a considerable proportion of the available reading materials was necessary before children's free choice became operative. As far as reading games and apparatus are concerned, infant teachers usually accept that children should use them in a particular sequence, rather than in random order which would nullify their graded levels of difficulty. Yet in certain infant schools this principle is not accepted for books.

I believe we need to develop a form of procedure halfway between that of children's unrestricted access to a miscellaneous collection of books and complete reliance on a basic reading scheme under the teacher's direct control. Once motivation to learn to read is aroused not only are small amounts of instruction valuable but graded practice is also necessary. This can best be arranged by ensuring that at every stage a child can be guided to choose books and equipment from a selection appropriate to his level of attainment. Both the miscellaneous collection and the graded collection of books are necessary. For the latter, the teacher needs to select certain simple books at different levels and arrange them on different shelves or mark them with distinctive bindings so that every child can always know where to find something of interest which both he and his teacher realize he will be able to read with a fair degree of success.

Many of the books already mentioned can be selected to fulfil this purpose. So can the supplementary books of many look-and-say reading schemes, for example *McKee Platform Readers* (Castley), *Janet and John Supplementary Books* (O'Donnell and Munro 1951), *Happy Venture Library Books* (Flowerdew and Schonell) or *Beacon Booklets* (Grassam 1957); and also the supplementary books of certain phonic approaches, for example, *Gay Way Red Stories* etc (Boyce 1959), *Royal Road Miniatures, Royal Road First and Second Companion Books* and *Sounds and Words Stories*. The child who has read the particular preceding basic book and is able to recognize the appropriate sight words or grasp the relevant phonic rules, as the case may be, can be left free to choose his own supplementary book and read it for himself. The phonic supplementary books can also prove valuable for the child who has been reading a look-and-say scheme and whose teacher has introduced incidental phonic words, providing the child is given access to them at the appropriate stages. Both look-and-say and phonic supplementary books wisely chosen and introduced as part of a plan of graded practice provide perfect opportunities for individual choice within a structured framework. Yet how often one sees these very books being used in two opposing and equally inappropriate ways.

The progressive teacher often displays simple supplementary books from many schemes for children's free choice. Then children, not fully prepared for them, pick up these books at random and, finding them too difficult, quickly discard them. We should realize that although supplementary books from different look-and-say reading schemes may look of equivalent simplicity, this is not so. The overlap of words between one scheme and another is not nearly so great as one might imagine. The more formal teacher, in contrast, often uses a different procedure. She insists on hearing the child read all the supplementary books in a reading scheme. What a waste of opportunity for individual choice!

Neither of the extreme forms of procedure seems to me to be entirely successful. To have every step of reading tuition dominated by the teacher can crush the eagerness of the young child, deprive him of the pleasures of freedom of choice and sap his initiative. On the other hand, complete freedom for the child to try to read materials which the teacher knows to be too difficult for him seems to be merely structuring a frustrating situation for the child. I believe that subtle arrangements made by the teacher to ensure the child's inevitable success with the books he chooses to read or the reading games which he plays would represent the most practical form of freedom likely to ensure individual learning. Accordingly, although the selection of reading books and equipment to form graded collections at different levels of difficulty is not an easy task, I am certain that it is important for us to devote more attention to it.

Summing up

There are many advantages to be gained when the emphasis in beginning reading is on pupil learning rather than on teacher instruction. Yet the creation of a school environment designed to promote motivated, individualized learning should not lead to the conclusion that all instruction should be taboo. In fact, I am certain that the ideas now being developed in our progressive primary schools will soon become discredited if they are accompanied by an acceptance of the idea that it is no part of the role of a teacher to teach.

The freer the school environment from the child's point of view, the more carefully must the teacher have structured it, particularly with regard to learning to read. There are three main reasons for this conclusion. First, English is not a regular language and therefore does not lend itself so easily to discovery methods of learning as do mathematics and science. Secondly, as heuristic methods of learning can only be fully developed when facility in reading and writing has been acquired, the creation of some structure in the process of learning to read and write becomes even more important in progressive schools. Thirdly, the position of changing staffs in primary schools strengthens the need for a certain amount of structure in reading tuition.

Three broad ways of structuring the reading environment have been suggested. First, systems of regularizing the written code or of drawing attention to the existing rules should be carefully appraised rather than discarded out of hand as inappropriate, particularly for progressive schools. Secondly, in both formal and informal schools teachers need a master plan for reading tuition; the latter probably having even more need of it than the former. Thirdly, all reading materials need selecting in the light of how they will encourage children to help themselves. Procedures for the use of these reading materials should be so planned that children's freedom of choice will operate within a framework of graded stages.

References

BLEASDALE, E. & W. (1967) *Reading by Rainbow* Moor Platt Press

BOYCE, E. R. (1959) *The Gay Way Series* Macmillan

CARVER, C. and STOWASSER, C. H. (1963) *Oxford Colour Reading Books* OUP

CASTLEY, D., FOWLER, K. and CARSTAIRS, S. *The McKee Platform Readers* Nelson

DANIELS, J. C. and DIACK, H. (1957) *The Royal Road Readers* Chatto & Windus

THE PLOWDEN REPORT (1967) *Children and their Primary Schools, Vol. 1: The Report* HMSO

FLOWERDEW, P. and SCHONELL, F. *Happy Venture Library* Oliver & Boyd

FRY, E. (1967) The diacritical marking system and a preliminary comparison with i t a in: DOWNING, J. and BROWN, A. L. (eds) *The Second International Symposium* Cassell

GALT *Basic Word Lotto* (N.692)

GALT *Key Words Lotto* (N.940, N.941 and N.942)

GALT *Key Words Self Teaching Cards* (N.970 and N.971)

GATTENGO, C. (1962) *Words in Colour* Educational Explorers

GRASSAM, E. H. (1967) *The Beacon Readers* Ginn

GRASSAM, E. H. (1966) *Phonic Workbooks* Ginn

JONES, J. K. (1967) *Colour Story Reading* Nelson

JONES, W. R. (1965) *Step Up and Read* ULP

MAIL, A. (1966) *Springboard Readers* Warne

McNally, J. and Murray, W. (1962) *Key Words to Literacy* Schoolmaster Publishing Co

Melser, J. (1960) *Read It Yourself Books* Methuen

Moxon, C. A. V. (1962) *Remedial Reading Method* Methuen

O'Donnell, M. and Munro, R. (1951) *Janet and John* Nisbet

Parker, D. H. and Scannell, G. (1963) *Reading Laboratories* Science Research Associates

Piers, H. (1966) *Mouse Books* Methuen

Pitman, J. (1959) *The Erhardt Augmented (40-sound 42-character) Lower-case Roman Alphabet* Pitman

Randell, B. (1966) *Methuen Caption Books* Methuen

Reis, M. (1962) *Fun with Phonics* Cambridge Art Publishers

Ryder, E. (1957) *Stories for Me* Macmillan

Southgate, V. (1968) *First Words* Macmillan

Southgate, V. and Havenhand, J. (1959) *Sounds and Words* ULP

Stott, D. H. (1962) *Programmed Reading Kits* McGraw-Hill

Sullivan, M. W. (1963) *Programmed Reading* McGraw-Hill

Taylor, J. and Ingleby, T. (1961) *Reading with Rhythm* Longmans

Taylor, J. and Ingleby, T. (1965) *This Is the Way I Go* Longmans

D

3   Teaching beginners to read: USA

JOSEPHINE B. WOLFE

Director of language arts research, the Graduate
School, University of Scranton, Pennsylvania

Paper presented at Third Annual Conference of UKRA Cambridge
1966, first published in *Reading: Current research and practice*

Teaching beginners to read, whatever their age, is a subject of
sensational publicity nationally and internationally among students
of reading, teachers of young children and the public. Although
many studies have been done and are being done in the area of
beginning reading, it is unfortunate that the publicity—like most
publicity—rarely reports the concerns and/or any factual information in an understandable style.

Teaching beginners to read

Without equivocation, *every young child can learn to read.* In fact,
it is unquestionable that some children at age five, perhaps one in
fifty, already have begun to read before entering school. At the same
time, one would not quarrel with the premise that *every child should
learn to read* so that he may become an effective citizen in his society.
Therefore, it is apparent that our concerns about teaching beginners
to read should be focussed on the 'when' and the 'how' rather than on
the 'can' and the 'should', remembering that a good study should
be longitudinally designed and conducted in an 'unfragmented'
manner. Such an approach is being attempted in the USA. During
the past two years, projects involving between 20,000 and 30,000
children have been and are being sponsored by the Cooperative
Research Branch of the United States Office of Education with Dr
Guy L. Bond serving as director and Dr Robert Dykstra serving as
associate director. Since both gentlemen are staff members at the
University of Minnesota, Minneapolis, this institution was selected as
the coordinating centre for the projects. While it is difficult to draw
specific conclusions and implications from such an endeavour at this
time, several observational outcomes and personal reactions can be

made from reviewing the descriptive literature and from visiting some of the situations where the projects are on-going.

1 The project directors, the teachers, and the over-all staff members of the various projects have grown professionally. They have gained much from the experience of being involved in the projects and by sharing and comparing the procedures, the results, and the conclusions of the studies. In other words, the research programme has proven to be a valuable in-service technique because, in most cases, the teachers of the control group regularly attended as many in-service professional meetings as did the teachers of the experimental group to learn more about the instructional materials being used, teaching techniques, the instructional needs of children and teaching beginning reading in general.

2 There appears to be no one method for teaching beginning reading which is so outstanding that it should be used exclusively.

3 There are greater variations among the teachers within the methods than there are between the methods.

4 The use of a multiplicity of approaches and materials appears to be more effective than a single approach accompanying a single set of materials.

5 Wherever the *Language Experience Approach* supplements or complements another approach, results appear to be exceptionally good. Of course, this can be expected, since the *Language Experience Approach* is a natural approach by which children can experience all phases of language—listening, speaking, reading, and writing.

A step-by-step description of the natural approach

Naturally, with language improvement being basic to all areas of language, the *Language Experience Approach* appears to be a 'perfect' informal technique for improving a child's ability to read. Since it is an informal technique, it appears to be the best technique to use as an adjunct to any of the so-called formal reading programmes. Therefore, let me describe this natural approach step-by-step.

Step 1 Prepare the children for dictating their experiences by discussing common experiences as a group. Common experiences may include such areas as 'pets', 'trips', 'safety rules', and 'science experiments'.

Step 2 Have the children discuss their reason for developing their experiences, keeping the discussion brief, lively, and worthwhile.

Step 3 Be sure that the children agree on a general type of record to be used for recording their language experiences. The experiences may be recorded in various forms, such as narra-

Josephine B. Wolfe

tions, list of plans, diaries, news stories, reminder stories, what-we-know stories, what-we-want-to-know stories and stories related to vocabulary development activities.

Step 4 Guide the children in agreeing on a title for the language experiences that are to be recorded. For example, the central idea of the experiences may be expressed by a word or a short phrase.

Step 5 Prepare a preliminary draft of the language experiences with the children. Complete sentences are not always appropriate. Paragraphs, phrases and lists of words may be used, depending upon the purpose and the skills being developed and/or maintained in the lesson.

Step 6 Guide the children in editing the preliminary draft of their language experiences.

Step 7 Provide follow-up activities that are related to the specific skills which are being developed in the lesson.

Step 8 If the language experience story is to become a permanent record, construct the language story into chart form. However, *all* language experience stories do not need to be recorded for permanency.

Which methods? What materials?

Which methods and what materials for teaching beginners to read have long been subjects of controversy and concern among the general public as well as the teaching public. Although studies have been made and are continuing to be made by competent investigators, confusion blooms. Such a feeling is understandable when one considers that it is impossible to compare materials, methods, and frequently the ideas of the eager publisher or the zealot exploiting his ideas. All makes for real uncertainty! Therefore, a pooling of the minds of those concerned would appear to suggest that *when* a young child is taught to read, by *which* methods and with *what* materials depends greatly upon a teacher's sensitivity of knowing *when* the child is ready and his competency in using at least a dual approach, one of the approaches being the *Language Experience Approach* to learning.

4 Early reading skills

GEOFFREY R. ROBERTS
Lecturer in primary education,
University of Manchester

This paper is a revised and combined version of two papers presented
at Sixth Annual Conference of UKRA Nottingham 1969, first
published in *Reading skills: Theory and practice*

Some points about learning a skill

Learning a skill is something more than mere habit formation in that
a habit usually requires a fixed response or sequence of responses,
whereas in performing a skill such as reading the reader must be
capable of adjusting his responses to the fine variations in the print.
For example, he must distinguish between the sounds of 'ough' in
'thought' and in 'though'. This demands a critical and flexible
approach on the part of the child.

The type of teaching that helps a child to take up a critical
position when trying to read words is not one which requires a
rapid and immediate response from the child (Roberts 1968, Kagan
1965), and neither is it one which passes on information from teacher
to child in a formal way brooking no questions about the rectitude of
the teacher's word. Rather, it is one in which the child is encouraged
to discuss the possible, and even the impossible, alternatives. In
order to accomplish this, the teacher and child must allow themselves
time for reflection, and in many cases the teacher should show the
child how she would tackle the problem, so that the child will see
that the teacher herself has to work things out. This may take up
considerable time, it may even seem laborious to the teacher, but it
is the only way to create a flexible approach to word identification
in a language which contains so many sub-categories and irregularities of spelling.

The distribution of practice

For a long time I have been worried by the haphazard way in which
we have distributed the practice periods in learning to read. Many

schools, even the better ones, consider that a period of time lasting from twenty to thirty minutes a day should be allocated by each child to reading. Why is this so? Why only once per day? Is this the optimum distribution of practice in learning the skilled behaviour involved in reading? I have the feeling that a more likely answer is that by general concensus it has been agreed that there are certain basic skills which should be taught and that the easiest way to apportion time is to allocate to each skill one section of time per day per child. This performs a neat cycle to the teacher's day and satisfies everyone's conscience. But in the field of psychology there are some pertinent experiments which should cause us to reconsider the distribution of time allocated to learning to read.

The problem examined in these experiments is 'massed' versus 'distributed' practice and the research is reviewed by G. F. Reed (1968). It is obvious that reading as a skill is too complex to revert to massed practice—that is, it cannot be learned at one session, no matter how long, because fatigue and boredom would intervene. However, reading can be equated in part to several sub-skills (Roberts and Lunzer 1968). Each of these sub-skills can be treated to some extent as an entity and several can be dealt with separately in single sessions of learning. Moreover, it is important that they should be thoroughly taught at the time when they arise, e.g. 'ight' as it occurs in several common words should be learned thoroughly by the child at one session. Why maintain, as many teachers by their actions do, the practice of half or quarter teaching something, merely on the excuse of the presence of other intervening factors, such as other facets of the reading process or other activities?

Nevertheless, these sub-skills are an integral part of a wider skill, so they must occur in relatively close proximity to the other sub-skills and in relation to the whole composite skill. There is guidance from research about the spacing of these periods. Kientzle (1946) demonstrated that beyond a certain period of rest nothing was gained. At the same time we have some evidence (Travis 1939) and our own experience suggests that the length of the learning session is more crucial than the length of the rest period. If you look realistically at the children in your class, you will admit that seldom if ever can they concentrate on any aspect of learning to read for twenty minutes, let alone half an hour. Most of that time would be wasted dreaming, looking around, pretending to work!

So, taking these two points together—length of learning session and length of intervening rest period—it would seem advisable to shorten the periods allocated to teaching reading and to increase their frequency. These may be anything from two to ten minutes according to the task and may or may not include practice of particular sub-skills. In this way a child will return to reading in some form —new learning or practice as the case may be—several times a day.

Furthermore the length of the learning and practice sessions, and the time intervals between them, should be varied according to the task and the learner. This is quite feasible within the type of educational practice where several types of activity are occurring simultaneously and where there is a genuine integration of subjects and skills in the learning process.

The organization of the classroom

Most people will agree that one of the distinguishing marks of a good teacher is the ability to organize a class. And if we look more closely, we will find that there is a pattern and rhythm to the teaching which enables the teacher to avoid unnecessary effort. Unfortunately pattern and rhythm do not come easily to all teachers and it may be considered a criticism of our training establishments that once they abandoned the Herbartian steps they also abandoned any obligation to present the trainee with a formula within which and from which he could operate and develop.

First, I shall deal with pattern. All that I have written and said about reading is based on the assumption that the teacher makes herself available to help individual children and small groups of children at various times during the day.

Now it is obvious that this is impossible if forty children are learning to read at the same moment. Therefore in a class of children where the majority are at the stage of learning to read, it seems logical that the work of the class should be arranged so that not all the children are participating in reading simultaneously. The problem is how to avoid the 'chicken on the midden' effect, where all sorts of things are happening at once and where it is not easy for the teacher to control effectively all the learning situations. Furthermore, this type of situation may impede learning; many adults find it difficult to concentrate on a book amidst other people's activities, some of which involve movement and noise. The answer must surely be either the open plan school with bays allocated to various pursuits so that the different activities are separated from each other, or the adaptation of this principle within the confines of the closed classroom. This can be done within the classroom by setting up areas to which the children go to pursue different activities. For example, a reading area, a mathematics area, an English area, an art and craft area and other areas can be created as the need arises. All that has to be done is to pull out cupboards, bookcases and tables so that they stand at right angles to the wall and bays have been created in which work of a specific nature and under appropriate conditions of equipment, noise and movement, can take place. Furthermore the teacher will easily see whether or not each child is participating in the desired activity. The 'motivational pull' of these areas will act in

Geoffrey R. Roberts

the same way as an attractive dress salon to women: the children are in the reading corner, therefore they feel that they should be reading. All that is required of the teacher is that she should know in advance what in general she is going to expect her children to do that day. She must also of course be prepared to move away from the outmoded and irrelevant idea of a desk based child.

My second point refers to rhythm. If a teacher has not formulated her own particular rhythm then she may find Whitehead's cyclic process of learning (1962) useful. He suggested that there were three stages; romance, precision and generalization. The stage of romance is akin to a period of motivation, where each item of learning is presented to the learner in the most favourable circumstances. The teacher should try to imbue the task with an air of excitement and the child with enthusiasm. But this is one of the fundamental features of teaching, you may say. Yes, but do we always do our utmost to bring excitement to every task? The child invariably comes to these tasks, in the first place, full of enthusiasm; it seems a pity that so many have this enthusiasm squashed by unimaginative teaching and a thoughtless lack of involvement on the part of the teacher.

The stage of precision is where the child learns a particular item or aspect of reading. At this stage, the child learns the sub-skills of reading; he also learns to interpret all aspects of the form and meaning of written language. The work at this stage can take a variety of forms, but the attachment of the name precision to this stage reminds us to be more precise and discriminating in the tasks we set and in the standards that we require.

Finally, the stage of generalization is the point at which the child applies and uses what he has learned. This may take the form of an oral response to a word; it may involve interpreting a particular sentence structure; or it may require the child to read a passage or a book. This stage may occur several times during a short lesson, as indeed will the whole cycle in this case, or it may occur only once at the end of a lesson. This is the stage at which the child reaps the benefits of his learning; he enjoys using his newly learned skills.

There are numerous ramifications of the cyclic process, but the main reason that it has been raised in this paper is that it offers a formula, which can serve as a constant reminder to the teacher that every aspect of the work of teaching a child to read is of fundamental importance and if a part is neglected then it will be that much more difficult for the child to achieve proficiency.

Criteria for an early reading programme

It is suggested that there are three basic components which must be considered when preparing a programme of early reading instruction and guidance. They are the task, the child, and the teacher. The child's mental and physical capabilities and the content of the task determine the limits of the work, whilst the teacher manipulates the methods and procedures within these limits. Therefore, although we cannot say that she is of overriding importance in the learning situation, we can say that her decision and methods will crucially affect the way in which the subject matter is arranged and presented. Also, her decisions will affect the opportunities which the child has to react favourably or unfavourably to the task.

In order to avoid the confusion which would result from a consideration of all three components simultaneously, each one will be examined in isolation.

The task

Table 1 presents the schematic representation of the task facing the teacher. It should be borne in mind that reading is skilled behaviour and it involves facility in language and the interpretation of symbols. There are three aspects of language: phonic, syntactic and semantic.

Retaining these established facts in mind, whatever the stage of reading ability under consideration, the next thing to decide is the sub-skills which make up the complete skill of reading.

One of the earliest skills a child must acquire when starting to learn to read is to recognize that the different letters vary in shape and that the shape of each letter is invariable. This can be achieved in a variety of ways—alphabet books, playing with wooden letters, matching individual letters, tracing with the forefinger letters made of glue and sand—much of it incidental and unstressed as a part of learning to read. This can be as much fun as counting and chanting, rhyming and sing-song. However, there should be as little vocalization of the individual letters as possible. Any vocalization that does take place should be within the context of a meaningful word or closely associated with a familiar word.

The other sub-skills are enumerated below. The order in which they are acquired by the child does not necessarily follow exactly the listed order. Naturally, the teaching method will influence the order, although it cannot alter it radically because many of the later sub-skills depend on the acquisition of the earlier ones. The child must learn, in one way or another the following:

1 That the printed text tells a story or gives information, i.e. that the visual symbols convey a language message.
2 That the various shapes of letters and words are cues to the various sounds we make when speaking, although the child need not be able to identify specific letters or words at this stage.
3 That there is an *exact* correspondence between the order of

sounds spoken and the left to right sequence of *words* as printed —with the spaces between printed words corresponding to (possible) minimal pauses in speech: ə, kæt, sæt, ɔn, ə, mæt = a cat sat on a mat.

4 To differentiate visually between the letter shapes: i and p, t and m, b and d, and so on to include all the letters.

5 To identify letter shapes by their sound: c=/k/, a=/æ/, tae =/t/.

6 That there is an approximate correspondence between the left to right sequence of the letters as written and the temporal sequence of phonemes (sounds which make up the word) c⟶a⟶ t=/k/⟶/æ/⟶/t/.

7 To differentiate visually between the digraphs (ea, ai, ch, sh, ie, etc).

8 To identify the digraphs by their sound: they must learn the various alternatives, e.g. 'ea' in beat, idea, beautiful, ocean, great.

9 To form a meaningful word by synthesizing, in their correct order, meaningless vocal syllables: /ai/, /den/, /ti/, /fai/ = /aidenti : fai/ (identify).

10 To differentiate frequent letter strings, e.g. -tion, str-, spr, -ing, un- etc.

11 To identify these letter strings by their sound: -tion = /ʃən/; -ing = /iŋ/.

12 A variety of strategies for forming and recognizing unfamiliar polysyllabic words.

13 To respond with increasing facility to all the demands made in strategies 1 to 12 so that the whole process becomes more and more automatic, effortless and fluent. (Taken from G. R. Roberts (1969) *Reading in Primary Schools* Routledge & Kegan Paul).

This enumeration of the sub-skills of reading is in effect a breakdown of the subject matter, so that the full significance of its contents can be determined. It is not intended as a teaching programme; it is something that the teacher should keep in her mind so that she can see the complete pattern of learning emerge.

Once the separate contents of the task have been determined, it is necessary to consider the order, the method and the emphasis in which the contents are presented. For example, many of the common words of English contain digraphs. Should these be introduced at the outset, or should the child concentrate upon words containing single vowels in the first instance, and, if so, what about hard and soft vowels? How are words to be introduced, individually or in sentences, and how are they to be learned, by contrasting them with other words or by summation? And, finally, is the set of readers to form the basis of the programme, or is it to be supplementary to the programme?

The child

There are several points about the child which must be related to the task. The subject matter must be arranged to suit the child's mental capacities, which will consist of shifting proportions of intuitive thinking and concrete operations. These will fall neatly into the pattern of a preparatory stage and a full learning to read stage. But the child's mental capacities are not the only constraint upon our manipulation of the subject matter. Receptivity of the child to learning is an important consideration. Motivation and background are factors which will determine the child's reaction. And part of this will be the interests of the child (see Table 2).

The teacher

The basic decision which the teacher has to make is whether reading is caught or taught. If the teacher believes that learning to read just happens, then her approach will be fully incidental, although few would deny the need to plan an environment of activities, interests and motivational devices which will guide the child through the stages of learning to read. If, however, the teacher decides that a child must be taught to read by a conscious effort on her part, then a carefully graded programme must be prepared in which specific predetermined methods allow her to intervene in an incidental manner or in which the work is executed more or less according to a time schedule.

The answer to this decision will determine the part played by the teacher—initiator or counsellor—and her preference for one or the other must in turn affect her choice of method.

References

KAGAN, J. (1965) Reflection-impulsivity and reading ability *Child Development* 36

KIENTZLE, M. J. (1946) Properties of learning curves under varied distribution practice *Journal of Experimental Psychology* 36

REED, G. F. Skill in LUNZER, E. A. and MORRIS, J. F. (1968) *Development of Human Learning* Staples Press

ROBERTS, G. R. and LUNZER, E. A. Reading and learning to read in LUNZER, E. A. and MORRIS, J. F. (1968) *Development in Human Learning* Staples Press

TRAVIS, R. C. (1939) Length of practice period and efficiency in motor learning *Journal of Experimental Psychology* 24

WHITEHEAD, A. N. (1962) *The Aims of Education* Benn

Geoffrey R. Roberts

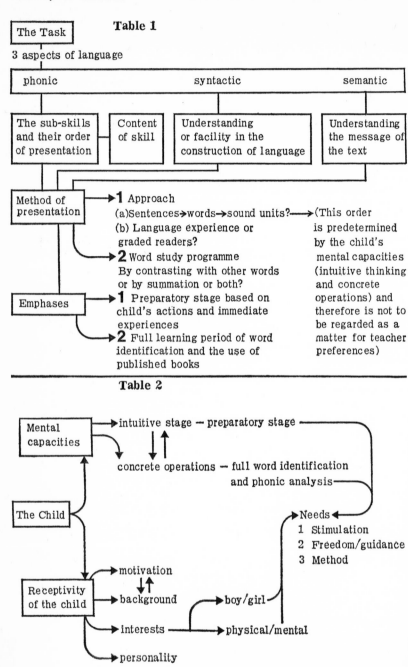

Table 1

The Task

3 aspects of language

phonic	syntactic	semantic

The sub-skills and their order of presentation	Content of skill	Understanding or facility in the construction of language	Understanding the message of the text

Method of presentation

1 Approach
(a) Sentences→words→sound units? → (This order
(b) Language experience or graded readers?
2 Word study programme
By contrasting with other words or by summation or both?

Emphases

1 Preparatory stage based on child's actions and immediate experiences
2 Full learning period of word identification and the use of published books

is predetermined by the child's mental capacities (intuitive thinking and concrete operations) and therefore is not to be regarded as a matter for teacher preferences)

Table 2

Mental capacities → intuitive stage — preparatory stage
concrete operations — full word identification and phonic analysis

The Child

Needs
1 Stimulation
2 Freedom/guidance
3 Method

Receptivity of the child
→ motivation
→ background
→ interests → boy/girl
→ physical/mental
→ personality

5   The intermediate skills

JOHN E. MERRITT
Professor of Educational Studies,
Open University

Paper presented at Sixth Annual Conference of UKRA Nottingham
1969, first published in *Reading skills: Theory and practice*

The first essential in reading is the ability to recognize individual
words on the printed page; that is, the ability to respond to the individual printed word as to the spoken word. If we cannot recognize
the individual words we just cannot read. It seems appropriate, therefore, to designate those complex skills upon which word recognition
depends as 'primary skills'.

A mere mastery of the primary skills does not of course, represent
the ability to read. Comprehending, evaluating and organizing
new facts, impressions and ideas—these are the very essence of reading. We might in fact wish to define reading as 'thinking within the
context of the printed page'. This definition, however, would exclude
the primary skills. What such a definition covers, in effect, is what
we might well term the 'higher order skills'. These are obviously
quite different in kind from the primary skills and their development
poses a separate set of problems for the teacher.

But what of fluency? Where does this fit into the picture? After
all, there are many children who can achieve high scores on word
recognition tests, and who can even comprehend what they so pain-
fully read, but who read haltingly—often one word at a time. That
is to say, they achieve a satisfactory standard in terms of primary
skills and higher order skills, but they are still not efficient readers.
There are other children, often intelligent children, who read fluently
but with little comprehension. In fact, even you and I often read a
passage quite fluently—then realize that we have not understood a
word, although mostly we read fluently and also with comprehension. On the one hand, then, it would appear that fluency involves
more than primary skills, essential as these are, for the ability to
recognize words is no guarantee of fluency. On the other hand it is
clear that the skills which underpin fluency are relatively independent

John E. Merritt

of higher order skills, for it is possible to read fluently without comprehension.

Many writers include both primary skills and higher order skills when discussing fluency. This is an unnecessary confusion, for there is now ample evidence that there exists a separate set of skills which provide the essential basis of fluent reading. These are the skills to which I have referred elsewhere (Merritt 1969) as 'intermediate skills', and I would suggest that an understanding of their nature is essential if we are to develop more effective procedures for developing reading ability.

I should like to stress at the outset that the skills to be described do not represent new discoveries in any sense. The object of this paper is merely to draw together a number of ideas from various sources in a systematic way so that the essentially homogeneous nature of the intermediate skills may be recognized. This, it will be seen, leads to a much better understanding of the reading process itself and should, one may hope, lead to improvements in our teaching of reading.

Let us now consider the four basic questions which have arisen in the foregoing introduction and address ourselves to them in some detail:

1 Are there really such skills as 'intermediate skills'?
2 What is the essential basis of the intermediate skills?
3 How do the intermediate skills function as part of the reading process?
4 What are the implications for teaching?

Question 1 Are there such skills as intermediate skills?

Consider the following three texts and decide which can be read with the greatest fluency:

Text A
The great obstacle the schools face is the simple fact that a court order is required to get anyone into them. This is because an approved school involves an enforced stay for up to three years for training and treatment. The liberty of the subject is involved and therefore the courts regulate the matter.

Text B
The simple school the courts get is the great fact for a court stay is required to face into them. This involves because an approved obstacle is an enforced matter for up to three years of training and subject. The liberty that the treatment is involved and therefore the schools regulate the order.

Text C

school simple the The courts fact is great get to required is face the for court a involves stay This because an matter obstacle approved anyone them into an enforced is up to for three training and years of is treatment involved subject The liberty the that the therefore and school order regulate the.

Of these three passages, it can readily be demonstrated that the easiest to read is Text A. It is read slightly faster than Text B and much faster than Text C. It can also be learned most easily. Text C is hardest on both counts, and Text B falls somewhere between. Why is this so?

Text A is normal prose and makes sense. The words follow in the sort of sequence one would expect. Text C is the same set of words as in Text A but set down in random order.

In Text B the words are the same and the sentence structures are much the same—but adjectives have been switched in position, nouns have been interchanged with other nouns, and so on. The result is that the passage reads almost like normal prose, but makes as much, or as little, sense as the now well-known sentence; 'Colourless green ideas sleep furiously.'

If fluent reading was simply due to the operation of primary skills, Text B would be no easier to read than the random words in Text C. Again, if comprehension provided the essential basis for fluency, Text A would be read very much faster than Text B.

These passages in fact demonstrate quite clearly the decisive difference between reading separate words (using primary skills), reading fluently with comprehension (using higher order skills) and reading fluently with little or no comprehension.

The case that some kind of reading skills operate above the level of primary skills and below the level of higher order skills is obviously substantial. It receives further support when the nature of these skills is examined in some detail.

Question 2   What is the essential basis of the intermediate skills?

The reading of material resembling English to a greater or lesser extent has been studied extensively in the last two decades. Among the texts used are those described as 'approximations to English'.

It is a simple matter to construct texts which approximate more and more closely to English by adopting a procedure based on probability of occurrence, or co-occurrence of words in normal English prose. In the following example, the words were simply chosen at random from a dictionary:

Zero Order   Combat callous irritability migrates depraved temporal prolix alas pillory nautical.

John E. Merritt

In this next example words were chosen at random from a prose text, so that frequency of occurrence is reflected in the selection:

First Order   Day to is for they have proposed I the it materials of are its go studies the hour of the following.

Some words tend to go together quite frequently in normal prose, whilst other pairs are unusual, 'dark' and 'night' for example go together frequently, as do 'filing' and 'cabinet'. This frequency of co-occurrence is known as 'collocation'. The next example, therefore, reflects this tendency for words to collocate in pairs in normal English prose:

Second Order   Goes down here are not large feet are the happy days and so what is dead weight what many were constructed.

Of course words do not just go together in pairs. In the next example the selection of each word reflects the probability of its following the previous three words:

Fourth Order   We are going to see him is not to chuckle loudly and depart for home. (These examples are from G. A. Miller 1957).

Texts can thus be constructed at a variety of levels, or 'orders of approximation to English'.

It has been found with such texts that increasing the order of approximation to English leads to a tendency to improvement on certain kinds of task, e.g. reading aloud, recalling after an interval, filling in missing elements and typing. Even from casual reading of these examples it is evident that the higher order approximations are read more easily than are the lower order approximations and these gains continued until something like a tenth of approximation is reached.

Now these findings are very interesting but their significance cannot be understood without a study of what it is that produces the effects we have noted. Transitional probabilities—the probabilities relating to the co-occurrence of the words—do not tell us very much. They merely provide one level of description: a purely statistical level. We must examine the relationships between the words in a number of ways if we are to understand what we have been considering.

Epstein (1961) set out to study the influence of syntactic structure independently of meaningfulness and independently of word co-occurence. He did this by contrasting sentences of nonsense syllables such as the following:

1 The yigs wur vumly rixing hum in jegest miv.
2 Yigs rixing wur miv hum vumly the in jegest.

1 and 2 consist of the same set of nonsense syllables, plus two functional words which have no referential meaning: 'the' and 'in'. In both cases the nonsense syllables have grammatical tags, such as *-ly* on adverbs and *-s* on plural nouns. The only difference between

sentences 1 and 2 is that whilst the former is readily seen to be grammatically structured, the latter is in random order.

In a carefully controlled experiment, Epstein found that his subjects took significantly less time to learn sentences of Type 1 than they took to learn sentences of Type 2. From this and other related experiments it can be seen that the ability to respond to syntactic sequences is an important aid to learning. It seems highly likely that the actual reading of such material is similarly facilitated by the ability to respond to syntactic sequences, and that this is one of the features to which we respond in reading approximations to English.

Two other types of text used by Epstein were as follows:

3 lazy paper stumbled to shallow trees loudly from days
4 loudly trees paper from days lazy shallow stumbled

Both of these are meaningless sentences and the level of collocation is very low. Whereas 3 is syntactically structural, however, the words in 4 are randomly ordered.

Needless to say Type 1 sentences were most easily learned. (The reader should consider these results in relation to his assessment of the Texts A, B and C presented earlier in the discussion of Question 1.) Clearly the syntactic features are important irrespective of the transitional probabilities that exist between the individual words. Syntax is, as it were, brought in accidentally and by the back door in the construction of purely statistical approximates to English.

It is interesting to note that the syntactically structured nonsense syllables of Type 1 were as readily learned as the randomly ordered real words of Type 4 sequences. The importance of the phrase unit in sentence processing was demonstrated by Herriott (1967).

Perhaps all of this seems a little laboured. It is always wise to adduce evidence, even when dealing with what seems obvious, for all too often things are not what they seem. Nevertheless, there seems little doubt of the importance of syntactic structures in fluent reading, although more direct evidence is still required.

What we have found so far is that approximations to English provide a tool for demonstrating the importance of sequence in reading. It is the ability to respond to various kinds of sequence which characterize the intermediate skills. But more refined tools are needed to identify the different kinds of sequence which may be involved, as well as their relative importance. What follows is an attempt to isolate some of these types of sequence and the effects of their interaction.

1 *Letter sequences*

a i -BCDE *ii* AB-DE *iii* ABCD-
b i -CEGI *ii* AD-JM *iii* AEIM-

E

John E. Merritt

In these examples it is perfectly easy to fill in the missing letter from our previous knowledge of the alphabetic sequence and our observation of the intervals between the letters in each sequence. Our experience of the alphabet is that the sequence is invariable so we can be absolutely confident in our judgment.

If, however, there are many possible sequences, as in our written language, we become less confident. Let us see what happens, then, when we introduce a degree of uncertainty into the pattern. We can do this by considering the following letter sequences as representing sounds.

2 *Phonemic sequences*

a ---apstibal   *b* Pru---tical   *c* Cadigul---

Imagine these are words which you have not previously enountered and try to guess the missing sounds. You will notice that the range of possibilities is still distinctly limited. (To be purely phonemic, of course, it would be necessary for the sequences to be presented orally with, say, a tapping noise to indicate the number of missing sounds.)

Now, would everyone, young and old, able or less able, give the same range of possible answers as you produced yourself? If not, would they all give such different answers that no general pattern could be perceived? Or would the answers tend to be limited in number and similar in principle? The reader should note his own solution and then try the sequences on children and/or adults in such numbers as he finds necessary in order to arrive at a conclusion.

If the items are presented as unfamiliar words with letters (or sounds) missing—and, indeed, even without this clue—you will find that the alternative solutions will tend to be limited in number and similar in principle. Why?

Because, just as we are familiar with the alphabetic sequence, so we are familiar with certain kinds of phonemic sequence. We expect certain sequences of sounds to occur or not to occur at the beginning of words, in the middle of words, or at the end of words. The length of the word affects what we expect in any given position, as does the stress pattern determined by the spelling. All the possible combinations are not equally likely to occur. Some, in our experience, are very common; others are less common. If each individual you could conveniently test was to write down all possible solutions in order of probability there would not doubt be a marked similarity between the various lists. This is because your subjects would all belong to the same speech community and have had roughly similar experiences in terms of the phonemic sequences in the language they have heard and use.

66

3 *Word sequences (collocation)*

    a Bus...............   *b* Good ....   *c* Try ....

Asked to supply the missing word in the above examples, 'bus stop', 'good luck' and 'try hard' would be found to figure fairly frequently among the various possible alternatives. 'Bus carburettor', 'good haystacks' and 'try synthetics', whilst quite unexceptionable as collocates, are, as we saw earlier, unlikely to be offered. Transitional probability, therefore, is not to be dismissed as unimportant. It is one of the factors which assist fluency.

Taking words that occur with very high frequency in speech and writing, Atkinson (1967) found that even in children's writing the lowest number of different collocates to follow a 'key word' (after MacNally 1962) was 94. This was the number of different words bound to follow the word 'that'. There were 696 different collocates for the word 'the'. On the other hand, certain pairing did occur sufficiently frequently to be worthy of note. 'And we', 'I was', 'in the', 'of the', 'was a', were among the high frequency pairings. Merritt (1968) found that when these key words were presented in a random sequence it took much longer for children to read the text than when the same words were presented in a highly collocated sequence. These findings would appear to refute the statement by Robins (1967) that for such words ('the', 'a', 'if', 'when' and so on) collocation is not a relevant part of the statement of their use.

Significant as these findings may be for very common words, it seems likely that the vast majority of words have so many collocates that collocation by itself is not likely to offer much assistance to the reader. Before leaving collocation, however, let us just notice the effect of combining collocation and a very small additional cue:

4 *Collocation plus structural cues:*

    a Bus c--------.   *b* Good l---.   *c* Try h---.

Immediately any additional cues are given, in this case the initial letter of the missing word plus word length, the range of possibilities becomes severely restricted. The interaction between collocation and what is called in programmed learning a structural prompt is clearly much greater than the influence of either cue in isolation. Not, for example, that c--------, l---, or h--- by themselves produce no instant response, for the number of possibilities is very much wider than when the constraint of a preceding word is present. Similarly, there were quite a number of possibilities when the cue word was simply followed by a space in examples 3a, b and c. Clearly the whole, in this case the actual combination of word and letters, is greater than the mere sum of the parts.

These observations are consistent with the findings of Pollack

John E. Merritt

(1964). Pollack, however, used whole sentences with varying amounts of structural cueing. The inclusion of a whole sentence introduces additional factors which will be dealt with below.

5 *Grammatical structure*

a .... exist.   b They ....

In 5, we can see that a plural noun, or certain pronouns may complete the sentence, i.e. both form and class of the missing word are restricted by the grammatical structure.

In 5b, we note that only a verb can fill the empty slot, and that it must be plural—if there should be a separate plural form. Tense, on the other hand is not determined, except that there is no extra slot available for an auxiliary verb, and this does limit the possibilities to some extent.

In any incomplete construction, then, the grammatical features limit the range of words that can be inserted into the empy slot in terms of form and class. Sometimes the degree of limitation may be slight, whilst in some cases only a very limited range of possibilities may be left open.

6 *Semantic field*

a Yesterday, Tom Smith went to Swenston by ....
b Tom Smith went to the bus stop and got on the ....

In example 6a, as in examples 5a and 5b, grammatical structure determines the form and class of the missing word. In this case, the missing word must be a noun, so the area of choice is at least limited to the extent that all non-nouns are excluded. Likely collocates of the word 'by' relegate some of these nouns to low levels of expectancy but this still leaves the area of choice very wide. However, a mere glance at the example above shows that choice is in fact restricted mainly to nouns representing certain forms of transport. In example 6b, the choice is even more restricted and alternatives to the response 'bus' would be rare. Clearly, the additional information comes from meaning—but how?

In order to gain a little insight into how meaning operates in this sort of situation let us note that 'Tom Smith' obviously refers to a member of the class of male human beings and he may well be Anglo-Saxon in origin or culture. What we are likely to say about him or think about him is therefore restricted by our experience of Anglo-Saxon males. The term 'went' relates to travel or transport. Thus our expectancies are based on our experience relating to kinds of transport. Swenston is evidently a geographical location and is possibly a populated area. It has a western rather than an oriental flavour. Expectancies relating to camel or elephant transport, therefore would be less likely than for other modes of transport. Our association of each word with other items in the semantic field to which this word belongs makes certain pairs of associations more likely than others. This is similar to collocation except that we are here concerned with associations between groups of categories of words within which the items may be said to belong to the same semantic field, rather than with pairs of single words. 'Man—travel—city—by ....' can now be seen as a stimulus which, as a result of previous experience, can produce such expectancies as train, car, bicycle etc. This represents a massive restriction of possible responses, and to the extent that this occurs, one may predict increase in speed of word recognition and hence of fluency (Morton 1964).

Let us note that 'Swenston—(by)—travelled—Tom Smith ....' on the other hand, could have elicited quite a large number of associative responses, e.g. 'gratefully', 'quickly', 'tried', 'too' etc (Carroll 1964). In example 6a, therefore, whilst it might have seemed at first that semantic field played the dominant role, since its introduction reduced the area of choice so massively, we can see that this was largely due to the important restrictions already imposed by grammar and collocation.

Let us take a final look at examples in which a variety of cues can be seen operating in combination:

7 Combined cues

 a Tom Smith went to Swenston by b--.
 b Tom Smith went to Swenston by --a--.
 c Tom Smith went to Swenston by --r.
 d Tom Smith went to Swenston by ----pl---.

In these examples few competent readers would respond with words other than 'bus', 'train', 'car' and 'aeroplane', respectively. As in example 4, a careful examination shows that the limitation cannot be attributed to any one cue, or to a simple addition of cues, but to the effect of their interaction (Pollack op. cit, and Wilson 1964).

The enormous influence of the interaction of cues, as distinct from their separate contributions, is not at first easy to understand. Fortunately, a simple model makes the reason patently clear.

Let us suppose that we have an individual with a very limited vocabulary. Let us assume that his vocabulary is, in fact, restricted to the words shown in the box below. Let us also suppose that he can respond to grammatical features. This means that, somehow or other, his brain is capable of sorting out words in the way represented schematically on the diagram.

Consider the possibilities available to this reader given the following sentence: a big, bonny bo

From the point of view of sentence structure it is highly unlikely

John E. Merritt

that anything other than a noun would follow two successive adjectives. This reduces the choice to those words in the noun row, i.e. to twelve words. From the point of view of letter sequence, the choice is restricted to the nine words in the 'bo' column.

	a	bi / \ bo	i	
article	a			
adjective	artistic accurate athletic	big bizarre binary	bold both bonny	imperturbable impressive ineffable
noun	angel aunt arch	bin biscuit bicycle	boy book bottle	idea item igloo
verb	attempt ask applaud	bind bisect bid	bounce bowl boggle	identify illuminate impart
preposition	at	by		in

But, when the two criteria are put together, 'noun' plus 'bo', the choice is clearly not 12+9=21 words. The choice is restricted to those words which satisfy the criteria on *both* counts, i.e., the 3 words at the intersection of the 'noun' row and the 'bo' column.

If we were to add collocation, or semantic field, to the diagram, the choice would be reduced even further. It would reduce to one word, 'boy', with a higher degree of confidence. Thus, every additional criterion massively reduces the area of choice and increases confidence in accurate prediction.

Even with a very large vocabulary, the ability to respond to the sort of sequences outlined above permits the reader to predict subsequent words and phrases with a high degree of confidence. And the more familiar the sequence presented, the more accurate the predictions will become. So much is clear from the reader's own experience in tackling the examples provided.

We can now see that the essential basis of the intermediate skills is the ability to respond simultaneously to a variety of kinds of sequence. Just as we can respond simultaneously to a variety of attributes of a single object, so we can respond to a variety of attributes of a speech sequence. Thus we can respond to a speech sequence at the level of sound, syntax and meaning simultaneously just as we can respond to a ball in terms of its roundness, speed and hardness simultaneously at the time of catching it in flight, making whatever adjustments are called for by each attribute.

We can now look more closely, in the case of the intermediate skills, at the nature of the response itself.

Question 3   How do the intermediate skills function as part of the reading process?

Let us summarize what we have discovered up to this point. What we have found so far is that one of the responses to a word is the anticipation of the next word. Similarly, one of the responses to a letter or a phoneme is the anticipation of the next letter, or the next phoneme. One of the responses of a group of words, syntactically structured, is the anticipation of the form and class of the next word. Word meanings, too, determine the kinds of word we may anticipate.

The anticipation is based to a large extent on transitional probability—the frequency with which these items or classes of items have followed each other in our previous experience. Thus the interaction of all the different cues produces a massive curtailment of possibilities, and even when restriction to a single word is not achieved, the probabilities create a hierarchy within the small range of words that are left.

Now there is a great deal of psychological evidence to show that speed of visual recognition is increased as the area of search is reduced. One would hardly have expected otherwise. The anticipations we have been considering do precisely this—they reduce the area of search. It is evidently for this reason that recognition of each successive word is speeded up when context cues are used effectively in fluent reading.

This immediately moves the emphasis in teaching reading to the development of all those skills which lead to accurate anticipation. We do not, of course, abandon the primary skills. What we must realize, however, is that to develop these whilst neglecting the intermediate skills is to teach reading in a thoroughly unbalanced way.

Let us take the argument a stage further. If we are anticipating on a basis of many cues that one or a very small number of words may follow, we are, as it were, arousing in the brain a set of models of some kind against which to match each successive unit we perceive. The act of reading therefore appears to be one of prediction and model-matching. This makes a sharp contrast with the concept of word building which most people would entertain in thinking of word recognition.

The intermediate skills then, function in advance of the recogni-

John E. Merritt

tion of individual words by making readily available to the reader a limited number of possibilities against which each successive word may be checked. Because they provide so much information, only the briefest inspection of the predicted word is often necessary. Missing words, missing letters or misspellings then provide little hindrance to the fluent reader, as is demonstrated in the following passage:

If yuo are a fl--nt reodur yu wlll heve no difticllty reoding th:s.

Sometimes an incorrect word is predicted and failure to check carefully leads to an awareness of error some letters later. In this case, the word incorrectly read has contributed to an anticipation concerning the later words which is then found to be inaccurate. Intermediate skills have an additional function in reading then, in that they assist in the discovery of errors of word recognition, errors to which they themselves may contribute.

Yet another function of the intermediate skills is that they facilitate the recognition of words not already in the sight vocabulary. How else could children learn to read new words in the face of the anomalies of English spelling? Try for example to determine what this word says, using the sort of phonic rules available to children: baced.

It is the combination of intermediate skills with the unreliable cues provided by the spelling that assist the child to solve the problem. In the following context the child should have no difficulty: Tom is my very baced friend.*

Finally, let us note what has been implicit in an exposition which has been devoted largely to the effect of the intermediate skills on reading successive words.

In so far as the intermediate skills relate to sequences they are concerned, we may suppose, not merely with the anticipation of each successive word, or successive slot, but with the anticipation of groups of words and sentence structures. We may also suppose that as more of any given sentence is read, its completed form will be anticipated with increasing confidence. Again, the concept we must have of this process is one of prediction and model matching, not some sort of building operation once all the individual bits have been collected. And if the child cannot anticipate the pattern of the sentence then we may expect his comprehension to be commensurately reduced (Loban 1963).

In summary we may say that intermediate skills simplify the problems of word recognition by activating a limited number of possible models against which the visual stimulus, i.e. the printed word, can be checked. This includes models of sentence structure

*The word of course is *best*. The spelling adopted here uses sound-symbol relationships of very high frequency, eg **a**ny ni**ce** pass**ed** etc.

72

within which the words can be organized to permit their subsequent comprehension.

NB It must be noted that certain rather complex issues have not been pursued in this analysis. What has been presented has been selected as being most likely to be helpful to the practising teacher.

Question 4   What are the implications for teaching?

Just as concentration on the primary skills leads to an unbalanced programme, so an excessive emphasis on intermediate skills and neglect of the higher order skills would lead to an unsatisfactory diet. Indeed, in making the foregoing analysis I suffered considerable discomfort as I thought of pencils being sharpened ready for the task of preparing mechanical exercises for children to perform like so many well trained monkeys! It is the old story. An area is analysed and many teachers will painstakingly follow the analysis in the construction of their programme. What I would suggest is the very reverse. Decide what sort of educational experiences young children should have, then, within this context, decide how best to develop the individual skills as the opportunities can be created.

On this cautionary note we may attempt the task of considering some detailed procedures for developing the intermediate skills. We must hope that in doing so we shall not ourselves stray so far from the routes between productive educational cases that we get lost in the desert of arid drills!

There are two aspects to be considered. One is the language experience of the reader. The other is the language of the material read. The greater discrepancy between the two, the more difficult the reading becomes. Whereas the emphasis has previously been placed on the vocabulary of reading books, it is evident that we must now pay much more attention to language structure (Strickland 1962). If the patterns of language structure are not familiar to the child he cannot correctly anticipate. If he cannot anticipate with reasonable success then he is habituating himself to neglecting context cues and consolidating habits of word by word attack. By so doing he is learning, positively, not to read fluently.

Once again, a laboured point. But the busy teacher is liable to forget that the child is learning something with every breath he takes and with every word he reads. Unsupervised, he is as liable to consolidate bad habits as he is to establish good habits. In reading, unfortunately, he often has more opportunities to learn the former.

It is clearly essential to develop the child's effective experience of language as a first priority so that he can cope with a variety of texts. Such experience should be a central feature in any curriculum and without it many children will be severely handicapped in all their learning. The problems of providing effective language experience however, although central, will not be dealt with here, for they present a general educational problem and require more extensive treatment than can be encompassed in this paper. We must, alas, restrict ourselves to more mundane matters—a consideration of reading texts, and the child's interaction with these texts.

Commercially produced printed texts

With regard to the commercially produced printed texts, there is no obvious reason why children of almost any age should not be as concerned about their suitability as we are. Neither is there any obvious reason why they should not be allowed to assess texts for themselves. On the one hand, the assessment of texts is a big job, and the busy teacher really has not got the time to do it thoroughly without help. On the other hand, genuine involvement in the task means increased motivation for the pupil as well as increased insight into the problem.

But what techniques can be used for assessing the readability of texts. There are a number of statistical formulae for assessing readability and an interested teacher may wish to try these. A more promising technique, however, is that of the 'Cloze procedure'. All that this entails is the deletion of say every tenth word in a sample of the text. The children then try to guess the missing word. The percentage of correct guesses provides an estimate of the difficulty of the text for the individual child, or, if averaged, for a given group of children. The children can prepare the texts for each other and do virtually all the work. They can then form their own opinions as to what sort of percentage of correct responses renders a book readable.

Every aspect of this exercise—from the preliminary planning to the final analysis—provides opportunities for educational experiences of the highest order. The sensitive teacher will not need any elaboration on the possibilities which this situation provides.

In terms of our immediate objectives, all the available reading material can be assessed for readability over a period of time—backed by the teacher's personal judgment on the basis of the evidence provided by the children. The information may be stored so that the children or the teacher can refer to it at any time.

Other sources of reading material

Much of the printed material currently available is unsatisfactory from many points of view for disadvantaged children—and even for more fortunate children. One of the best sources of reading material is of course the work of other children. Many of the projects undertaken by children provide for more satisfactory reading than the textbooks covering the same ground. Apart from being more meaningful, because they can be interpreted in terms of the children's own experiences, the patterns of language structure are much better matched to the patterns used by other children.

The exchange of material of this kind between schools is due for an enormous expansion in the next decade and can be justified on broad educational grounds (cf Merritt 1966). The opportunities it provides for stimulating effective reading and a genuine interest in reading and language are wide (cf Leybourn 1968).

Whilst providing every opportunity for the development of higher order skills, exchanges of this kind provide material that is ideal from the point of view of the development of intermediate skills. All the context cues inherent in such material are of the kind that can be aid to elicit anticipatory responses on the part of the child. Obviously, his chances of predicting from a context written by a child of similar age and experience are much higher than they are when reading material written by an adult. When adult material is predictable it is all too often condescending or banal.

It will be some time before there is sufficient material of this kind available in every school to make a significant impact on reading. However, all such material should be retained, stored and indexed for ready retrieval (an important exercise in its own right), and this will provide the basis for a resource unit which will improve in quality over the years as successive classes work over the material, edit it, and substitute superior work.

The child's interaction with the texts

The sorts of activity already proposed will almost certainly produce a greater improvement in intermediate skills than any specific teaching procedures are likely to provide. This does not mean, however, that specific procedures are unnecessary. On the contrary, such procedures are essential for sharpening imperfectly established concepts and for refining skills as yet crudely formed. If they fail to do this it is because the procedures are badly designed, badly timed, or too crudely implemented.

It is my intention here merely to draw attention to some procedures which seem to be most relevant to the development of intermediate skills, but it will always be the teacher's job to select, and to ensure that he does not fall foul of the criticisms listed above.

1 The Text B response

Children at the secondary stage, and many primary schoolchildren, are perfectly capable of participating in a little experiment in which they compare their fluency, and ease of recall, using texts of the kind presented in the discussion of Question 1 at the beginning of this paper. In discussing the results of such an experiment, designed by the children themselves, one child said that Text B reminded him of most textbooks he read in school! This needless to say provided an

impeccable beginning for a discussion of the reading process, and
the ways in which reading might be improved. We should surely
interest children in the nature of the reading process itself. This
particular experiment is one excellent way of doing so.

2 Sentence completion

Research by Loban (1968) showed that almost all children used all
six basic sentence patterns. Their difficulties arise in handling complexities within these basic patterns. One of the most important
things for children to learn is that single words, and groups of words
may be functionally equivalent, e.g. that a noun phrase has the same
function as a noun, that a verb phrase has the same function as a
verb, and so on.

In order to establish a learning set of this kind it is essential that
children should have ample opportunity for seeing that sentences
may be completed in a variety of acceptable ways. Exercises which
provide such opportunities, rather than those to which there is a
single correct solution, are more likely to be of most value. The more
the children discuss their various solutions under the teacher's
guidance, the more likely it is that they will develop the necessary
insight and linguistic skill.

There are two ways of approaching this problem. One is to start by
deleting the smallest parts of a sentence, i.e. single words, letting
children fill in the gaps with as much elaboration as they wish. The
other is to begin by deleting larger units, e.g. subjects or predicates.
There is a good reason for suspecting that the latter (i.e., deletion of
larger units) may be slightly preferable, for the deletion of the subject of a sentence, or the predicate, helps the child to see the fundamental structure of the sentence.

Recent work by Clark and Begun (1968) has shown the importance of left to right processing of sentences, although a different
form of processing (hierarchical processing) does occur at the same
time. Their research confirmed the view that the linguistic unit which
occurs first in the sentence is the most important thematically. This
means that the deletion of the first part of a sentence restricts the
possible endings to a much greater extent than deletion of the second
part restricts the possible beginnings. This might mean that deletion
of predicates provides an easier task for children than does the deletion of subjects.

The object of all this is not, of course, to teach grammar in any
formal sense. The formal teaching of grammar has never been shown
to increase competence in either writing or reading. The object is
simply to increase the child's sensitivity to sentence structure.

3 Cloze Procedure

This may be used as a teaching tool, as well as for the purpose of

assessing texts. The reader might like to complete the following
examples (Cloze procedure: non-selective deletion):

a *Tenth word deletion*
  Looking around the dining room as we finished lunch
  had to agree that the teenage girls all looked   the same to me.
  Some were spotty, some fat,   quite dishy. But which ranked
  as deprived and which   was a judgment I would hesitate to
  make.
     Answers: I: much: some: depraved

b *Eighth word deletion*
  No one I met in the approved   system even accepted that
  such a distinction   . The public row which developed around
  the   of the teenage girl at Swenston who   alleged to
  have had an affair with   married man turned primarily on
  this point.   girl had done nothing wrong in law   why
  should she be punished?
     Answers: school: existed: committal: was: a: The: so

c *Sixth word deletion*
  As an argument it has   the approved schools pretty sore.
       is, they argue, a complete   of their role—yet a
  assistant prison governor now working   child care could say
  to   : 'Oh, I know they're   to be for treatment and
       , but you can't get   from the fact that the   is
  there, and rightly.'
     Answers: left: It: misunderstanding: former: in: me:
                 supposed: training: away: stigma

The increase of difficulty with higher frequency of deletion is
fairly clear. It would seem to be a good idea to start children off on
the easier texts, then increase the frequency of deletion so that they
are constantly challenged, but never humiliated, by the level of
difficulty.

Again, children should gain absolute approval for wholly acceptable responses. The 'correct' answers may certainly be produced, but
they should be critically evaluated. It will quite often be found that
a child's offering is actually superior to the original, and this discovery can be highly motivating for the child.

Discussion of results is of the utmost importance in this exercise
as has been suggested by Schneyer (1965). This can be individual,
or it can be a class exercise. In the latter case, less able children will
often find unexpected opportunities for gaining approval, for with
the sentence being read aloud from time to time they can often
produce perfectly satisfactory solutions even with more difficult
material. This exercise, incidentally, can be as stimulating for adults
as for comparatively young children.

Although investigations of this kind of exercise have been concerned with developing comprehension, the abilities called into play are clearly those we have termed intermediate skills. Comprehension requires much training in addition to that which would be provided by this sort of exercise. There is no reason, of course, why one should not go on to provide this additional training using the same material. Indeed, this would seem to be a very sensible course. But that is another story.

As a variation, structural prompts may be inserted, e.g. initial letters or digraphs, dashes to indicate the number of letters etc. This has the disadvantage of eliciting a convergent, rather than a divergent response. It is not advisable therefore to give such cues until the children have acquired the habit of responding to functional equivalence, as evidenced by their ability to supply words of appropriate form and class. Once they can do this however, the training to pay strict attention to the structural prompts should pay dividends in the development of reading accuracy.

Once accuracy has been well established it may be worthwhile to introduce a speeded exercise — on the other hand, I suspect that well-conceived training in the use of intermediate skills, together with an actual need to read more quickly, is likely to produce the best results. This, however, is a matter for thorough investigation rather than speculation.

4 *Highlighting techniques*

The use of bold face for highlighting key words, and the underlining or italicizing of phrases, have been demonstrated as aiding comprehension and retention respectively (cf experiments by Dearborn, Johnson and Carmichael (1949) and Klare, Malory and Gustafson (1955), cited in Spencer (1968)). Colour highlighting would no doubt be equally effective. The underlining technique seems the most practical for the reader to consider.

A good test of a child's ability to recognize the structure of a sentence would be to get him to underline those aspects of the construction he has been learning in sentence completion tasks. His efforts can then be checked by other children who are at the same stage of development. Again, group discussion, sensitively handled, may be of great value.

Once a set of texts has been prepared in this way, they can be read by children at a lower level of development. For these children the underlining provides a cue for recognizing the structure of the sentences and provides supplementary experiences to run parallel with sentence completion exercises at the same level.

Summary

Identification of the intermediate skills and understanding of their contribution to the reading process leads to a more precise understanding of the function of different kinds of teaching procedure. It also permits a more accurate assessment of the needs of the individual child. Although a beginning has been made in the development of diagnostic instruments (Merritt 1968), the best diagnosis is that which derives from the observation of a knowledgeable teacher noting the performance of children on well-designed material. It is hoped that this paper will contribute to the teacher's understanding of this area of skill—and to his understanding of his pupil's reading needs.

References

ATKINSON, D. (1968) A study of the written vocabulary of children of high and low socio-economic groups *Diploma dissertation* Durham Institute of Education

BLOOMER, R. H. (1962) The Cloze Procedure as a remedial reading exercise *Journal of Developmental Reading* 5

CLARK, H. and BEGUN, S. J. (1968) The use of syntax in understanding sentences *British Journal of Psychology* 59, 3

EPSTEIN, W. (1961) The influence of syntactic structure on learning *American Journal of Psychology* 74

HERRIOTT, P. (1967) Phrase units and the recall of grammatically structured nonsense *British Journal of Psychology* 58, 3 and 4

LEYBOURN, M. J. (1968) A simple language experience programme in *ACE Forum on Teaching Reading in junior and secondary schools* Ginn

LOBAN, W. D. (1963) The language of elementary school children *NCTE Research Report* 1

McNALLY, J. and MURRAY, W. (1962) *Key Words to Literacy* Curriculum studies 3 Schoolmaster Publishing Co

MERRITT, J. E. (1969) Developing competence in reading comprehension in *Improving Reading throughout the world* International Reading Association

MERRITT, J. E. (1969) Reading skills reexamined *Special Education* 58, 1

MILLER, G. A. (1951) *Language and Communication* McGraw-Hill

MORTON, J. (1964) A model for continuous language behaviour *Language and speech* 7

POLLACK, I. (1964) Interaction of two sources of verbal context in word identification *Language and speech* 7

ROBINS, R. H. (1964) *General Linguistics: an introductory survey* Longmans

John E. Merritt

Ruddell, R. B. (1965) The effect of oral and written patterns of language structure on reading comprehension *The Reading Teacher* 18

Schneyer, J. W. (1965) Use of the Cloze procedure for improving reading comprehension *The Reading Teacher* 19

Spencer, H. (1968) *The Visible Word* Lund Humphreys

Strickland, R. G. (1962) The language of elementary school children *Bulletin of the school of education* Indiana University

Wilson, T. W. (1964) The effect of method, type, position and size of letter deletion on syllabic redundancy in written English words University of Georgia Dissertation available from University Microfilms Inc, 313 North First Street, Ann Arbour, Michigan

6 Reading through the grades

ELIZABETH THORN
North Bay Teachers College,
Ontario

Paper presented at Fourth Annual Conference of UKRA Nottingham
1967, first published in *Reading: Problems and perspectives*

My purpose in this paper is to comment on *what* must be achieved
through modern reading instruction, and to offer some suggestions
for the development of a total school reading programme to meet
these ends.

That improvement in current practice is needed, and has been
needed, is self-evident. While the entire history of reading instruction has been one of criticism, evaluation and change, the changes
have not always kept pace with the demands placed upon reading
by society. In recent years there have been renewed efforts to
improve reading instruction and raise the literacy level of the western
world.

Of major importance is the current trend to promote reading programmes through all the grades, to acknowledge that we can no
longer assume that reading skills have been mastered when a child
has been in school for three years, to recognize that infant teachers,
junior teachers and secondary teachers are equally teachers of reading. In addition, there is a new concern with reading in the total context of language development which has led to emphasis on the
thinking skills of reading rather than the mechanics of word perception.

A total school reading programme can only be explored in the
light of the objectives of the whole curriculum—hopefully, objectives
which are changing in accord with modern needs. For generations
the purpose of education was to have the pupil remember what he
was told or had read—'to acquire a body of knowledge.' Today's
purpose is to have the pupil develop ways of thinking through his
own problems; problems he faces as a student and problems he will
face as an adult.

Our technological society places a tremendous emphasis on this
ability to think; the person with a low level of thinking ability finds

his job taken over by a machine. The schools have met the demands for a thinking populace by developing new programmes in science, in mathematics, in geography—programmes based on principles of inquiry and discovery, programmes placing primary emphasis on the ability of the individual to think through a problem. Modern curricula recognize that in the face of the 'knowledge explosion' the school's task cannot be to teach children the sum total of knowledge but to teach them how to cope with it.

Reading has a vital role to play in this kind of education. The question that arises is whether or not reading instruction has moved in harmony with the advances in other areas. Has reading instruction focused attention on thinking? On ideas rather than words?

Teachers of reading must recognize the new demands being placed on reading and adjust instruction to meet them. The answer does not lie in debating the values of one alphabet as opposed to another, or the phonic method as opposed to the whole word method. Rather we must broaden our scope and consider the role of reading itself in life today, a role that is changing, that is going to change.

I have heard it said that reading is on its way out—that before long the content of books will be recorded and listened to rather than read. This may be, but I am not prepared to accept it, if for no other reason than that only reading allows communication while at the same time providing escape from the world of noise we live in. I am more in accord with those who feel reading is being re-placed rather than replaced. Our public librarians note, for example, that their young patrons tend to use books more and more as sources of information, as research tools; much more of their reading is directed by a specific purpose; less time is spent 'just reading' than was common in the past. Yet is this not to be expected when they have ready access to television, motion pictures, record players, radio? When sports and club activities are zealously organized for them? We cannot deny that these are essential and valuable parts of our culture; we cannot suggest that children are wrong to turn to them for some of the satisfactions that we as youngsters found in books. And yet there are still only twenty-four hours in a day. Some adjustments must be made. Teachers cannot say to today's young people, 'You must use reading as I have used it.' We must lead them instead to identify its place in their world—a world of television and space exploration; a world that has no place in its work force for the illiterate; a world that cannot afford an unthinking and unknowing population.

Dr Francis Chase (1964) has referred to the two levels of illiteracy threatening the world today. An obvious problem is the illiteracy of hordes of people in underdeveloped countries; perhaps the more serious problem is what Dr Chase describes as 'the higher level of illiteracy.'

The higher illiterate can absorb and repeat ideas found on the printed page but he has not developed the ability to relate these ideas to the life around him. He does not engage in the kind of dialogue which will test the relevance of what he has read to his own personal experience, to the lives of those he meets, or to the behaviour of individuals and social groups in general. He does not know how to bring about the conscious interplay between ideas previously encountered and the content of what is being read at the moment. He does not raise the sharp questions which probe the content of reading for meaning, test it for accuracy and penetration, and weigh its implications for himself and for society. He cannot entertain ideas which are at variance with his preconceptions of the 'nature of things', or see other individuals, groups and nations in any light except that of his own self-interest. He lacks the courage to consider ideas which seem threatening to cherished beliefs or vested interests. He is unable to enter appreciatively into values, modes of behaviour, and points of view arising in cultures other than that in which he has been nurtured. In short, for the higher illiterate, reading is not an invitation to reflective thought. It does not arouse an active process of relating the abstractions on the printed page to persons, events, and institutions of the real world; it does not lead to an internal reorganization of ideas previously received or the establishment of receptivity to other new ideas; and it does not become a seizing of the present moment to extract from past experience insights into the future. (Chase 1961)

It would seem that Dr Chase has outlined the true worth of reading in our lives and presented a challenge to all of us as teachers, a challenge to cultivate the process of reflective thought so that all our students read or experience sharpens their perception of the world.
To accomplish this, a first essential is a thoughtful reading programme encompassing all school grades. The five- or six-year-old beginning to read is just as capable of reflective thought as is the adult—if he is provided with reading experiences that fit into his conceptual framework. Indeed, it is vital that he be taught so that he accepts reading in this role from the very beginning lest he develop habits of reading mechanically, unthinkingly. The college student, too, needs and profits from reading instruction that promotes reflective thought. It seems folly, at any level, to assume that a reader faced with new experiences and new reading challenges will be able to meet those challenges and engage in the kind of thinking demanded by the material and the situation as adequately without instruction as with it. It would follow that the school should accept the responsibility for providing for all students in its charge

the necessary reading instruction to facilitate a meeting of minds between children and authors.

In contemplating the organization of such a reading programme the key words must be 'continuity', 'sequence', and 'integration'. 'Continuity', in that important skills and abilities are given recurring emphasis throughout the curriculum. For example, if we agree that a reader should learn to evaluate the accuracy of what he reads, it is essential that from month to month and year to year he be given continuing opportunities to practise and develop this ability. 'Sequence' is similar to, but more than, continuity. Sequence refers to the importance of having each application of a skill build upon the previous one, increasing the breadth and depth of that application. It steers us away from the danger of repeating an activity over and over again with material at the same level of difficulty, steers us away from producing 'good readers of easy material' and ensures growth towards maturity in reading. 'Integration' refers to the importance of teaching skills or subjects, not in isolation, but as a part of a child's total experience. This is especially true in reading instruction, for language (hence reading) is the unifying force that ties together all that the child thinks and feels and is. Reading is not, cannot be a subject isolated either from the mainstream of language development or from its true content which should be found in the child's experience. Reading instruction must become a part of each activity of the day.

It is obviously going to be difficult to organize something as personal as language and reading on a 'grade' basis. Continuity, sequence and integration are essential—but for each individual. We need not have 'grade' programmes just because we have signs on classroom doors saying first grade or fourth grade or seventh grade. Nor do we necessarily have a completely individualized pattern of instruction. Within any class, groups with common interests, abilities, needs, will take form and the teacher will capitalize on this in her instruction. But we cannot fit children into grade moulds. When I speak of first grade or fourth grade programmes, I will be referring to a level of reading development rather than the work of a particular age group.

A major concern during the period of initial reading instruction is the introduction of reading as a *thinking* process, and the maintenance of instruction at this level, during the early stages when the mechanics of word perception must be mastered. For the beginning reader, words are often a barrier to meaning rather than the instruments of it; and the teacher's response too often is an isolation of words, even of letters, and emphasis on these rather than on the derivation of meaning from symbols. This problem need never arise if reading is recognized as just one aspect of language development and the school programme is planned in relation to each child's experience and his level of language growth.

The child's experience in his own world is the only firm foundation for beginning reading instruction for it is from his experience that he derives meaning for language symbols. His pre-school experiences are supplemented and extended by in-school experiences and through the use of oral language integrated into a single conceptual framework. This consideration of experiences enables children to build listening and speaking vocabularies and facility in using them for expression and reception of ideas. Such facility in oral communication is the first step towards writing and reading.

Writing demands that the children assemble their ideas and have them recorded in an organized form. The beginner, of course, is unable to transcribe, but with the teacher as secretary, the young composers, either individually or in groups, can dictate and watch their ideas being recorded in written form—and as these are read they recognize the relationships between oral language, written language and reading. They recognize that what they can say, can be written; and that what is written can be read.

Children read their own compositions, and as they do, build up a store of sight words. The function words of English (such as you, are, it, the, why, is, now) are learned readily because of their frequency of use. Other words are remembered because of their high interest. Each child, through his own writing, builds up a personal sight vocabulary.

Because of the strong meaning the written material holds for the young authors, they become adept at using context clues early in their reading development. Under the teacher's direction they learn principles of phonics and word structure as the need arises, learn them in a meaningful situation for immediate practical application rather than for rote memorization. In this way the mechanics of word recognition become an integral part of the reading activity without ever violating the supremacy of *meaning* in the reading act.

Children following such a programme become deeply imbued with the feeling that reading and interpretating ideas are one and the same. When they begin to read books they maintain this point of view and demand from people who write for them the same lucidity that they found in their own writing.

These children are authors themselves. They have debated, evaluated, compromised as the ideas of their group were shaped into written form; they have learned to acknowledge the rights of their classmates to differing opinions and still maintain their own; they have had their ideas questioned both before and after being recorded; they have learned that the words on a page are nothing more than the representation of someone's ideas. Because of this background they do not hesitate to demand *meaning* from, and to question every writer. They expect that the ideas offered will enrich their experience but they accept that they meet writers, as they have met classmates, who have little to say and say it in a very pedestrian manner; they expect to meet writers, as they have met classmates, who have a superior store of information on a particular topic, or who are difficult to understand. And they do not hesitate to question and criticize authors even as they have been criticized. They learn to read critically from their earliest reading experience.

The literature provides plentiful evidence of the potential of young readers for critical reading. As they try to integrate new ideas gained from reading with their past experience and knowledge, they frequently end up questioning both. They note details that don't 'fit'. They refer to authorities, both people and books, for clarification. They learn to evaluate those authorities. Such development, however, requires careful direction by the teacher. Critical reading presupposes accurate word perception and a thorough understanding of the literal meaning of the author; it presupposes that the reader has carefully interpreted the author's ideas, has recognized his mood, tone, purpose, his inferences and his implications. And it presupposes that the reader recognizes that his own background knowledge must be adequate before he can evaluate what someone else has written. The world is full of people condemning without knowing. Teachers should give priority to developing a sense of responsibility for soundly based criticism, criticism that is evaluative rather than petty and destructive.

The development of this quality of critical reading demands fine guidance and a high level of questioning skill on the part of the teacher. She must be certain that her pupils note accurately the facts, the details presented by the author, but avoid focussing her questions at this level. Instead her questions should be such that the children are required to *use* these details rather than simply recall them: questions that expect them to recognize the author's implied meanings, and base inferences on what he has said; questions that expect them to relate the author's ideas to their own experience and to form judgments about their validity; questions that ask them to comment on what was written: the author's choice of words, his style of writing, his accuracy, what he has said.

Last winter one group of third grade children read a story from their reader about two Eskimo boys participating in their first seal hunt. The story dealt with the reactions of one of the boys as he made careful preparation for the great day and finally set out with the adults. It described how carefully he followed the procedures that should have led to success, how he stoically endured the grim cold through a day of waiting—and then watched his friend catch a seal. Throughout it was obvious that Alunak was doing all the right things, that it was just the luck of the hunt that no seal came his way.

His friend was not a clearly defined character, but just the author's instrument for playing on Alunak's feelings, for leading him to say to himself on the way home, 'Now Nagasok is a hunter, and I, Alunak, am still a boy.' The teacher chose to focus on this statement in the group discussion of their reading. Essentially the problem posed for the class was, 'Was this a valid way of determining the boy's worth to his community?' Finding the answer required a careful consideration of the Eskimo culture, as revealed by the author and as known to the children. It lead them to ponder where the author's sympathies lay. It demanded a close study of story detail to determine whether Alunak had been worthy of success. And it gave full play to individual views, illustrating well Chases's contention (1964) that

> the interaction with, or response to the content presented will vary enormously, reflecting differences in temperament, imagination, sense of identity and self-esteem, and many other factors.

But withall, no matter what the value of a free-wheeling discussion, the teacher made sure that the children came to grips with the thoughts of the writer, that their consideration of the topic did not take place in isolation from the views presented in print.

The requirements so far outlined for a primary reading programme could be met using children's compositions and a 'good' school reader. (By 'good' I mean one that offers children a variety of materials of sufficient literary quality to merit close study, and presents concepts that provide food for thought.) However, it was mentioned earlier that first and foremost we must help children to find a place for reading in their lives. To do this we must provide a stimulating selection of books in every classroom from kindergarten onwards and teach children to use them to satisfy their own needs. Becoming a reader will not be the result of pressure to read from parents or teachers. Rather it will result when the pupil feels that reading will advance his own self-esteem or serve his own interests. In a discussion of motivation in reading, Jenkinson says:

> Curiosity, the desire to know and then hopefully to understand, appears to be innate in human beings.... The thirst for understanding, the need to know and master the world in order to feel safe in it, is everywhere evident in child behaviour.... The development of languages helps the child to organize and systematize his knowledge and to find relationships and meanings. When the child learns to read, the opportunities to satisfy his curiosity become almost limitless, since through reading he can assimilate the discoveries of others and can use their classifications

It is the duty of the teacher in all grades to engineer the classroom environment so that the child's 'need to know' and the wisdom of 'those who know and have written' meet face to face. And it is her duty to ensure through her basic instructional programme that the child has the essential skills to extract from the books what he needs. This assumes a classroom where children are *free to learn*; where discovery and inquiry are paramount; where the teacher is not the only, nor even the major, source of information. It means a classroom where children as groups or individuals are encouraged to become involved in their own interests, to recognize their own questions and to satisfy their own curiosity. Teachers who give their pupils such freedom in pursuit of learning would have had a supporter in Samuel Johnson:

> A man ought to read just as inclination leads him; for what he reads as a task will do him little good.

It is to be hoped that teachers foster the inclination towards the imaginative and the adventurous that is a part of childhood and a part of reading. This aspect of literature should not be neglected in any well balanced programme.

A good beginning programme lays a foundation for successful reading. A continuing programme through the middle and upper grades is essential to guide the students towards maturity in reading. It will not differ markedly from that of the primary years. The reading process is the same and the skills employed by the skilful reader are essentially the same in sixth grade as in first grade. The change takes place in the level of difficulty of the materials which are read.

In the middle and upper grades, however, there should be a more intensive study of the interpretation skills themselves. While a first grade pupil can read 'The Little Red Hen', and select the main idea fairly readily, the problem facing the senior student reading 'Hamlet' is quite a different one. It would be well if he were cognizant with techniques that would enable him to break the total down into manageable units and find the central thought. Students, then, must come to understand the functioning of interpretation skills —what are the qualities of a valid inference? How can the author's purpose be detected? How can propaganda be recognized? In what situation is a judgment rather than a conclusion formed? How does a judgment differ from a conclusion? And so on. In addition the increasing amount of content material to be read requires a keen understanding of the specialized application of reading skills in the various subject areas. The school programme should also involve reading for everyday living: reading a newspaper; evaluating advertisements; reading instructions; reading contracts; insurance papers, etc.

Both continuity and sequence are thus built into the reading programme as recurring use is made of each interpretation skill, but with greater breadth and depth as the material increases in difficulty.

The middle and upper grade programme (ages nine to thirteen) is a continuation of the primary programme (ages five to eight) in other key respects. Certainly it is important that as children advance through school, curiosity and a spirit of inquiry still provide the chief motivation for reading; and that children read for pleasure as well as for information. And it is equally important that the emphasis on total language development continues. Oral language is the basis for reading in senior grades as surely as in first grade.

> The reading programme that recognizes the true nature of language ... provides opportunities ... for students to enrich their vocabularies, to use words precisely and to clarify their thinking as they listen, speak, read and write. Since there can never be much critical thinking if students are not involved in a living, sharing of ideas, they must be encouraged to discuss what is said or written. From guided discussions emerge hitherto unrecognized problems that establish purposes for further reading, thinking and discussion. This process leads to a general clarification of issues.... As the teacher listens, she identifies gaps in language, knowledge and experience that need to be filled in at a later time. (cf Gordon 1965)

Note the power that is attributed to oral language, in building meaningful vocabulary, in developing precision of expression, in helping children integrate new knowledge with old, in revealing pupil needs to the teacher, and perhaps most important, in fostering the ability to see new questions arising from reading. Written language too is still a vital force in promoting the organization and clarification of ideas gained from reading. The pattern of simultaneous language and conceptual growth that marked the beginning of the school reading programme should be equally evident in the final grade.

With such a reading programme we might hope for young people leaving our schools agreeing with Untermeyer that there are two reasons for reading. The first is to escape from the routine of everyday living, to leave this realistic world for an unrealistic one. But the second and most important is ... 'not to escape the world but to accept it, and to more than accept it, to participate in it—to use books as a means of sharing, of recognition, to enter the world with a greater awareness'.

References

CHASE, F. S. (1961) In the next decade *Controversial issues in reading and promising solutions* Proceedings of the annual conference on reading, 23 University of Chicago Press

CHASE, F. S. (1964) Meeting individual differences in reading in *Meeting individual differences in reading* Proceedings of the annual conference on reading, 26 University of Chicago Press

Elizabeth Thorn

JENKINSON, M. D. (1964) The role of motivation in reading in *Meeting individual differences in reading* University of Chicago Press

GORDON, L. G. (1965) Promoting critical thinking in FIGUREL, J. A. (ed) *Reading and Inquiry* IRA conference proceedings, 10 Newark, Delaware: IRA

UNTERMEYER, L. (1965) What Americans read and why in FIGUREL, J. A. (ed) *Reading and Inquiry*

7 Utilizing the learners' experience in reading comprehension

H. ALAN ROBINSON
Professor of Reading, Hofstra University,
New York

Paper presented at Fifth Annual Conference of UKRA Edinburgh
1968, first published in *Reading: Influences on progress*

There is an island in the ocean where in 1914 a few Englishmen, Frenchmen and Germans lived. No cable reaches that island, and the British mail steamer comes but once in sixty days. In September it had not yet come, and the islanders were still talking about the latest newspaper which told about the approaching trial of Madame Caillaux for the shooting of Gaston Calmette. It was therefore with more than usual eagerness that the whole colony assembled at the quay on a day in mid-September to hear from the captain what the verdict had been. They learned that for over six weeks now those of them who were English and those of them who were French had been fighting on behalf of the sanctity of treaties against those of them who were Germans. For six strange weeks they had acted as if they were friends, when in fact they were enemies... Lippman, 1922).' Walter Lippman's *Public Opinion* began with this story called 'The World Outside and the Pictures in Our Heads.' He noted that whatever we believe to be a true picture we treat as if it were the environment itself. As we perceive our world so we decide how we shall act.

'Students use their experiences to understand the world about them whether we are involved in stimulating them or not. Man is essentially an organizing creature responding to much of the stimuli in his environment, trying to understand the clues that he notices and making for himself a picture of reality as he sees it. Perhaps our role is to help him improve on his organization of what he notes and interprets. For without doubt, as students build pictures in their heads of the world as they perceive it, so they will act (Robinson, 1966).

What kind of experience, then, should we help students to use and what help shall we provide? Let us view the possible answers to the questions within a framework consisting of three parts: first, environmental; second, linguistic, and third, instructional.

Environmental

If we are to help students use their experiences we had better be acquainted with their experiences. Too many teachers feel they live in a different generation and therefore do not understand this present generation. A teacher cannot and must not so reason. A teacher needs to become familiar with the present experiences of the students with whom he is involved. Obviously the experience does not have to be first-hand. The male teacher, for example, does not need to let his hair grow down to his shoulders or wear boots (unless he so desires), but the teacher must possess the perception, wisdom and curiosity to investigate the world in which the student lives. The teacher needs to know enough about the experiences of the student so that he can ask the right kinds of questions which will permit the student to make use of these experiences. The teacher must also be able, at least partially to understand the answers and help relate them to the learning situation.

The teacher should honour, not depreciate, the environment of the student. We cannot tell today's youth that they are wrong and that our generation is superior. For, indeed, we behaved, with different patterns, in like manner. We fought for our independence and rebelled against the establishment. And, in fact, our behaviour today shapes the environment of today's youth. We have hardly learned to profit by the experiences of others. Can we help our children?

It is difficult for teachers to honour environments very different from their own. For some, who may have grown up in very different strata of society than those in which they find their students, the difficulty may be acceptance of a stratum labelled 'lower class.' Of course, as soon as the word 'lower' is used, whether vocally or non-vocally, there is a negative connotation. Actually, the teacher is concerned with, 'Can I really accept, can I really allow the student to bring his experience to the classroom?' 'What if he talks about something he 'shouldn't' be talking about in the classroom?' Of course, the questions teachers then have to ask themselves are, 'Is there a 'shouldn't—' And if there is a 'shouldn't', what are teachers going to do about it? How are they going to control it? Teachers will have to resolve such questions. For if we are going to capitalize on the experiences of students and let them use their environmental experiences in learning, we must be concerned with knowing and honouring their environments. Strangely enough, those teachers sometimes most uncomfortable are those teachers who themselves come from the very strata of society in which they find their students, but they have moved from that strata of society to the next. They do not want to accept the experiences which they themselves have had and now reject.

If we can learn to honour and understand the background environment of students, we ought to encourage oral comprehension before we proceed to reading comprehension. We ought to fill up the chalkboards with their recorded experiences. At this oral level, we should stimulate students to reflect the life about them. We can, of course, build from the life about them many things for them to read. But in addition to giving them many opportunities to fill up chalkboards relating their experiences and putting in print areas of their experiences, we can learn what kinds of published reading materials will relate best to their experiences. We need to know them as beings who have had experiences in a particular environment. Then we need to use the experiences they relate to us in the teaching situation.

We need to ask the right kinds of questions. Some students respond only to questions. Also, many students will appear not to have had many experiences unless the teacher is able to ask the right kinds of questions. The right kinds of questions begin with, 'what', 'where' and 'when'. But, the right kinds of questions must progress to 'how' and 'why'. The right kinds of questions must get the student to think about his experiences because experience is not only what he has done, it is also his involvement and evaluation of what he has done. When we ask for the student to reflect his experience, we are not asking only for what it is, but what he thinks about it. In other words, where does he place a given experience in his whole framework of experience, and what kind of meaning does it have for him. Some students will have experiences in the back of their heads which they are reluctant to bring forward. Sometimes, some of these potent experiences, when finally brought forward through sympathetic discussion, make a student do more thinking than he has ever done before in his life.

Getting the pupil to use his experience in improving reading comprehension also means that many and varied kinds of reading selections must be utilized. Reading cannot be considered a subject but rather a learning process in the total school curriculum. Reading comprehension is improved when students are provided with the kinds of stimuli that will permit them to relate their experiences to their reading. We do not help students comprehend if the material has little relationship to their experience, and hence does not permit them to make use of experience when they look at the printed word. We need also to consider individual students or specific groups of children in relation to their backgrounds: their environmental experiences. If we are going to use a basal reader, does this basal reader permit them to bring their experiences to bear on the material? Does the city child best understand rural stories? Does a boy relate to stories about daily family life? We do, of course, want to enhance experience and move it forward, but at the very beginning stages of learning (whether in the early grades or in starting a new subject), it is impossible for any individual to bring experience to bear on what he is reading when he just does not have it.

We should capitalize on the use of non-print or audiovisual materials in the classroom in addition to asking the right kinds of questions and providing many suitable kinds of reading materials. If we are going to help students to get something from their experience to bring to reading comprehension, the experiences must have some potency and immediacy. Audiovisual materials help in vitalizing experiences. Students cannot go on trips continuously. But potent experiences can be brought to the classroom through non-print materials. The single concept film or film strip, for example, permits brief but powerful experience in the classroom which should be followed by adequate discussion to help students prepare to use the experience as they turn to reading.

The teacher must be careful in utilizing audiovisual materials to develop readiness and purpose for an activity. In the past, and let us assume not in the present, all teachers in a school were scheduled to see a film no matter what was going on in a particular classroom. Obviously to be a worthwhile experience the material should be an intrinsic part of the curriculum.

Experience building is certainly not limited to audiovisual materials. To use experience one must have experience. To help the student use experience wisely, readiness and purpose-setting should be preliminary steps to involvement in the experience, whether vicarious or realistic. A given student will have many experiences which he brings to the classroom that were somewhat purposeless and accidental. In the school setting he should be helped to become prepared for purposeful experiences.

One educator tells the story of the time a mother paid careful attention. The educator said, 'Your child needs more experiences. Do not try to force him to read orally at home and worry him about words, but visit some of the parks, museums and other attractions in your city to build experiences.' The conversation took place on a Friday. On Monday the mother called and said, 'We have been to the Museum of Science, the Museum of Art, two movies, two restaurants and we went to a hotel—is this enough?'

Hence, in order to help students use experience, we must prepare for the experience, direct it, and limit it. Obviously all students will accumulate varied experiences, but we must also provide directed experiences which will relate to the school curriculum. In this way we can help a student make use of what he has learned. We cannot expect too much from transfer of learning. Most students who have an experience learned in one situation, do not transfer well when confronted with a totally different situation. The best transfer takes place when the situation to which the student is going closely resembles the situation from which he came. A chief problem, of course, is that we often provide a curriculum very different from the experiences of the learner. He therefore finds great difficulty in relating his background to what he is supposed to be learning in school.

Linguistic

We must honour the language of today's student. To laugh and scoff about some of the terms that are being used, and to be unwilling to make use of them in certain situations is unrealistic. To feel that there is a teacher's language and that the teacher must never use the student's language is dishonest. We ourselves use many languages. 'Play it cool,' for instance, is an expressive term and probably, just as colloquialisms in many languages, say better something that a student of today wants to say than combination of other words that may be used. Teachers do not need to make 'play it cool' a part of their daily conversation. But there may be times when it is appropriate when just such identification with the student is important in his knowing that the teacher knows his language.

The students' willingness to use his experiences will depend in great measure on his confidence in the classroom environment and the teacher with whom he is working. If that teacher defeats him by saying, 'This is school. You can talk that way outdoors, but not in class,' then the teacher is depriving of him of a tool which he must use to bring his experiences to the classroom. This is particularly serious in so-called disadvantaged inner-city situations where teachers are very fearful of the language the child is bringing to the school. And well they might be in terms of traditional concepts of school language. If one walks down the street in the inner-city or ghetto area of any of our cities, one hears curse words as a normal part of speech. What does a teacher do when the student brings them to school? Can a student bring his experience to the classroom without making use of the language which was involved in those experiences? Must the teacher take a totally different view of his role in working with these children?

Probably the teacher's job is to teach the student a second language, and really, it is another language. But to say to the student, 'The language you are using is no good—do not use it—I want you to use something else,' is ridiculous. In many instances he does not know something else. Then how can he bring his experience to the even stranger printed page?

I remember a boy I taught who, I believe, was from Iran. He was a very smart young man, but in class he did very poorly in his use of and recognition of vocabulary words in sentences and paragraphs. Yet, on his standardized reading test he did well in vocabulary. This, I found, he was able to do because he had memorized the dictionary. He could give you synonyms, but he did not know what either word really meant in usage. Sometimes perhaps we do this to our students by asking for rote learning. We do this because we are fearful of their language and we want them to use the 'good' classroom language. They then use words unbacked by experiences and attempt to verbalize with little meaning for them, but to give satisfaction to teachers.

Linguistically speaking, we must help students look carefully at the language on the printed page to differentiate between what they know because they have had experience with the concepts, and what they do not know. They must be brought to realize that the total context of the printed page is much more important than any single word and that their own back-ground experiences can help them figure out unknown words. We often say that printed words on the page will help in figuring out an unknown word. This is not quite true. It is the background experience of the reader which will help him figure out the unknown word. If his background of experience permits him to know the other words and what they mean, then it will help him figure out the word in context.

Linguistically speaking, it seems that the most important strategy in helping the student figure out an unknown word is through the use of context. The most important strategy a student should learn is to make use of his experience background to unlock the unknown word. If the student cannot unlock the meaning of that unknown word through the context, then he might proceed to inspect the beginning consonant, look at the other consonants in the word in collaboration with the context, and then maybe, if essential, work on the vowel sound which is the most elusive of all. In the long run, word attack skills coupled with experience will help him get that unknown word. We can also help him by having him look at patterns of sentences and patterns of paragraphs. Remember, man is essentially an organizing creature. He not only picks up isolated experiences, but he picks them up and tries to put them together like a jigsaw puzzle. He will come up with whatever seems logical to him at that given time.

The student can organize his experiences linguistically. For instance, when he sees 'the', 'a', 'an' ,or 'my' in a sentence, he can be certain that the next word or so will be the name of something or someone. Then he realizes that when he finds the name of somone or something, the word after that will not be the name of someone or something but will more likely name an action. A knowledge of paragraph pattern and selection organization can enhance comprehension. When the student reads, he must bring his experience to bear in order to understand. But, if we and he can also organize these ideas, then he has a great chance of enhancing his reading comprehension.

Instructional

The learner's experiences will shape his objectives both within and outside school. Educators must consider the experiences of learners as we organize objectives for instruction, as we prepare materials, and as we organize learning situations and teaching procedures.

The curriculum must permit the student to reflect ideas from his background. Maybe, for instance, the teacher's objective of having a disadvantaged city youngster in a pre-primer by December is unrealistic. Maybe this goal needs to be altered. Maybe the goal is to have this learner be able to use functional sentences in the second language by December rather than even look at the printed page. Or, the goal might be that he can look at some printing, but it had better be in his language at this point. We cannot adhere to the goals we have traditionally set up in the curriculum without reason.

We must inspect and evaluate the kinds of materials we are asking students to read. The materials need to make sense to them in terms of the goals we and they are establishing. For some students it might be important to understand immediately that they can reach a concrete reading goal after they have been in the first grade a few months. For example, such a concrete goal might be reading the sentence, 'I will take a piece of candy.' When mastered, the teacher permits the pupil to take a piece of candy out of a box. Maybe this goal for some individuals is more important than the abstract goal that we often set in the reading situation. Maybe this kind of reading material for him is more important because it is closer to his experience background. As, of course, his experience background broadens, the goals can become more abstract. They may become more abstract as we do more in the classroom, and outside it, to help the student make use of his experiences, by helping him to bring his experiences to bear on what he is reading, and in accepting those experiences as valuable. He should, then, be able to move from a very concrete satisfaction obtained by reading to the more abstract satisfaction obtained through reading.

Today's experiences are altogether too broad and varied for the teacher to be able to stand in the classroom and give information. Lectures on the content of today will be dead tomorrow. We must aim at training the student to use reading as a tool for his independent learning. Hence it is crucial that he use his experience to unlock meaning.

Teachers can help students by teaching five steps in reading comprehension. Step one, the literal area of reading comprehension, is the student's engagement with the printed page as it is. A student looks at the words the author gives and is able to relate back or parrot back what the author says. This cannot be done without his making use of his experience, obviously, for the words are empty shells without his experience filling them. This is the simplest level and if we provide him with those materials which will enable him to make use of his experience, he will be able to do it fairly easily.

Step two is the interpretive level which requires that the student read between the lines. He must find the implications of the author. Now again, we not only have to provide him with purpose, but we have to provide him with the materials that will permit this. I have investigated several second grade content area books, particularly in social studies and science, and there seems to be a dearth of passages where there are any implications at all. Yet we talk about this as an important skill. We must get our authors to build in these kinds of thinking processes so that a student can bring his experience to bear on the printed page and can do some thinking about his experience and the author's experience. Finding such implications, which is making inferences on the part of the reader permits a dialogue beyond the literal level, between reader and writer.

Step three, the evaluation level, is what we might call critical reading. In order to read critically, he has to develop criteria on which to base his thinking. Therefore, this step provides opportunity to help the student firmly organize his experience so he can develop these criteria. He cannot evaluate merely isolated experiences; rather, he has to bring them together in categories, classify them, and develop criteria on which to base his thinking. This takes much work in thinking about the difference between fact and opinion, in making inferences and drawing conclusions (and differentiating between inferences and conclusions). The first two steps are involved for the student must understand what the author says in order to ask himself what it really means. Then the student will question what the information means in relation to his experience. He will have no way of relating his past experience to the new unless he has been able to develop some criteria.

Step four, the integrative step, is when the student makes the information a part of himself. He has read literally. He has made his inferences. He has evaluated and now he either discards all of it, discards some of it, takes some of it, or takes all of it and puts what he wants or needs into the whole bag of other experiences. Thus he develops further experiences.

Step five, the utilization level, is where he can use experiences gained in reading to do something. When what he does is new or different for society or for himself, the utilization might be called creative reading. A reorganizing of ideas, a repatterning, the acquisition of new insights are creative uses of experiences.

Concluding remarks

Since all students have had experiences, since all have organized them in one way or another the teacher's role, then, is to capitalize on what they have done and help them to improve their ability to use their experiences in relation to what they read. Most important, however, we must help students learn to use their experiences and help them renew their ability to gain new experiences and use them as they mature. As John Gardner says so well in his excellent book called *Self Renewal* (1963), 'When organizations and societies are young, they are flexible, fluid, not yet paralyzed by rigid specialization and willing to try anything once. As the organization or society ages, vitality diminishes, flexibility gives way to rigidity, creativity fades and there is a loss of capacity to meet challenges from unexpected directions' '... Every individual, organization or society must mature, but much depends on how this maturing takes place. A society whose maturing consists simply of acquiring more firmly established ways of doing things is headed for the graveyard—even if it learns to do these things with greater and greater skill. *In the ever-renewing society what matures is a system or framework within which continuous innovation, renewal and rebirth can occur*' 'The ultimate goal of the educational system is to shift to the individual the burden of pursuing his own education.'

References

GARDNER, J. (1963) *Self Renewal* New York: Harper & Row
LIPPMAN, W. (1922) *Public Opinion* New York: Macmillan
ROBINSON, H. A. (1966) *Reading: Seventy-five Years of Progress* S.E.M. No. 96, University of Chicago Press

8   Learning to listen

ROBERT FARRAR KINDER
English and Reading Consultant
State Department of Education, Connecticut

Paper presented at Sixth Annual Conference of UKRA Nottingham
1969, first published in *Reading skills: Theory and practice*

Possibly because we know children have been using their ears since
birth, we seem to think that hearing is synonymous with listening and
we take it for granted. Possibly because we have not discussed these
subtle and complex skills as much as other language skills, we tend
to stress them less in school programmes. A new concern for development of specific skills in this area seems to stem from new
teaching devices and from a fresh look at the world in which our
pupils live. These changes are interrelated.

Tape recorders and listening stations are relatively new in the
classroom. But for most pupils the close relatives of classroom audio
devices, radio and television, are familiar forms of communication.
Such classroom equipment helps bridge the gap between the pupils'
real world and their school world.

But the fact that pupils are accustomed to receiving information by
listening does not mean they have really developed this ability. If
the goal sought is learning, listening is more significant than hearing.
One of the challenges for today's schools is to develop a programme
to increase proficiency in listening.

Goals

Two basic goals of a listening programme are to help pupils acquire
skills necessary for enjoyable, thoughtful and profitable listening
experiences; and to develop attitudes that encourage continued
self improvement in these skills, even beyond school.

To implement these broad goals, teachers need to identify the
teachable skills and to specify the understandings and the attitudes
the school will promote. Then they must decide at what school level
each skill, understanding and attitude will be introduced, emphasized and reinforced.

Skills
Some of the skills that we might consider are:

1 listening attentively
2 perceiving and remembering enough details to form an accurate impression
3 searching for order among details
4 suspending final judgment until provided with sufficient evidence
5 listening in a way that makes others comfortable
6 relating details heard to one's own experiences, including reading
7 listening at times primarily to a speaker's ideas and only secondarily to the way he expressed them

Understandings
Some concepts we might consider are:

1 listening can be a source of pleasure and enjoyment as well as a source of information
2 listening requires active and immediate self-involvement
3 listening provides impressions coloured by many factors: the receiver's past experiences, his prejudices about certain words and objects, his physical well-being
4 suspending final judgment until provided with sufficient evidence
5 listening is part of a three-way process involving speaker, message and receiver
6 good listeners encourage improved speech
7 the expressed reaction of listeners controls the quality of the content of mass media

Attitudes
Some attitudes that seem worthy of consideration are:

1 the desire to derive meaning from what one hears
2 the desire to supplement what one hears with added information from one's own experience, from ideas expressed in print
3 the curious questioning of what one hears
4 respect for the ideas of others

Instructional programme

Planning
Sources of information for teachers are the pupils' listening and the professional literature on the subject. Teachers can conduct directed observations of pupils in classrooms, as well as in non school settings.

How successful are pupils in listening to follow directions?

How long is their attention span at various grade levels when listening to a story? An explanation? Information about a particular topic?

Robert F. Kinder

To what extent do pupils question what they have heard? Relate this to what they have read.

What are the pupils' radio and television habits? Preferences?

Teachers can administer standardized tests of listening comprehension and they can construct and administer informal inventories of pupils' listening. All these yield clues as to which aspects need stress at what level.

Organization

Compelling ideas provide organization for the listening programme. A particular aspect of these skills is singled out for instruction and practice as needed but is then put back into the framework of meaningful learning. This organization places high priority on the need to create stimulating day-to-day activities that provoke pupils' needs to listen with increasing competence. The exact subject matter will be partially dependent on current offerings on radio, television and in the community: theatres, lectures etc.

Improvements in listening support improvement in the other language skills. For example:

1 A pupil who has improved his ability to generalize accurately about information he has heard may find it easier to generalize about information he has read.

2 A pupil who has improved his skill in remembering details he has heard tends to find it easier to include accurate, vivid details in his writing.

For this reason teachers should be aware of sub-skills common to listening and viewing or reading speaking, or writing.

Methods

Practice in listening should be purposeful. Teachers should make sure children are listening *for* something, not just listening.

A classroom discussion in which one pupil talks and others listen is highly appropraite at times. Pupils need increased skill in listening actively; for example, listening to follow a speaker's train of thought, or to contribute something relevant to what has been said, or to raise questions. These are skills of meaningful discussion which pupils will continue to perfect as adults. But each pupil needs many more opportunities to perfect these skills than can be provided by class discussion alone. We should consider other techniques such as:

1 small group discussions
2 classroom demonstrations
3 illustrated talks ('show and tell' in early grades)
4 oral reading, puppet shows, and plays and television productions

Pupils can participate meaningfully in evaluating and setting goals for their listening. They might discuss and then list what they consider to be the characteristics of a good listener in a class discussion or a successful viewer of a television show. The class might also draw up a list of needs in listening on which pupils want to work next.

Materials and equipment
All teachers have at their disposal the means for instruction in listening, including:

1 pupils and other people engaged in a variety of activities
2 different kinds of noises
3 many pupils who talk

Most teachers have additional devices they can use to improve listening, includir the overhead projector, film and filmstrip projector, record player, tape recorder, listening stations, television set and radio. Suggestions for a variety of ways in which the materials and equipment might be used and which aspects of what skills might be emphasized at various levels of school are invaluable to teachers. Teachers are urged to answer this question: What appropriate learning experiences utilizing radio, television, motion pictures, overhead projector, tape recorder are suggested for various grade levels?

Conclusion

Today listening is a primary language tool in each person's life. Some experts estimate that most people expend more than fifty per cent of their language skills time in listening. Moreover, evidence seems to demonstrate that increased proficiency in listening also supports increases in the other language skills of speaking, reading and writing. For these reasons school staffs are urged to build and maintain strong listening skills development programmes for all their pupils now.

9 Listening skills and reading performance

MARY WOOTTON MASLAND

Department of Otolaryngology, School of Medicine, Columbia University, New York

Paper presented at Fifth Annual Conference of UKRA Edinburgh 1968, first published in *Reading: Influences on progress*

The peculiarly human activity which we call reading would seem at first thought to be largely a visual affair. It is only when one reflects on what those patterns of letters which we call words represent that the auditory aspect of reading becomes apparent. What the patterns on paper represent, of course, is *spoken* language. The chief medium of communication between speaker and listener is the spoken word, meant to be received by the ear and brain of the listener. All the years before a child learns to read, he has been bathed in a sea of sound, out of which has crystallized, slowly at first and then by leaps and bounds, his native language, its vocabulary, its linguistic forms and grammatical patterns until, at about age six, he is not only able to pronounce almost all the sounds correctly, but can use many hundreds of words. Also, as Templin (1957) has shown, he is at home with almost all the grammatical forms used in his own environment of family and neighbourhood. For most children, all this has happened by ear, before the visual code to his language is formally presented to him, in the form of the first steps in learning to read. Some children, however, arrive in the schoolroom not nearly as well equipped as others to make the auditory-visual translation or integration which learning to read represents. Ingram and Mason (1968) have done a follow-up study on a group of language-retarded children and a control group. They found the language-retarded children significantly below the controls in reading achievement. Flower (1965) has commented on several aspects of auditory dysfunction which seem to underlie some aspects of reading disorders. The present discussion is concerned mainly with exploring some of the possible sources of difficulty in learning to read, particularly for those children who have deficiences in auditory function.

It should go without saying, particularly in the United Kingdom, where the Ewings (1947) at the University of Manchester, and others have stressed the importance of early detection of hearing impairment that any degree of loss of hearing acuity can and does impede the development of speech and language. Certainly, if the sense organ, the ear, is not in a condition, because of injury or disease, to receive and transmit sound accurately, one can presume that the child receives only a muffled or distorted message. If the deficit is great, strenuous and special methods will be needed to teach the child to talk. If the hearing deficit is moderate or affects only certain frequencies, particularly the high frequencies, or if it is only recurrent, it is much more likely to be unnoticed. However, language learning can and does suffer because, among other effects, the distortion or lack of clarity of the speech sounds makes it very difficult for the child to learn new words and language forms with accuracy.

Important as good hearing acuity is for normal language acquisition and performance, there are other auditory functions which are perhaps just as important in learning spoken language and possibly more important in learning to read. Among these are auditory attention, discrimination (Dykstra, 1966), memory (Johnson and Myklebust, 1967) and the ability to process and store auditory information (Hardy, 1962). There are several aspects of attention which merit separate consideration as follows:

Attention

1 listening, or *focusing* attention on auditory events;
2 *maintaining* attention to auditory events;
3 *scanning*, which involves monitoring the ongoing stream of language, while maintaining alertness towards relevant details;
4 *shifting* between focus on details and a more generalized attention to the stream of auditory events.

All of these aspects of auditory attention have relevance to the classroom; first of all, whether a child is able to pay attention to what is said, i.e., to listen; secondly, whether it is possible for him to keep on listening until the particular message he needs to hear is finished; third, whether he is able to pick out of the ongoing stream of language the identifying details of the speech sounds which make up a particular word, and fourth, whether he is able to shift his attention smoothly between sharp focus and generalized awareness and back again. All these aspects of attention are also important in the visual sphere and a weakness in any one of them, whether for auditory or visual events, or both, might be a significant factor in impeding learning to read. In the early stages of learning to read there must be required a blending or integration of auditory and visual elements. Is it possible that such integration involves simultaneous attention to each? Making the auditory-visual association seems very difficult for some children. Birch and Belmont (1964) have pointed out the impor-

Mary W. Masland

tance of ability to make such an auditory-visual integration to good reading performance. It seems reasonable to ask clinicians, teachers and parents to observe the degree of competence with which a child can pay attention to auditory events. From infancy on, it has been an important factor in his learning of oral language, which is the foundation of written language. The recognition of aberrations of attention to auditory events may help point out subtle auditory and language deficits in children who are having trouble learning to read.

Discrimination

Ability to distinguish fine differences between sounds (e.g., 'pen' and 'pin,' and 'cap' and 'cat') is possessed by children in varying degrees. De Hirsch, Jansky and Langford (1966) reported that the Wepman Auditory Discrimination Text was one of ten tests of a predictive battery which did identify in kindergarten those children who would have difficulty in learning to read. Dykstra (1966) investigated the relationship between auditory discrimination and reading achievement and found that, of seven measures of auditory discrimination, five were significantly related to later reading performance.

Memory

Another great stumbling block to the smooth acquisition of reading skill may be a deficiency in auditory memory. Such weakness in auditory memory function may appear in one or several of the following forms:

1 Memory for phonetic detail, i.e. *what* is heard in terms of the smallest units of auditory information, the phonemes.
2 Memory span, by which we mean not only duration of auditory attention in time, but also the number of bits of auditory information which can be stored within a given time. Rate of intake of auditory information is obviously determined by these two factors.
3 Memory for sequence, or the order in which auditory events are recalled.
4 Memory for *patterns* of phonetic detail, as well as the prosodic patterns of rhythm, stress and inflection.

It is important to recognize that some children are much better than others at storing and recalling auditory information and that in almost every classroom there are some children who have extraordinary difficulty in this respect. They may have trouble remembering the details of what they have heard, or the sequence in which they have heard it. It is a common finding that such children have been late in developing language, even though intelligence and hearing may be normal. Spoken language has in many cases ceased to be a problem by school age, although some children still lag in articulation and linguistic competence. The task of learning to read may place new stress on the weak auditory memory abilities of these children since evocation of auditory details and patterns is required for decoding from the visual to the auditory details and patterns is required for decoding from the visual to the auditory mode. Learning to integrate the two may be very difficult for some children weak in auditory memory. However, with special help, early in the learning process, the visual clue may become a tremendous help in remembering a sound. As de Hirsch et al (1966) have pointed out, kindergarten and early grade teachers can be taught ways of observing auditory behaviour and providing auditory training, so that the children who have particular difficulty can be given special attention and help.

A teacher, in observing the auditory behaviour of one of her pupils might ask herself:

Does he hear well? When he has his face turned away from me, or when there is a lot of competing noise in the classroom, does he catch what I say? If I speak in a soft voice, when he cannot see my face, can he tell me what I have said? If not, it may be well to have his hearing tested and, if there seems to be a question about his auditory acuity to refer him for a medical check-up.

Is his auditory attention easy to attract and hold? Can he focus his attention on auditory events, such as stories, and keep listening until the story is over?

Is he good at detecting fine differences in phonetic detail or does he have trouble distinguishing the difference between words that sound alike, for example, 'cap' and 'cat'. If so, his auditory discrimination of sounds may be poor.

Does he often make mistakes in saying words which he can *imitate* perfectly? When he reads, does he sometimes substitute a word which bears some phonetic resemblance to the proper one, but does not make sense? He may have a poor *memory* for phonetic detail.

Does he understand a spoken message as long as it is brief, but make mistakes or seem confused or negativistic when it is relatively long? Auditory attention span may be too short to allow him to take in the full message.

Does he have trouble remembering in what order sounds follow one another in a word, or make the mistake of putting words or sounds in the wrong order when asked to give a message or recite a passage of poetry, or to learn a new word? Does he 'scramble' the order of letters in words he is reading, spelling or writing?

Does he seem to comprehend well when verbal messages or instructions are given him slowly, but fail to comprehend when the teacher's rate of speech is too fast for *him*, even though it is not too fast for most of his classmates? His rate of processing of

Mary W. Masland

auditory information may be slower than average. There may be some relationship between rate of auditory intake and speed of early reading, in children of this kind.

For most of the difficulties outlined above, Johnson and Myklebust (1967) present excellent strategies for observation and training.

Careful testing of children referred to speech clinics because of delay in speech or language development, to learning clinics because of significant delay in reading or to child guidance clinics because of undesirable behaviour may often reveal auditory problems. Analysis of psychological and language testing should provide a profile of a child's strengths and weaknesses in various modalities with a variety of tasks, such as the WISC and the ITPA provide. The latter is particularly useful for highlighting differences between auditory, motor and visual abilities. The answers to such basic questions as to whether reading problems associated with deficiences in auditory function may be based in special genetic patterns, in failure of auditory-visual integration in the nervous system, in dysfunction of the mechanisms of attention or in other conditions, all await further research. In the meantime, we will do well to be acute observers of the learning behaviour of children in pre-school, kindergarten and the early school years, creative in our efforts to solve problems as they arise by prompt and specific educational measures and careful in devising properly controlled studies to evaluate the results of our efforts.

References

BIRCH, H. and BELMONT, L. (1964) Auditory-visual integration in normal and retarded readers *Am. J. Orthopsychiatry* 34

DE HIRSCH, K., JANSKY, J. and LANGFORD, W. (1966) *Predicting Reading Failure* New York and London: Harper and Row

DYKSTRA, R. (1966) Auditory discrimination in beginning reading *Reading Research Quarterly* 1 (3)

EWING, I. and EWING, A. (1947) *Opportunity and the Deaf Child* London: University of London Press

FLOWER, R. (1965) Auditory Disorders and Reading Disorders in: *Reading Disorders* edited by Flower, R., Gofman, H. and Lawson, L. Philadelphia, Pa.: F. A. Davis Co

HARDY, W. G. (1962) Human Communication—ordered and disordered *Volta Review* 64

JOHNSON, D. J. and MYKLEBUST, H. R. (1967) *Learning Disabilities. Educational Principles and Practices* New York and London: Grune and Stratton

MASON, ANNE (1968) Follow-up of educational attainments in a group of children with a retarded speech development, and in a control group in CLARK, M. M. and MAXWELL, S. M. (eds) (1970) *Reading: Influences on Progress* UKRA

TEMPLIN, MILDRED C. (1957) Certain Language Skills in Children Minneapolis: University of Minnesota Press

10 Stimulus models for teaching reading

HARRY W. SINGER
Professor of Education, University of California,
Berkeley

Paper presented at Fifth Annual Conference of UKRA Edinburgh
1968, first published in *Reading: Influences on progress*

Because the term 'model' has multiple meanings, it has been suggested that the term be defined whenever it is used (Kingston, 1965).
Therefore, I shall begin by explaining what I mean by the term
'stimulus model.' Then I will review some relevant studies based
on various methods of teaching reading to tease out their educational
consequences. Finally I will present a model constructed at the fourth
level and will use this model to evaluate methods for initiating reading instruction. I shall conclude with some hypotheses and suggestions
for further research and teaching.

Definition of terms

The term 'model' refers to (a) the identification of the general skills
and abilities or working system that the average individual can use
or mobilize in response to a printed verbal stimulus; mobilization of
this working system may occur when the average individual is recognizing a word, associating meaning to a word or phrase or sentence,
or responding to a question that deals with interpreting, inferring
and integrating ideas presented in a paragraph or in an entire story
and (b) the general organization and interrelationships among these
skills and abilities. In attempting to make these variables and
relationships explicit, the objective is to use the model to deduce
explanations of reading behaviour and to formulate testable hypotheses that will augment our understanding of the development of
reading ability. Eventually this augumented understanding of the
nature of reading ability should result in pedagogical implications
for the improvement of reading achievement.

The term stimulus refers to the unit of print emphasized in the
initial stage of reading instruction; more broadly, stimulus refers to
the method or to the scope and sequence of emphasis on printed

material in the process of teaching reading. In the history of American Reading Instruction (Smith, 1965), 'the unit of initial instructional emphasis has varied by increasing in a surprisingly systematic way from the letter (alphabet method) to word parts (phonics and structural methods) to the whole word (word method) and finally to the sentence and paragraph (experience chart method) (Singer, 1965a).

Although the experience chart method and basal readers have long dominated the American scene (Austin and Morrison, 1963), considerable experimentation in methods and media for initiating reading development has occurred in the last five years. This experimentation is due to the following reasons: the impact of linguistics upon reading instruction; innovations in media of instruction, such as television teaching and programmed instruction; increased competition among publishers for the burgeoning school market; and increase in financial support, particularly from federal funds, not only for innovation but also for evaluation of instructional strategies and materials. As a consequence of the emphasis and support for innovation of methods and materials for teaching reading, the stimulus unit *now* emphasized in American classrooms covers the entire continuum from the letter unit (phoneme-grapheme correspondence) to the paragraph or whole story approach.

Chall (1967) defines the stimulus or methodological continuum as varying along a dimension of emphasis with 'coding' or word recognition at one extreme and 'meaning' at the other. She places 'systematic phonics' programmes which tend to start out with a synthetic phonics approach, separately from connected reading at one extreme of the continuum. Next on the continuum are the linguists and modified alphabet approaches. Towards the meaning end of the continuum are intrinsic phonics programmes which stress sight words and meaning. Closest to the meaning end of the continuum are the programmes which stress the look-say approach and emphasize thought or meaning, but tend to teach no phonics. This methodological continuum defines the current Great Debate in American reading instruction (Chall, 1967). Some people think that the question in the debate is which method is best. But teachers and researchers know that regardless of which method is employed, the range of achievement in the typical classroom is approximately two-thirds of the chronological age of the children in the group (Bond and Tinker, 1967). At the end of the first grade level, this range is about two years and at the sixth grade level it is about seven years. Consequently, the more significant question for both scientific and pedagogical purposes is: what are the educational consequences of each method of teaching reading? To approach an answer to this question, we shall begin by reviewing three pertinent studies.

111

Harry W. Singer

Review of selected studies

In 1922, Buswell, using an eye-movement camera for assessing symptoms of central mental processes in reading, compared results of a phonic method with a method that emphasized meaning or content. The results indicated that the phonic method tended to promote left to right sequence and word pronunciation, while the meaning emphasis fostered concern for the content, but a slower degree of progress in word recognition and rhythmic eye-movement behaviour or sequential reading. Buswell also plotted the eye-movement behaviour of a cross-section of an average group of pupils selected from each grade level. From these data, he concluded that there was a common route to the goal of maturity in reading, around which individuals vary.

Agnew (1939) also reported that differences in methodological emphases resulted in differential effects in oral and silent reading. On word recognition and oral reading, the phonics-emphasis group was superior to the non-phonics emphasis group, but on silent reading, the two groups were about equal. These results suggest that the combination of abilitites used or mobilized for oral reading placed a greater premium on a phonics subskill, but for silent reading a quantitatively and/or qualitatively different combination of subabilities was mobilized in which phonic abilities had less weight and other subabilities had greater weight.

A similar conclusion can be reached by careful reading of the largest methodological study ever undertaken in the United States. In this study, Bond and Dykstra (1967) compared five methodological emphases (initial teaching alphabet, basal plus phonics, language experience, linguistic, and phonics combined with linguistics) against a basal reader approach. For comparison criteria, they used word reading, paragraph meaning, spelling and word study skills, as assessed by subtests of the Stanford Reading Achievement Battery. Although Bond and Dykstra recognized that there are serious methodological flaws in the design of the First Grade Study, such as non-comparable samples, their findings at least suggest hypotheses for further research. In general, Bond and Dykstra found that the non-basal instructional programme tended to be superior to a basal programme when assessed on the criterion of word recognition skills at the end of the first year of reading. However, when non-basal programmes were compared on the basis of comprehension, the differences were less consistent. The programmes superior to the basals in development of word recognition skills, as assessed by Stanford 'word reading' and Fry's phonetically regular and Gate's random sample of words, were it a, basal plus phonics, linguistic, and phonics-linguistics, but *not* the language experience approach. The programmes that were superior to basals in development of comprehension—were basal plus phonics and phonics-linguistic programmes.

Apparently, more emphasis upon phonics and linguistic elements than usually encountered in a typical basal reader programme *and* inclusion of meaning or connected reading enhances not only word recognition skills, but also comprehension.

From these results we can formulate the hypothesis that the various stimulus emphases result in models or readers whose skills on the average are developed differently. In one method, word recognition skills may become initially better developed than word meaning, while in another programme the results might be just the opposite. This inference would explain why in some of the First Grade Studies comprehension could still be equal even though the subskills in the two programmes are differentially developed. This hypothesis should, of course, be tested. A longitudinal investigation might be conducted, using the six stimuli or input emphases of methods of teaching reading on comparable samples. It would then be possible to test the hypothesis that differential inputs of methods of teaching reading result, at least initially, in different models or general working systems for attaining speed and power of reading. It would also show whether the differences are lasting or whether convergence of the models tend to occur. Until this study is conducted, we can obtain an idea of the kind of models that might result from systematic variation of input stimuli or methods of teaching reading by inspecting a model constructed at the fourth grade level. This model was based upon a general method of teaching reading since the children in the study had been taught by a variety of methods. In general, they had migrated to California from other states and had also moved about from one California school to another; consequently, they had been exposed to a variety of methods of teaching reading.

Fourth grade model

This model was constructed by administering a battery of 36 tests to an average sample of fourth graders. The variables used in the study were selected because previous research had demonstrated that they were correlated with speed or with power of reading. In addition, some variables were included because they had theoretical significance. The purpose of the study was to determine by the statistical means of substrata analysis the most parsimonious set of variables that would tend to account for the maximum amount of variation or degree of individual differences in speed and power of reading. Also, the study sought to test the following hypothesis: 'General reading ability is a composite of "speed" and "power" of reading, and that underlying each component is a multiplicity of related and measurable factors' (Holmes, 1954).

The results of the study confirmed the hypothesis and were constructed in a model. This model, whose construction is reported in

Harry W. Singer

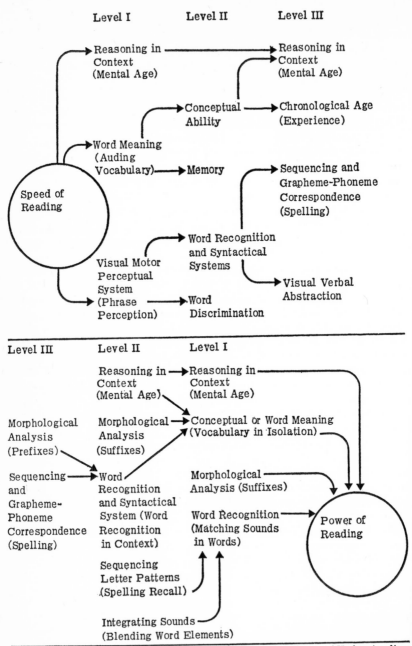

Simplified Design of Systems for Decoding, Reconstructing, and Understanding Written Material, Based Upon Statistically-Determined Model. (Singer, 1962, 1965b; Holmes and Singer, 1966)

detail elsewhere (Singer, 1962, 1965b; Holmes and Singer, 1964, 1966), is shown in the figure. However, the statistically-determined per cent contributions to the variance of the particular criterion or subcriterion have been omitted and generic or factor names for the selected variables have been added.

Next to the generic names, in parentheses, are the names of the particular variables selected from the intercorrelation matrix by the Wherry-Doolittle represent factors in the linear prediction equation for the particular criterion or subcriterion. Thus, for predicting the variance in the criterion, Power of Reading, which was assessed by the Gates Reading Survey subtest, Level of Comprehension, are mental age (reasoning in context), vocabulary in isolation (conceptual or word meaning ability), suffixes (morphological analysis), and matching word sounds or ability to sound out whole words (word recognition). At the second level, for predicting the subcriterion of Vocabulary in Isolation, mental age and word recognition in context (word recognition and syntactical systems) precipitated from the analysis. Accounting for variance or individual differences in the subcriterion of Matching Sounds in Words are spelling recall (sequencing letter patterns) and blending word elements (integrating sounds). At the third level, the subcriterion of word recognition in context could be predicted from prefixes (morphological analysis and spelling ability (sequencing and grapheme-phoneme correspondence. This use of the Wherry-Doolittle multiple correlation technique for successive analyses of the criterion and subcriteria is known as substrata analysis (Singer, 1965c).

For predicting the criterion of Speed of Reading, also assessed by a subtest of the Gates Reading Survey, are reasoning in context (mental age), word meaning (auding or listening vocabulary), and visual-motor perceptual system (phrase perception). At the second level of analysis, underlying the subcriterion of word meaning are conceptual ability and a memory factor. Accounting for variance in visual motor perceptual systems are word recognition and syntactical systems (word recognition in context) and word discrimination. At the third level analysis, reasoning in context (mental age) and chronological age (experience) are the predictors selected in the multiple prediction equation for Conceptual Ability. For predicting the subcriterion of Word Recognition and Syntactical Systems are sequencing and phoneme-grapheme correspondence (spelling recognition) and visual verbal abstraction.

Implications

The model has implications not only for a theory of reading, but also for the methodology and pedagogy of reading (Singer, 1962, 1965e). The model indicates that a complex set of factors can be mobilized for attaining speed and power of reading. From the model, it can readily be seen that some of the same factors underly Speed and Power of Reading. However, the set of factors underlying these major components of general reading ability are not identical. Consequently, in switching from Speed to Power of Reading or vice-versa, the average individual reorganizes his general working system and mobilizes a somewhat different organization of subskills and capacities. The model also suggests why different methods can be successful in developing children into readers: althought different methods emphasize different subskills, they may include all the factors shown in the model, perhaps only varying the timing and the sequence of introduction of word recognition, word meaning, and reasoning in reading techniques (Heilman, 1961). Hence all the necessary subskills and abilities are probably developed in each method, but with a different degree of emphasis. Through a combination of these subskills and abilities, individuals taught by different methods could be equally proficient in attaining speed and power of reading.

The model also indicates that an instructional programme for developing an average reader from a beginning to a fourth grade level of reading ability would have to incorporate into the curriculum all the educable factors shown in the model *plus* other factors that are not included in this model but which may also be necessary in the various development stages of reading. For example, knowledge of letter names is important in learning to read at the first grade level (Bond and Dykstra, 1967), but do not show up in the fourth grade model because at the fourth grade level almost all, if not all, children at this level know all the letter names. Included in the programme would be at least three subsystems: decoding or word recognition, word meaning, and reasoning-in-context (interpreting, inferring, and integrating ideas). Also, there should be some alternation from power to speed of reading so that the subskills and abilities for both of these components can be developed to their fullest potential as children progress through school (Singer, 1965d). Until more developmental evidence is adduced, the curriculum for reading instruction must also depend upon a logical analysis of the hierarchial structure of reading ability. That is, the curriculum constructor, whether a writer of basal material or a school supervisor or a classroom teacher or a remedial reading specialist, must make an analysis of the behavioural objectives of instruction, decide on the necessary sequence of substeps for attaining these objectives, and then provide the educational experience or stimuli input for developing them in pupils. An example of such a hierarchical structure has been worked out in the area of reading (Gagné, 1965). This structure needs to be developed into a reading programme and empirically evaluated, perhaps by statistical procedures similar to those employed for the model at the fourth grade level.

Furthermore, the model can be conceived as a cross-section of variables to employ as a minimum set of objectives to attain in reading by the fourth grade level. These objectives can also be used as evaluative criteria for determining whether or not the various methodological emphases or types of stimulus inputs along the decoding-meaning continuum stress development of necessary variables for attaining speed and power of reading. Those programmes towards the decoding end of the continuum tend to emphasize or facilitate development of word recognition abilities, but not word meaning and reasoning-in-context abilities, while those at the meaning end of the continuum tend to stress acquisition of word meaning and reasoning-in-context, but not word recognition abilities. The model indicates that all three of these components, word recognition, word meaning, and reasoning-in-context, are interrelated and are mobilized in combination for the attainment of speed and power of reading.

As more cross-sectional analyses are done at the primary grade levels with comprehensive evaluative criteria, we will be able to determine to what extent variation in stimulus input results in the development of common routes and variation around the common route to maturity. Also, we might ascertain whether different known groups, such as slow versus fast and least versus most powerful readers at the elementary level differ in their pattern of reading development and hence require different curricula or whether only the *rate* of development of general reading ability is different from group to group. Evidence at the high school level suggests that the patterns of reading development of known groups *are* different and hence require differential curricula (Holmes and Singer, 1966). An example of what such a differentiated curriculum at the first grade level might involve can be gleaned from the first grade study. Bond and Dykstra (1967) reported that poor beginning readers tend to benefit more from a highly structured programme as presented in basal readers while good beginning readers could achieve better from a less structured programme as occurs in an individualized reading programme.

Although pupils can and do learn to read successfully by means of a variety of programmes, we cannot conclude that any one programme will do as well as another for all children. On the contrary, the evidence tends to suggest that we need a differentiated programme, beginning as early as the kindergarten level to meet the reading needs of children (Singer, Balow, and Dahms, 1968). Indeed, over-emphasis upon a particular method may be detrimental to the development of reading ability in children. For example, Burt and Lewis (1946) concluded from a large scale remedial reading study conducted in England that a *change* in method of instruction from emphasis upon one input mode to another, such as auditory to kinesthetic or kinesthetic to visual or auditory to visual, and so forth, was the most significant factor in improving the reading of their pupils. Perhaps the improvement in reading resulted not just from a Hawthorne Effect or from matching stimulus input to the modal dominance preferred by the child, but in developing a more adequate and more flexible system of subabilities with the child.

Experimentation now going on in England and the US and elsewhere in stimulus models for teaching in the initial stages of reading development is having the salutory effect of providing teachers with differentiated curricula. Until we discover criteria for matching these curricula to individual differences or for using the curricula to *stimulate* children's development, particularly for educationally deprived children, teachers must *not* champion only one method and only one model, but instead be cognizant of all the available stimulus models and be willing to use any methods and materials which will enable all of their pupils to develop to their maximum potential in speed and power of reading.

References

AGNEW, DONALD C. (1935) The Effect of Varied Amounts of Phonetic Training on Primary Reading *Duke University Research Studies in Education* No. 5 Durham, N.C.: Duke University

AUSTIN, MARY C. and MORRISON, COLEMAN (1963) *The First R: The Harvard Report on Reading in Elementary Schools* New York: Macmillan

BOND, GUY L. and DYKSTRA, ROBERT (1967) The Co-operative Research Programme in First-Grade Reading Instruction *Reading Research Quarterly* 2

BOND, GUY L. and TINKER, MILES A. (1967) *Reading Difficulties: Their Diagnosis and Correction* 2nd Edition New York: Appleton-Century-Crofts

BURT, CYRIL, and LEWIS, R. B. (1946) Teaching Backward Readers *British Journal of Educational Psychology* 16

BUSWELL, GUY T. (1922) Fundamental Reading Habits: A Study of Their Development *Supplementary Educational Monographs* No. 21 Chicago: University of Chicago Press

CHALL, JEANNE (1967) *Learning to Read: The Great Debate* New York: McGraw-Hill

GAGNE, ROBERT M. (1965) *The Conditions of Learning* New York: Holt, Rinehart and Winston

HEILMAN, ARTHUR W. (1961) *Principles and Practices of Teaching Reading* Columbus, Ohio: Charles E. Merrill

HOLMES, JACK A. (1954) Factors Underlying Major Reading Disabilities at the College Level *Genetic Psychology Monographs* 49

HOLMES, JACK A. and SINGER, HARRY (1964) Theoretical Models and Trends Toward More Basic Research in Reading *Review of Educational Research*

HOLMES, JACK A. and SINGER, HARRY (1966) *Speed and Power in Reading in High School* US Department of Health, Education and Welfare: Office of Education. A publication of the Bureau of Educational Research and Development. Superintendent of Documents, Catalogue No. FS 5.230:30016. US Government Printing Office, Washington, D.C., 20402

KINGSTON, ALBERT J. (1965) The Use of Models in Research in Reading in: FIGUREL, J. ALLEN (ed) *Reading and Inquiry. Proceedings of the Annual Convention of the International Reading Association* Newark, Delaware: International Reading Association 10

SINGER, HARRY (1962) Substrata-Factor Theory of Reading: Theoretical Design for Teaching Reading in: FIGUREL, J. ALLEN (ed) *Challenge and Experiment in Reading. Proceedings of the Annual Convention of the International Reading Association* New York: Scholastic Magazines

SINGER, HARRY (1965a) Conceptualization in Learning to Read in: THURSTON, ERIC and HAFNER, LAWRENCE (eds) *New Frontiers in College-Adult Reading. Fifteenth Year Book of the National Reading Conference* Milwaukee, Wisconsin, 53233: The National Reading Conference Inc

SINGER, HARRY (1965b) Substrata-Factor Evaluation of a Precocious Reader *The Reading Teacher* 18

SINGER, HARRY (1965c) Symposium on the Substrata-Factor Theory of Reading: Research and Evaluation of Critiques in: FIGUREL, J. ALLEN (ed) *Reading and Inquiry. Proceedings of the Tenth Annual Convention of the International Reading Association* Newark, Delaware: International Reading Association

SINGER, HARRY (1965d) A Developmental Model for Speed of Reading in Grades Three Through Six *Reading Research Quarterly* 1

SINGER, HARRY (1965e) *Substrata-Factor Reorganisation Accompanying Development in Speed and Power of Reading* Final report on Project No. 2011, US Office of Education

SINGER, HARRY, BALOW, IRVING H. and DAHMS, PATRICIA (1968) A Continuum of Teaching Strategies for Developing Reading Readiness at the Kindergarten Level in: FIGUREL, J. ALLEN (ed) *Forging Ahead in Reading. Proceedings of the Twelfth Annual Convention of the International Reading Association* Newark, Delaware: International Reading Association

SINGER, HARRY (1969) Theoretical models of reading *Journal of Communication* 19

Harry W. Singer

SINGER, HARRY and RUDDELL, ROBERT (1970) *Theoretical Models and Processes of Reading* Newark, Delaware: International Reading Association

SMITH, NILA B. (1965) *American Reading Instruction* Newark, Delaware: International Reading Association

WHERRY, R. J. (1947) The Wherry-Doolittle Test Selection Method in: GARRETT, H. E. *Statistics in Psychology and Education* New York: Longmans, Green and Company

MEDIA AND MATERIALS

11 Teaching reading through the medium of i t a

JOHN DOWNING

Professor of Education, University of Victoria,
British Columbia

Paper presented at Third Annual Conference of UKRA Cambridge
1966, first published in *Reading: Current research and practice*

i t a—a simplified and regularized writing-system

Abbreviations such as i t a carry a great deal of meaning for so
few letters. Furthermore, when the system they represent has been
the centre of controversy as i t a (initial teaching alphabet) has
been for several years, these initial letters become the focus of
many more meanings. The reality of the original idea is in danger of
being forgotten because the abbreviation is at least one step away
from the original phrase, and these extra meanings become associated with the almost magical letters. Indeed, some over-enthusiastic
supporters of i t a do appear to regard it as a potion or elixir which
will cure all their pupils' ills. In contrast, there are some opponents
of i t a who appear to regard it as the blackest of black magic.

To escape from this aura of extra meanings around i t a let us
introduce the initials s r w s and begin afresh. This will help us to
put i t a in perspective. An 's r w s' is a *simplified and regularized
writing-system*. The spoken language is a system of sounds produced
in air. This system of air can be represented on paper by a system
of symbols in ink. Such a system of ink is what is referred to in
linguistics as a writing-system. A simplified and regularized writing-
system is one in which the code for the spoken language has been
made more simple and more regular than that of the traditional
writing-system.

Such s r w ss have been proposed for English over and over again
during the past four centuries. Pitman's (1961) i t a is thus a modern
example of a long line of development. Also, i t a is only one of
many s r w ss competing for teacher's consideration at this present
time. Some of these rival s r w ss also have initials, *e.g.* E N W is
English the New Way (cf. Cortright, 1966; Laubach, 1964), W E S is
World English Spelling (cf. Simpler Spelling Association, undated),

D M S is the Diacritical Marking System (cf. Fry 1966). Other s r w ss of current interest to teachers of reading in English are Wijk's (1958) Regularized English, Malone's (1963 Unifon, Davis' (1964) New English Orthography, Gattegno's (1964) Words in Colour (see also Dean, 1966) and Jones' (1965) Colour Story Reading.

Nor does it seem possible to regard i t a as unique among other s r w ss as far as its characteristics are concerned, i t a has additional characters for those sounds of English which have no single letter of their own in the traditional writing-system for English—but so also did Hart's (1570) s r w s in the sixteenth century. i t a has regularized spellings for those words which are irregular in conventional orthography, e.g. cum, ruf, cof, but so also did Hart's system. i t a is specially designed to help children make a transition from i t a to conventional orthography. This is unusual but still not unique. Leigh's s r w s used in the schools of St Louis from 1866 also had this feature, which is referred to explicitly in the reports of Harris (1869), the Superintendent of Schools who began the experiment there.

What is exceptional about i t a is the extent to which its use has spread in English-speaking countries for teaching reading and writing and in other countries for the teaching of English. i t a is particularly widely used in Britain and the United States. In Britain, by the beginning of 1966, some 1800 schools were using i t a as compared with only twenty schools in the first year of the experiment in 1961. Probably i t a's superior progress, in comparison with other s r w ss is chiefly due to an important feature of the original British i t a research plan. Before the research began the University of London Institute of Education and the National Foundation for Educational Research in England and Wales (1960) issued a pamphlet appealing for support for the experiment which contained this important declaration:

NO COPYRIGHT

The particular alphabet used above may be obtained (in 12pt.) from The Monotype Corporation, 32 Fetter Lane, E.C.4.—Any designers' rights have been freed for all time for unrestricted use by all.

Steps were also taken to ensure that all British publishers had the opportunity to produce books in i t a for the experiment. This availability of a variety of books is peculiar to i t a. None of the other s w r ss has been able to provide this range of materials. A duplicated list of 170 titles published by many different publishers is available from the National Book League.

Thus i t a is an unusually successful example of an s r w s, although it must be admitted that this success may not necessarily be due to the specific features of this particular s r w s. The research so far conducted on i t a has not been concerned with developing the ideal s r w s. From the outset, i t a was the example of s r w s which it had been decided to use in the British experiment, although the more general concept of an s r w s for English seems to have been what the Minister of Education had in mind in promising her 'interest and goodwill' in reply to Dr Mont Follick's request that she should 'state her policy towards proposals by a competent research organization to investigate possible improvements in the teaching of reading by means of a system of simplified spelling' (Hansard, 7 May 1953). It seems appropriate, therefore, to bear in mind that i t a in our research needs to be regarded as a *representative* of s r w s's. From here on in this paper, I shall report our research on the particular system, i t a, but it should be recognized that we do not know whether the same or even better results could not have been produced by one of the other alternative s r w ss.

The i t a writing-system

Full descriptions of i t a have been provided in several publications by members of the Reading Research Unit, e.g. Downing (1965b), McBride (1965), Mountford (1965). Here, I shall give only a very brief summary of the three main features of i t a for the teaching of beginning reading.

1 *i t a reduces the load of learning*

(*a*) i t a usually has only one print configuration for each English word, *e.g.* ɖɑb only (not *Dab*, *DAB*, *etc.*).

(*b*) i t a usually has only one symbol for each phoneme (sound-unit) of English, *e.g.* ie only in pie, pien, mie, mienɖ, gie, gieɖ, hie, instead of a variety of symbols in traditional orthography (t o), *e.g.* 'pie', 'pine', 'my', 'mind', 'guy', 'guide', 'high', etc. ('Usually' but not always, only one symbol for each phoneme, *e.g.* both c and k are used in i t a for the hard sound at the beginning of words such as cat and kitten. Some other s r w ss have abolished c and are thus simpler than i t a. However, it is thought to gain in similarity to t o for transition purposes through such compromises with English spelling conventions.)

2 *i t a regularizes and simplifies the written code for English phonemes*

(*a*) Gross irregularity of the relations between sound and printed symbol is removed by i t a, *e.g.* the ambiguous o in 'done', 'gone', 'bone', 'one', 'women', is replaced by a coding which represents more systematically these different vowel sounds, thus, ɖun, gon, bœn, wun, wimen. (Gross irregularity but not all, *e.g.* e in rewaurɖeɖ represents a different sound to that common to reɖ, beɖ, feɖ, leɖ, seɖ, heɖ. This compromise is also made in the interests of easier transition to t o).

(b) The grouping operation which makes learning to read in English more complex than, say, Finnish, is largely abolished by i t a, *e.g.* the t o digraph ʧ in ʧhop, ʧheese, muʧh, etc., becomes a single character in i t a, thus ʧ in ʧhop, ʧheez, muʧh. The effect is probably even more important in words where the two parts of the letter group for a single sound are separated by another letter, *e.g.* ie in mine, dive, hide becomes in i t a ie as mien, ɖiev, hieɖ.

3 *i t a is designed to ease transition to t o*

The new i t a characters and the spelling rules of the overall i t a writing-system are designed to maximize transfer-of-learning from i t a to t o once fluency in the former has been achieved. This design for transfer rests chiefly on the finding that fluent readers use only minimal cues situated chiefly in the upper part of the line of print. (See, for example, the research of Paterson and Tinker, 1940.) Therefore, as far as possible the upper part of the i t a configurations of whole words are similar to the upper part of the t o configurations of the same words. Pitman has also suggested that the use of contextual clues is a necessary skill for easy transfer.

The British experiments with i t a

The Reading Research Unit has conducted a series of experiments on i t a, of which two are concerned with the effectiveness of i t a in beginning reading and later transfer-of-learning to reading in t o (traditional orthography).

Briefly, in the first experiment, begun in 1961, an experimental group using i t a for the first stages of learning to read was compared with a control group using only t o. In the analyses of results these two groups have been matched on non-verbal intelligence, verbal ability, age, sex ratio, social class, urban/rural location of the school, infants only or infants and juniors combined types of organization, size of school and pupil-teacher ratio. This scientific rigour has not excluded reality from the experiment. Every effort has been made to preserve real-life conditions in the experimental and control group classes. For example, the children began school at the usual age in Britain, i.e. five years, they were taught by the common eclectic or 'mixed' methods with phonics later rather than earlier, and they used the most popular basic reading series in Britain, i.e. the 'Janet and John' series (O'Donnell and Munro).

Experiences in the experimental and control groups (apart from the different writing-systems) were also matched. Thus both groups used the same basic reading series, the experimental group having 'Janet and John' in i t a and the control group having 'Janet and John' in t o. Also, from the very beginning attempts were made to ensure that any possible causes of Hawthorne Effect were matched in the two groups —although, of course, it must be admitted that it is uncertain whether these attempts were entirely successful. Some misconceptions seem to have arisen in the minds of some commentators on the methods of the British i t a research and these have been discussed in Downing (1965a) and Downing and Jones (1966).

In a second experiment with i t a, begun in 1963, matching followed similar lines to those described above except that the teacher's ability was also brought under control by the same teacher teaching both i t a and t o classes. This second experiment also serves as a check on the findings of the original study of 1961.

Results of the i t a experiments

The complete account of the results of the first i t a experiment, together with discussions of the research and its conclusions by other psychologists and educators, is provided in *The i t a Symposium* (1967). The results of the second experiment and the relating of its findings to those of the first study are presented in Downing (1967). Briefly, three main conclusions have been reached:

> 1 *i t a as a transitional writing-system for beginning reading and writing in English generally produces superior results in t o reading and in t o spelling by the end of the third year in school.*

This conclusion is supported by the following test results from the first experiment:

(a) On the Schonell (1956) Graded Word Reading Test administered in t o to the experimental and control groups at the beginning of the third year, the i t a pupils achieved significantly higher t o scores than did the pupils who had used t o from the beginning (see Table 1).

TABLE 1 *Results of Schonell's graded word reading test given in t o to both experimental and control groups*

Group	N	Mean	Median	Q_3-Q_1
Experimental	291	29.70	26.94	28.10
Control	291	24.39	23.31	24.32

Difference significant in favour of i t a group at 5 per cent level using Kolmogorov-Smirnov* (one-tailed) test.

$$\chi^2 \text{ (2 d. of f.)} = 6.59$$

* Cf. Siegel (1956)

John Downing

(b) On the Neale (1963) Analysis of Reading Ability administered in t o to both experimental and control groups at the end of three school years, the i t a pupils were significantly superior on all three measures, i.e. accuracy, speed and comprehension (see Table 2).

TABLE 2   *Result of Neale analysis of reading ability (Form B) administered in t o to both experimental (N=194) and control (N=194) groups at the end of three school years*

Measure	Group	Mean	Median	Q3–Q1	Kolmogorov-Smirnov χ^2(2 d. of f.)	Per cent Significance Level
ACCURACY	Experimental	38.97	38.28	27·21		
	Control	31.66	30.23	27.89		
					10.55	1
SPEED (words per minute)	Experimental	59.07	61.00	41.55		
	Control	51.59	49.39	43.57		
					9.29	1
COMPRE-HENSION	Experimental	14.77	14.24	12.01		
	Control	12.60	11.24	12.33		
					9.92	1

In the first experiment it was found that the superiority of the i t a group's ability in t o reading was most notable among the highest-achieving segment of the sample—those who 'learn anyway and, therefore, do not need innovations', according to some educators. The lowest-achievers, in contrast, seem to receive least benefit from i t a but this is probably due to the fact that they need much longer experience of i t a before showing the effects of transfer to t o reading.

(c) The t o spelling of the i t a pupils as measured by Schonell's (1950) Graded Word Spelling Test was found to be marginally better by mid-third year and significantly better by mid-fourth year (see Table 3).

This superiority of the i t a pupils in t o spelling was found to exist at all levels of achievement. Peters' (1966) independent finding that 'i t a-taught children, with their more systematic and economical attack, present a more receptive base for the teaching of [t o] spelling conventions' suggests also that there is a generalized transfer-effect arising from the i t a pupils' early experiences of the regularity of letter-sound relations in i t a.

TABLE 3   *Result of Schonell's graded word spelling test (t o)*

Group	N	Form A Mid-third Year			N	Form B Mid-fourth Year		
		Mean	Median	Q3–Q1		Mean	Median	Q3–Q1
Experimental	374	28.44	25.96	19.45	102	39.11	39.44	27.29
Control	374	25.34	24.69	19.72	102	32.25	32.08	21.78
Kolmogorov-Smirnov (one-tailed) test								
χ^2 (2 d. of f.)			4.49				6.25	
Difference			Not significant			Significant at 5 per cent level		

These findings on t o reading and t o spelling have not, as yet, been checked by the second experiment because it has not reached the appropriate stage in the testing programme.

> 2 *The success of* i t a *in improving* t o *literacy skills occurs in spite of an important setback in the growth of these basic skills at the stage of transition from* i t a *to* t o.

Subjective impressions of the stage of transition from i t a to t o suggest that it occurs without noticeable difficulty. However, the t o test results between the middle of the second year and the beginning of the third year of school showed that achievements in t o were poorer than they had been a few weeks or even months earlier on the same tests in i t a. This setback has been found again in the second i t a experiment. This was true, except for the speed of reading, even for the superior pupils in the i t a group. A study of these children's t o reading errors showed that they were not transferring in quite the manner originally envisaged by Pitman (1964). They appeared to be processing t o in smaller units than the upper half of the configurations of whole words. This may be due in part to a tendency to require transfer from i t a to t o at too early a stage, although this does not seem a satisfactory explanation if one considers that the errors studied were made by the higher-achieving pupils in the experimental group.

Thus, the superiority in the t o reading of i t a pupils occurs after a recovery from a setback at the transition stage. It is possible that this seback could be reduced in several ways, *e.g.* the timing of transition could be improved, new teaching techniques for transfer could be evolved, and better materials might be devised. Also, it must be remembered that i t a is an *ad hoc* s r w s which itself could be improved or superseded by some better s r w s. Burt (1962) clearly had this in mind when the i t a experiment was launched in 1961, for he wrote:

> Even supposing that these novel proposals turn out, on the whole, to be more effective than any of the earlier ones, it still would not follow that they are the best that could be devised.

If the idea of using an s r w s for the beginning stage followed by a transition to t o is to be carried further towards the optimum of efficiency, then a programme of research on shaping the s r w s device itself should have high priority in the next stage of this line of investigation. Even if i t a continues to be used unchanged for some time, more research is urgently required on teaching techniques and materials which will make better use of i t a's own potential.

The plateau or even regression at the transition stage in the i t a approach may be expressed in another way. If the children using i t a had not had to make a transition to t o but could have continued to use this s r w s exclusively, then almost certainly the development of their literacy skills would have continued to improve instead of being slowed down through the introduction of the more complex and irregular conventional writing-system for English. This brings us to the third and most important of the findings of our two i t a experiments:

> 3 *The traditional orthography of English is a serious cause of difficulty in the early stages of learning to read and write.*

This finding is supported by a great deal of evidence:

(*a*) Progress through the basic reading series 'Janet and John' was much more rapid in the i t a group, as is shown by Table 4. The second i t a experiment also showed superior progress in i t a classes.

(*b*) Significantly higher scores were obtained on all i t a tests of reading by the i t a pupils as compared with the t o test scores of the t o pupils. This is shown clearly by the results of two administrations of the Schonell Graded Word Reading Test (see Table 5) and one administration of the Neale Analysis of Reading Ability (see Table 6). In the second i t a experiment, too, the i t a pupils achieved superior results on these two tests.

(*c*) Markedly superior results in written composition and in the range of the written vocabulary found in the i t a group. These are reported in detail in Downing, Fyfe and Lyon (1967). This liberalizing effect of i t a on children's creative writing was emphasized by teachers in the first i t a experiment (see Downing, 1964) and it was also noted independently by Southgate (1963).

The most definite conclusion arrived at as a result of these i t a experiments is that the traditional orthography of English is an important cause of difficulty in learning to read in English speaking

TABLE 4   *Progress in reading basic reader series:*
percentage frequency distribution of reading primer reached

Reading Primer reached	After 1 yr. EXP. %	After 1 yr. CON. %	After 1⅓ yr. EXP. %	After 1⅓ yr. CON. %	After 2 yr. EXP. %	After 2 yr. CON. %	After 2⅓ yr. EXP. %	After 2⅓ yr. CON. %
Non-starters	6.6	5.2	2.2	0.3	2.1	0.3	0.7	0
At Books Intro. 1 or 2	55.0	75.9	28.8	54.5	15.6	35.4	9.4	25.9
At Book 3	17.8	15.7	12.8	17.2	7.8	17.1	5.0	19.1
At Book 4	10.9	2.8	14.5	13.3	5.1	12.0	4.3	11.2
At Book 5	4.0	0.5	8.1	7.2	3.0	4.5	2.5	6.1
Beyond Book 5	5.7	0	33.6	7.4	66.4	30.6	78.1	37.8
N	651	651	580	580	333	333	278	278
Median Primer Position	Intro. 1,2	Intro. 1,2	4	Intro. 1,2	Beyond 5	3	Beyond 5	4
Superior Group	ita		ita		ita		ita	
Kolmogorov-Smirnov (one-tailed) test χ^2 (2 d. of f.)	49.51		92.71		85.02		90.21	
Percent level of significance	0.1		0.1		0.1		0.1	

TABLE 5   *Results for Schonell graded word reading test given after 1 year*
and after 1⅓ years in i t a to i t a group and in t o to t o group

Group	N	After 1 year Mean	After 1 year Median	After 1 year Q3–Q1	N	After 1⅓ years Mean	After 1⅓ years Median	After 1⅓ years Q3–Q1
Experimental (i t a)	660	17.99	10.15	26.40	585	33.93	30.78	39.04
Control (t o)	660	6.61	4.02	7.61	585	14.74	12.23	18.56
Kolmogorov-Smirnov (one-tailed) test χ^2 (2 d. of f.)		91.79				166.91		
Per cent level of significance		0.1				0.1		

TABLE 6   *Results for Neale analysis of reading ability given after $1\frac{1}{2}$ years in i t a to i t a group ($N=459$) and in t o to t o group ($N=459$)*

Measure	Group	Mean	Median	Q3–Q1	Kolmogorov-Smirnov X^2 (2d of f)	Percent Level of Significance
ACCURACY	Experimental	24.79	23.44	25.84		
	Control	13.68	9.70	17.99		
					96.78	0.1
SPEED	Experimental	26.41	23.95	21.79		
	Control	24.77	20.62	21.50		
					7.00	5
COMPRE-HENSION	Experimental	6.99	6.48	7.28		
	Control	4.86	4.06	5.99		
					46.18	0.1

countries. Children in such countries are likely to become confused about literacy-learning tasks so long as t o is used for beginning reading. In other countries where an s r w s is used by all as the common convention for their spoken language, the task is likely to be easier, as has been shown by Hildreth (1965 and 1966).

The question which cannot be avoided here is whether the English-speaking countries should not replace t o by an s r w s, or at least begin to modify t o in the direction of simplification and regularization. The i t a experiments have shown incontorvertibly that an s r w s has major advantages for the beginning stages, but the gains are offset considerably by losses at the transition stage. Even though the net balance is a gain by the end of the third year of school, it seems obvious that the simplest way of avoiding the problems causing this regression would be to remove the necessity to transfer to t o by adopting some kind of s r w s as the common convention for English.

In the meantime, i t a remains a valuable means of circumventing the worst effects of t o at the crucial stage when it is so important to provide children with positive reinforcement for their first more academic explorations, i.e. in the initial stages of learning to read and write. But there is no room for complacency among the i t a enthusiasts either. If the use of the initial teaching alphabet as a transitional system continues to grow, as seems likely from current trends then further development of teaching techniques, materials, and even the i t a system itself should be pursued with urgency.

5 Recent developments in i t a

The main conclusions of research on i t a have been further strengthened by new evidence published since this paper was prepared for the UKRA conference at Cambridge. The Schools Council's report on i t a by Warburton and Southgate (1969) independently arrived at substantially the same conclusions. For example, it states: 'There is no evidence whatsoever for the belief that the best way to learn to read in traditional orthography is to learn to read in the traditional orthography. It would appear rather that the best way to learn to read in a traditional orthography is to learn to read in the initial teaching alphabet.' Also, even more recently Downing and Latham (1969) tested a sample of the children in the original British i t a experiments and found that i t a pupils remained superior in t o reading and t o spelling achievements even after 5 years at school, well beyond the transition stage. One conclusion however, requires amendment. It is known now with greater certainty that i t a does indeed help slow learners. A later analysis (by Downing 1969) of data from the i t a experiments has shown that the incidence of reading failure is reduced importantly (approximately 50 per cent) when i t a is the medium for beginning reading. In view of these findings it is not surprising that the use of i t a has continued to grow. In England by 1972 probably about 15 per cent of primary schools were using i t a, and it is growing in usage throughout the world, not only for beginning reading, but also for a number of other purposes, especially for teaching English as a second language and for remedial reading (cf Downing 1970). The next decade will probably see further growth as a result of the legacy of six million dollars which the late Mr Eugene Kelley who was president of Coca Cola of Canada has left to the i t a Foundation. The income is to be used to bring an understanding of the known benefits of i t a to a wider audience of teachers and parents.

References

Burt, C. (1962) Preface in Downing, J. A. tⳍ beε *or not to be* London: Cassell

Cortrigt, R. (1966) Another Simplified Spelling *Reading Teacher* 19

Davis, L. G. (1964) *K-a-t spelz Cat: The New English Orthography* New York: Carlton Press

Dean, J. (1966) 'Words in Colour' in: Downing, J. A. (ed) *The First International Reading Symposium, Oxford,* 1964 London: Cassell, and New York: John Day

Downing, J. A. (1964) *The i t a Reading Experiment* London: Evans, and Chicago: Scott, Foresman

John Downing

DOWNING, J. A. (1965a) Current Misconceptions About i t a *Elementary English* May 1965

DOWNING, J. A. (1965b) *The Initial Teaching Alphabet Explained and Illustrated* London: Cassell, and New York: Macmillan

DOWNING, J. A. (1967) *Evaluating the Initial Teaching Alphabet* London: Cassell

DOWNING, J. A. (1969) New Experimental Evidence of the Effectiveness of i t a in Preventing Disabilities of Reading and Spelling *Developmental Medicine and Child Neurology* 11

DOWNING, J. A. (1970) *i t a's Effectiveness in the Prevention and Treatment of Disabilities in Reading and Writing* London: Initial Teaching Alphabet Foundation

DOWNING, J. A., FYFE, T. and LYON, M. (1967) The Effects of the Initial Teaching Alphabet on Young Children's Written Composition *Educational Research* 9

DOWNING, J. A. and JONES, B. (1966) Some Problems of Evaluating i t a: A Second Experiment *Educational Research* 8

DOWNING, J. A. and LATHAM, W. (1969) A Follow-up of Children in the First i t a Experiment *British Journal of Educational Psychology* 39

FRY, E. B. (1966) First Grade Reading Instruction Using Diacritical Marking System, Initial Teaching Alphabet and Basal Reading System *Reading Teacher* 19

GATTEGNO, C. (1964) Words in Colour *Forward Trends* 8

HARRIS, W. T. (1869) *Fifteenth Annual Report of the Board of Directors of St Louis Public Schools*

HART, J. (1570). *A Methode or comfortable beginning for all unlearned, whereby they may bee taught to read English, in a very short time with pleasure* London

HILDRETH, G. (1965) Lessons in Arabic *Reading Teacher* 19

HILDRETH, G. (1966) Armenian Children Enjoy Reading *Reading Teacher* 19

The i t a Symposium (1967) Slough, Bucks: National Foundation for Educational Research in England and Wales

JONES, J. K. (1965) Colour as an Aid to Visual Perception in Early Reading *British Journal of Educational Psychology* 35

LAUBACH, F. C. (1964) *Learn English the New Way* Syracuse: N.Y.: New Readers Press

MALONE, J. (1963) *Unifon* A paper presented at the Conference on Perceptual and Linguistic Aspects of the Reading Process, Center for Advanced Study in the Behavioral Sciences, Stanford, California

MCBRIDE, F. (1965) *Teachers' Course in Writing in i t a Reading Research Document No. 6* Edinburgh: Chambers

MOUNTFORD, J. (1965) *i t a as a Grading Device, Reading Research Document No. 5* Edinburgh: Chambers

NEALE, M. D. (1963) *Neale Analysis of Reading Ability* London: Macmillan

PATERSON, D. G. and TINKER, M. A. (1940) *How to Make Type Readable* New York: Harper & Row

PETERS, M. L. (1966) The Influence of Certain Reading Methods in the Spelling Ability of Junior School Children (Abstract) *Bulletin of the British Psychological Society* 19

PITMAN, I. J. (1961) Learning to Read: An Experiment *Journal of the Royal Society of Arts* 109

SCHONELL, F. J. (1950) Graded Word Spelling Test B, in: SCHONELL, F. J. *Diagnostic and Attainment Testing* Edinburgh: Oliver & Boyd

SCHONEL, F. J. and SCHONELL, F. E. (1956) Graded Word Reading Test in: SCHONELL, F. J. *Diagnostic and Attainment Testing* Edinburgh: Oliver & Boyd

SIEGEL, S. (1956) *Non-parametric Statistics for the Behavioral Sciences* New York and London: McGraw-Hill

SIMPLER SPELLING ASSOCIATION (undated) *Simpler Spelling As a Teaching Instrument* New York: Simpler Spelling Association, Lake Placid Club

SOUTHGATE, V. (1963) Augmented Roman Alphabet Experiment. An Outsider's Report *Educational Review* 16

UNIVERSITY OF LONDON INSTITUTE OF EDUCATION and THE NATIONAL FOUNDATION FOR EDUCATIONAL RESEARCH IN ENGLAND AND WALES (1960) *Some reasons why we are initiating an investigation into the early stages of learning to read, when the matter to be read is printed in a special form alleged to be easy to learn and leading easily to a full reading skill* London: University of London Institute of Education

WARBURTON, F. W. and SOUTHGATE, V. (1969) *i t a: An Independent Evaluation* London: Murray and Chambers

WIJK, A. (1958) *Regularised English* Stockholm: Wiksell

12   Words in colour

JOAN DEAN
Chief Inspector for Surrey

A combination of two papers presented at the First and Second Annual Conferences of UKRA Oxford 1964 and London 1965, first published in *The First International Reading Symposium* and *The Second International Reading Symposium*

In discussing Dr Gattegno's reading scheme, *Words in Colour*, I should like to make two points clear from the outset. In the first place, this approach has not, to my knowledge, been the subject of any controlled experiments. The observations I make are therefore very much a matter of personal opinion, and as we all know, the factors in learning to read are so many, that personal opinion may not be a valid form of judgement. In the second place, I am not wholly convinced that this is a suitable approach for young children, although I have been impressed with the reading ability of the infant school children whom I have seen using it. They are undoubtedly in possession of skills not acquired by normal approaches to reading nor, I think, by the Initial Teaching Alphabet, although in fact the skills to which I am referring can be taught in other contexts than that of *Words in Colour*. My doubts about this scheme are not whether it will teach children to read efficiently. I have seen that it can; my doubts are about the formal learning situation which it imposes—a learning situation which is in some degree foreign to our best infant schools. However, it may be that improved materials for use with this scheme may make it possible to introduce it in a less formal way. In any case, I am convinced that the scheme has a good deal to offer in terms of remedial teaching and also that there are a number of ideas stemming from it which are valuable at any level and which are applicable with other approaches.

The more I see of the teaching of reading, the more aware I become that there are many satisfactory ways of doing it and that our methods must always be fitted to the particular children we are teaching. No one scheme has the answer for all children and we need to be open minded enough to examine new ideas put forward without emotion and with detachment and to abstract from them whatever is of value for our particular children.

Let us look at this scheme. It is a scheme which sets out to make English phonetically regular by using colour with letter shapes to distinguish the many signs from which English words can be built. Each of the sounds found in English is represented by a colour which makes its pronunciation clear to the reader. Thus the letter 'a' coloured white will be pronounced as in 'hat', but when it is coloured blue-green it will be pronounced as in 'spade'. The sound 'a' as in 'spade' will be coloured blue-green whatever the letters composing it. In 'great' for example, the 'ea' will be blue-green, in 'vein' the 'ei' will be blue-green, and so on.

This is a fairly simple and I think a good idea, but it is easy to see that if one merely presented it to children in its entirety it would appear so complicated that it would probably be of little value. Very often teachers examining the ideas behind this approach stop at this point, not realizing that the scheme, as Gattegno plans it, has many of the qualities of programmed learning, each colour and sound being introduced and used in such a way that it is easily remembered. The steps the children are asked to take are very small ones, but each step widens the range of sounds which the child can read and write.

This is very much a phonetic approach. Gattegno believes that we underestimate children and that they are capable of much more intellectually at five than we normally assume. The approach as he plans it makes no concessions to look and say or to word-picture associations. The reading books which go with the scheme are baldly phonetic, with no illustrations at all until the book of stories is reached. The work starts with the introduction, one by one, of five vowel sounds. One of the points about this scheme is that there is a sign for every sound and a sound for every sign. The first signs given are 'a' as in 'hat', which is white, 'u' as in 'hut', which is yellow, 'i' as in 'pin', which is pink, 'e' as in 'pet', which is blue, and 'o' as in 'pot', which is orange. The teacher tells the children the pronunciation of these and refers to them as 'the white one, the yellow one, etc.' The children build letter combinations with them immediately. In fact they may start by making letter combinations with the first two alone, getting curious sounds like 'au' and 'uau'. Much of this is done by a process which Gattegno calls 'visual dictation' which means that teacher and children take it in turns to point out successions of sounds from the written signs on the blackboard. The idea of repeating a sound is also introduced at this stage, resulting in sound combinations like 'eea' and so on.

Very soon the first consonant is introduced—'p'—the brown one. Consonants are never, in fact, pronounced by themselves but always associated with vowel sounds. The teacher tells the children that the white sound and the brown one together make 'ap'. She then goes on to ask them what the other sounds they know make with the brown one after them, and she may get 'ep', 'ip', 'op', 'up'. They

135

also build up the combinations of sounds the other ways round, getting 'pe', 'pi', 'pa', 'po', 'pu'. Once they have grasped the idea of this, they go on to combine them in as many ways as possible. One or two of these combinations make real words, of which 'pop' and 'pip' will be known to the children. Next 't' is introduced, the purple one, and quite a number of words become possible—'pit', 'pat', 'tip', 'tap', 'pet', 'pot', 'top'. One of the points of this scheme however, is to get children to read what is there and to become adept at combining sounds, as well as to read real words, so sound combinations are also pointed out. It is intended to encourage children to play with words and sounds and to be able to deal with them in a flexible way, as well as to encourage careful looking and discrimination by fine detail. The children work a good deal from the blackboard, following the words and sounds the teacher points out or pointing out words to each other. The visual dictation idea has the advantage that the children are being forced to see words pointed out in the right temporal sequence. When they point out words themselves for others to read, they discover whether or not they have the sounds rightly arranged, because if they are not pointed out in the correct sequence they do not sound right.

From the beginning children are asked to write down what they hear—i.e. to write from dictation. With young children this means that one must also deal with the beginning of writing. Gattegno does this by getting them to draw each letter in the air, imitating the way the teacher does it, and then drawing it smaller and smaller and finally drawing it in pencil on paper. This seems to work with most children, but it might be equally satisfactory to use letter-cards and let children select those they need from a group of cards.

Charts are also provided so that children can refer back to previous work, together with reading books which simply deal with the sounds the children are learning and words and sentences built from them. The charts and the signs written on the blackboard are in colour. Everything else is in black and white, and the children's own writing is in pencil. The colours of the sounds are established through work with them, and through a good deal of closing the eyes and making images of them. The teacher might start by saying 'What do these make?' 'the purple one, the white one, the brown one'. When she gets the answer 'tap', she may say, 'Now turn them round the other ways, so that the brown one comes first; what do they make now? 'pat'. Now put the blue in the middle instead of the white one. What have we made? 'pet'.

The next sound to be introduced is the dark lilac sound 's' as in 'is' together with the green sound 's' as in 'so'. The double letter 'ss' as in 'mess', is simply shown as another sign for the green sound 's' and is introduced at the same time and in the same colour. With these letters a good many words can be made and the children can begin to write sentences as well as words. With 'm', the dark orange sound, and 'n', the dirty pink, we have enough sounds to do a good deal. It is at this point that teachers using this scheme have found it valuable to start making books for their children. At first these have a fairly limited vocabulary, but this is true of all first reading books. Once the initial stages are passed, however, the possibilities multiply rapidly, and it is frequently possible to come upon a word which has special meaning for a particular child and to make a book for him, which can be used for others too. It is interesting to compare the texts with those of more orthodox reading books. Here is an example of a well-known page from 'Janet and John' (O'Donnell and Munro.)

> Come, little dog.
> Come and play.
> Come and jump.
> Jump.

Here is a comparable example from a book made by a teacher for use with *Words in Colour*:

> is it a teddy
> it is pat's teddy
> sit up teddy
> teddy sits up

One might venture to suggest that the second author was influenced by the first! What I am really pointing out, however, is that phonetically based books do not necessarily have any worse texts than books based on look and say. Both, of course, are a long way below the children's interests and conversation at this time. To me this is one of the main reasons for being interested in any method which will help children past the initial stages of reading as quickly as possible. Let me give you some more examples of these books, however. Here is one from what the teacher calls the third grade. The grading is simply determined by the sounds which have been covered. The previous example was from the first grade.

> I like to help mummy
> I can make my bed
> I can dress myself
> I can carry the plates
> I can set the table
> I can carry the cups
> I can tidy myself
> Mummy thanks me

Lastly, an example from what the teacher calls the fifth grade. The children reading this had been in school for a year, and they had used the scheme for about two terms, although of course some were much further advanced than others.

> ann has a red umbrella.
> mummy gave it to her for her birthday.
> ann was five a week ago but it has not been wet yet.
> ann is sad. she cannot take her umbrella in the street.
> daddy tells her it can be a sunshade and that makes her happy.
> she rushes to get her umbrella to show it to pat and tess.
> pat tells ann she is silly as it is not wet.
> tess likes the umbrella and she gets under it with ann.
> pat is cross and sulky so she goes home.
> suddenly wet splashes go on the umbrella, but it keeps ann and tess dry.
> it is daddy with his hose.
> everybody thinks it is a funny trick.

Throughout these early stages, the children's ability to write is limited. Gattegno is of the opinion that all other material should be kept from the children while they are learning with this approach. This means that the normal stimulus of books and the writing of simple sentences of interest to the children is ruled out. This I find difficult to justify, since in practice children learn to read in a variety of ways, whatever the scheme they appear to be using, and are daily seeing a great variety of reading material all about them. It would seem more profitable to pursue the two in parallel, making links as soon as the scheme allows it. Children writing sentences of their own choice to describe their pictures, for example, would at first copy or go over what the teacher had written at their dictation, just as they frequently do with other schemes. Gradually it becomes more and more possible for the teacher to point out the sounds the child knows, although by the time this can be done to any extent, the child has grasped the principle that the spoken word can be written according to a logical system, and he is prepared to tackle any word, whether or not he has learnt it. Once children have found a tool by which they may build words, they begin to write fluently. This comment has been made many times about the Initial Teaching Alphabet. It is equally true of *Words in Colour*. In both cases, of course, the need for genuine motivation for writing is there especially after the initial excitement of being able to put the spoken word into permanent form in writing has passed. It is important that we do not forget the need for motivation for both reading and writing in our interest in new ways of teaching reading. We have only to look at the way in which the slowest child learns to read words like 'chocolate' to appreciate the importance of this. One might also add that we should not forget the need for teaching mature skills of reading at a later stage. Too often we regard the teaching of reading as finished when the child has completed a reading scheme.

Just as I feel that a variety of opportunity for writing is needed with this scheme, so also I feel that there is a need for the wide variety of reading material suitable for the children at their level. Teachers should be just as ready as they usually are to answer the question 'What does this say?' When the child already knows some sounds, the teacher can make use of this. She can also see that a fair number of labels and display captions contain sounds which the children know or are soon to meet and that these are discussed. It is certainly evident that children using this scheme are delighted to recognize the sounds they know.

I spoke earlier of the need to consider the question of motivation for reading. Gattegno is of the opinion that there is sufficient intellectual stimulus in his material to motivate reading, and in some ways this is borne out in practice. Each step is simple and brings a measure of success, so that we have the effect met in linear programming of reinforcement of learning by success. This is only one kind of motivation, however. Gattegno comes out very strongly against the teacher-imposed kind of motivation, where the child endeavours to learn simply in order to please and gain approval. This is a point worth considering in many aspects of education. It always seems to me to be an admission of failure on the part of teachers to give stars, marks or prizes to primary school children—implying that the material we are asking them to work on is not sufficiently worth learning to offer its own reward. While I would not go along with Gattegno to the point of always refusing to tell a child whether he is right or wrong, and never praising at all, nevertheless we might do well to look for incentives to learning other than desire for approval. A child will learn to read if it is sufficiently worth his while to do so. If by reading he can take part in some activity of real interest to him, then he will leave no stone unturned in his efforts to decipher what is before him. For some children it may be that the possibility of reading stories is so attractive that they will do their utmost to sort out words. For others—usually these are in the majority—a much greater incentive is the opportunity for action. Thus, instructions for making things and recipes for cookery may tempt some children to read. This is not to deny the attractions of playing with words but to add to the incentives for learning. If one deals with words only, apart from experience, the danger is that understanding will be lacking. This, in fact, is one of the dangers of this scheme. Teachers in forward-looking primary schools are only too well aware of the way in which real experience and the beginnings of the basic subjects need to go hand in hand; that children only really absorb new words into their vocabularies when these are made meaningful to them through first-hand experience; that children who fail to learn have often been lacking in opportunities to handle materials and to play. It is difficult to pass on experience verbally at the early stages of school life and discussions about the meanings of words outside the children's experience may be of little value, even though they may be able to read them. This does not invalidate this scheme, however. It simply means that the teacher must be on the alert, watching to see that the work does not become second-hand—too much a matter of verbal facility without understanding. The problem is not peculiar to *Words in Colour* and it a. There are plenty of infant schools endeavouring to teach reading in a vacuum and wondering why they have non-readers. With a remedial group, of course, the situation may well be different, although the business of finding motivation is even more important. This scheme is particularly valuable in providing for a measure of success from the beginning, and thus helping to build up confidence.

The scheme continues introducing sounds one at a time and using them with those already known. Several ways of exploring the use of words are suggested. We all know the difficulty many children have in sorting out the right directional attack on words. Gattegno tackles this by encouraging children to look for words that can be reversed and to practise reversing them. The game of changing one word to another by changing a sign at a time is played with special rules which make it possible to add or insert a sign and to reverse the word as well. Thus one might get from 'must' to 'stop' for example, in this way:

'must', 'most', 'post', 'past', 'pass', 'pats', 'pots', 'stop'

One can, of course, think of much easier examples, which would be suitable at the early stages.

Another activity involves filling in gaps in words in as many different ways as possible. For example, one might give children the outline 'm——t', which could be filled in to make 'meat', 'meet', 'mint', 'mast', 'most', 'must', 'malt', and so on.

These games are undoubtedly valuable elements in this approach. They might well be played probably somewhere in the junior school, whatever the method used for learning to read. I very much doubt if we do enough to make our children really interested in words and the relationships between them. Games like Lexicon and Scrabble also offer something of the same kind and encourage and discrimination necessary in both sight and hearing for accurate reading, spelling and pronunciation.

There are a number of worries connected with this scheme, which are frequently brought forward. Teachers usually ask 'where can I get hold of so many different coloured chalks, and anyway will my children be able to distinguish such a variety of colours?' Neither of these difficulties is the problem it appears to be. Boxes of coloured chalks can in fact be obtained from the Cuisenaire Company, but as they are introduced carefully and systematically, it would probably be possible to use the same colour more than once without confusion. In any case new colours can always be obtained by going over a shape with two different colours and in practice this is what was happening in the schools where I have seen the scheme in operation. Neither is there much difficulty in discriminating between colours, again because of the way they are introduced. Naming colours is not a problem either, because in practice the children name them. In one of the schools where I have been observing, for example, the various greens are known as 'pretty green', 'dirty green' 'tree green', and so on. One might note in passing, that the ability to differentiate fifty different colours and to invent names for them is quite a useful skill in itself. As the colours are only used on the board and not in the children's books, and as a good deal of the work on the board is in white, colour is not a great problem. Nor does colour-blindness seem to be the stumbling-block one might expect it to be. Signs are recognized by their shapes as well as by their colours, and although the colour-blind child is at a disadvantage, as he must frequently be in other contexts also, he has clues other than colour to help him. As he must frequently use shape to help him distinguish things normally distinguished by colour, he is probably more aware of this than most children. There is no doubt that the colour element in this scheme is valuable, however. Children who cannot recognize sounds from the shape of the symbol representing them, are often able to remember them when given the colour. I think I am right in saying that children of infant school age will more often sort things by colour than by shape, given the choice. This would seem to be borne out in my observation of this scheme in action. On the other hand, I may be personally biased about this, because I have always thought of both letters and numbers in terms of colours, though not in the colours of this scheme. I find this a great help in spelling and I remember a word by its colours, though some of the colours may be rather ill-defined. I have also been interested in watching children working with this scheme to notice that they were often able to recall, with their eyes closed, words that they were unable to recognize in print, even though the printed letters were in colour. A child unable to read the word 'pat', for example, seems able to recall it in imagination when told, 'think of the brown one, the white one and the purple one'.

Another point which often worries teachers is that a regional pronunciation. There are indeed some problems caused by this, but in fact one is recording the sounds made, whatever these may be, so that a word may be written with one set of colours in one part of the country and with a different set elsewhere. In the south we would write 'us' using the yellow sign and the green one, but in parts of northern England it could be written using the khaki sign and the purple one. The teacher is then left with the problem of how far she should endeavour to get children to use standard pronunciation. What the scheme does do is to make both teachers and children more aware of what they are saying.

Capital letters are not introduced at the beginning of this scheme, but are dealt with later on, and the reasons for using them explained. This seems to work reasonably well and the children using this approach seem to be no worse than others in tackling this problem and are possibly rather better.

Another interesting point which emerges is that children have no difficulty in blending sounds. In this case this is probably because consonants are never voiced except with vowels. The sound 'p' for example is always given with a vowel, 'up' or 'pa', never 'p', which would in fact be written as the brown sign with the dark yellow sign, 'pea'.

What about the materials for this scheme? There are two teachers' books, *The Background Book* and *The Teachers' Guide*. The *Background Book* is of general interest and sets out to deal with the ideas behind the scheme and to explain how it came into being. *The Teachers' Guide* deals with the scheme stage by stage. There are a series of charts covering all the sounds. These look confusing at first, but in practice one is dealing with what is on them so systematically that there is no problem. They can be used as teaching material and as reference charts. One of the difficulties is the space they take up. There are twenty-one of them and they really need to be displayed for most of the time the scheme is being used, so that children can refer to them. Among the most interesting pieces of apparatus are the *Fidel Charts*. The word 'Fidel' is taken from the Amharic word for alphabet. These give all the letter combinations of the English language in colour, and are arranged according to sound. Thus one group of sounds, coloured dark orange, contains the sounds 'm', 'mm', 'me', 'mb', 'gm', 'lm' (which are all spellings of the sound 'm'). Some of the letter combinations give one a good deal of food for thought. When, for example, is 'u' pronounced 'f' (in 'lieutenant') or when is 'ui' pronounced 'oo' (in 'bruise')? This is quite an interesting summary of sounds, apart from this scheme. It is built up stage by stage in black and white for the children in the *Word Building Book*.

For the children there are three graded reading books. These come as something of a shock to teachers accustomed to attractive and well-illustrated reading books, because they are entirely in black and white and are not illustrated at all. It is also true to say that they contain no reading matter which is of interest to children in terms of subject matter. The first book, in fact, contains mainly sounds and single words with a few sentences. Between them they cover all the possible ways of spelling all the sounds that make up the English language. The children I have seen using them do not appear to find them as dull as one might suppose, but it is difficult to decide

a

u	i	a	o	a	e	u	a	I	a						oi
y	oh	e	ay	you	ee	y	aa							oi	oi
oe	ey	ho	u	au	eau	ea	i	ea						oy	
ou	ie	a	o	ey	ue	ei	au	igh							
oo	a	ow	i	eigh	ew	ie	e	ie					e		x
	u	au	io	augh	eu	i	ah	eye					ee		x
o		au	ca	ough	eue	eo		ye					ea		xe
ia		ou	ou	oo	ieu	oe		eigh					ie		xc
ay			ei	hau				is							
e			y	oa				ai				oo	ou		
ai			ai							u	ew	ui		
ei			ough						wo	oe	ough	o	qu	x	
ui			ie							ee	ui				
			iou						u	ue	ew				

																	x
e	a	o	o	e	o	u											
ie	oe	oe	hou	a	oe	you											
ea	ow	ow	ow	ai	ow	eau											
ai	ai	owe	ough	hei	owe	ue											
a	a	oa		ayo	oa	ew											
u	u	oh		ea	oh	eu											
		ew		et	ew	eue											
		eau			eau	ieu											
		ou			ou												
		ough			ough												

p	s	s	m	n	f	f	d	l	th	th	w	k	r	b	h	g	sh	ch	ch	ng	j	qu
pp	z	ss	mm	mn	ff	v	dd	ll			wh	kk	rr	bb	wh	gg	ch	ch	tch	n	g	x
pe	ge	se	me	ne	fe	ve	de	le				ke	re	be		gu	t	t	t		d	xe
ed	c	c	mb	kn	ph	lve				the		ck	rre	bu		gh	s				dge	xc
cht	ce	ce	gm	dne	lf	ed						ch	wr				ce		che		ge	
ct	zz	sw	mn	pn	gh	ld						c	rh				ss		sch			
	si			lm	gn							che	lo				sc					
bt		thes										lk	rrh				ci					
pt	x	st										qu	rt									
tte	sch	sc										que										
th	ps											cch										

143

whether this is because they are really involved with and enjoying the intellectual stimulus of sorting out sounds, as Gattegno says, or whether they are merely thrilled with being 'on a real book'. Perhaps there is an element of both. Gattegno purposely omits pictures in order to concentrate the child's attention on the words without the benefit of extraneous clues. He contends that you are not encouraging a child to look carefully at a word, if you enable him to guess what it is from the pictures with it. It is worth giving some thought to this point, although I would personally regard some pictures as legitimate clues. Certainly I was moved by the small boy who turned over the pages in the *Book of Stories* and said: 'up here there's a picture'. In all honesty, I must admit that I do not like these books. I think one might use much of the same material and arrive at a more interesting conclusion, a conclusion moreover, within the comphrehension of the children. As I have shown, a number of the teachers working with this scheme are in fact doing this. One of the advantages of the scheme is that children can use other reading material, once they have gone a little way. In practice, capital letters can be rather a nuisance, but once they start to read, this is fairly easily overcome.

In addition to the three basic books there is the *Book of Stories* already mentioned. This explains itself, but would be more useful, I think, if it were broken up into a number of smaller books, and of course, it needs multiplying endlessly. In case you imagine from my comment earlier that it is profusely illustrated in the manner of normal infant school material, I should add that it has nine drawings in black and white, showing the main characters in the stories. There are also work-sheets which suggest the kind of word-making games already mentioned. These too could well be made by a teacher, and they offer a number of useful suggestions. Most teachers who use them say they are too difficult. Gattegno replies to this by saying that we underestimate children, and when one looks at the content of some of the reading material we offer them at the moment, one feels he may be right!

The work of particular schools

I want now to describe briefly some of the schools I have seen using this scheme. I must emphasize again that the figures I can offer are those of teachers kept for their own benefit. Where there is comparison of groups, it is not a comparison of properly matched groups, and there has been no attempt to balance time and effort spent on this scheme with that spent on other schemes.

I have been watching work in one six-class infant school over a period of nearly three years. When *Words in Colour* was introduced it was very new indeed, and the headmistress decided to try it out with one entrance group only before committing the school to it. At that time the children in the other classes were using the Beacon phonic scheme. The new entrance class following the one using *Words in Colour* were given *Janet and John,* which was a new scheme to the school. We are thus in a position to make some comparison between the four groups using Beacon readers, one group using *Words in Colour,* and one group using *Janet and John.* I recently received from the headmistress a list of reading ages (Schonell Word Recognition Test) and a list of chronological ages for each group in the school, last summer term. If one looks at the average reading age for each class and compares it with the average chronological age, it becomes clear that all classes except the one using *Words in Colour* are reading at a level below their chronological age. The difference varies from −0.10 with the oldest group to −0.85 with the youngest. The *Words in Colour* group have a difference between chronological age and reading age of +1.61. It is difficult to decide how much weight can be given to this, however, because the school admits to placing a good deal more emphasis on *Words in Colour* than on any of the other schemes.

In another junior and infant school in a good residential area, the scheme is in use much as Gattegno suggests, and is used as the main reading scheme for all beginners and for remedial groups of older children who originally learnt by other methods. The school is a lively one and it provides a really good reading environment with plenty of books and many interests for the children. The speed at which they learn to read and write is impressive, and nearly all children read at levels above their chronological age. It is difficult to know how much to credit this to the scheme, since this sort of progress is not unusual in this kind of area. The ability to discriminate sounds and symbols and to play with words and to puzzle out new ones is very strong, however, and these seem to be the special gains from this scheme.

Another infant school in my area is using the scheme quite differently as a means of systematizing knowledge of sounds once reading has begun with a look-and-say scheme. The children work through the initial stages fairly quickly, because the material is really familiar. There is less emphasis on making images of the colours and the scheme is augmented with a lot of teacher-designed apparatus. For example, the children use sets of coloured letters and groups of letters to build words and sentences. Due emphasis is given to the play with words, and these children are good at this.

The scheme is also being used in some of our secondary schools with groups of children who are backward in reading. Dr Gattegno himself carried out some work in one school with a group of children aged twelve to fifteen who were failing in reading. These children were gathered together from a number of secondary schools and they spent two days solidly on work with this scheme. I have records

Joan Dean

only of the seven boys from the host school. These children had
reading ages ranging from 5.8 to 7.9 years, with an average of 6.7
(Schonell Word Recognition Test). At the end of the first day the
average reading age had risen to 7.2 years and at the end of the
second to 7.8. In every case the reading age rose on both days. The
report on this experiment comments particularly on the gain in confidence and the improvement in tackling the test. One of the boys
concerned summed up his reaction by saying, 'If I had another
couple of days I think I would have been able to read the news-
papers.'

Another secondary school using the scheme with remedial groups
made similar comments. The teacher in charge of the group reported
good progress in every case and in particular noted that the children
gained confidence because the scheme gave them the ability to help
themselves.

Assessment of the scheme

I would like to conclude by looking at some of the advantages and
disadvantages of this scheme. Let us look first at the points in
favour of it.

1 Colour really helps. Evidence of this has come from all the schools
   which have used it. It would seem to be worth considering the use
   of colour as a discriminatory device in any context where children
   are finding confusion.
2 Children appear to enjoy it because they can do something from the
   beginning. This is particularly true in the remedial situation where
   they can see how it leads to reading. They seem to enjoy the
   exercise of solving a problem which is within their capacity, and
   teachers using this scheme have remarked that their children do
   not like to be told a word, but prefer to puzzle it out for themselves. Dr Gattegno makes a great feature of the child doing the
   work and taking responsibility for his own learning. With this scheme
   this is possible.
3 It develops to a high degree the ability to discriminate sounds and
   letter-shapes. Experience with i t a has shown us that young children do not look carefully at words, but get a general impression.
   In one of the schools where we are using i t a in my own authority,
   there is one class where some of the beginners in reading are
   learning with i t a and others with ordinary print. The children
   read each other's books quite easily and do not appear to see very
   much difference between them. If children starting reading are
   relying so much on general impression and are ignoring detail to
   this extent, it surely means that at some stage of learning to read
   we need to pay attention to detail of sound and shape. We prob-

146

ably deal inadequately with this aspect of reading at present. *Words in Colour* makes both children and teachers very conscious of sound and the need for careful listening and careful looking.

4 It develops the ability to play with words and to see relationships between them. One group I watched started with the word 'ear', then added 'th' to the end of it, then added 'y', then changed the 'th' to 'l' and added 'p' to the beginning and so on. This seems to me to be a great enrichment of knowledge of language, which we should pursue, whatever the method of learning to read.

5 Children who have learnt to read by this method are in a position to review the possibilities of spelling for any word. Only experience will help them to choose the right spelling from the possibilities, however.

6 There are no blending difficulties because the consonants are always given with vowels and never by themselves.

7 The scheme is systematic. A good teacher will teach well whatever the method and the children will learn. She will gradually, through experience, learn to arrange her material so that time is spent efficiently. A less good teacher may be helped considerably when she is working with some material which helps her to cover ground systematically. In this case the 'covering' of knowledge of certain sounds is reinforced all the time by continual building with them and the relationship between symbol and sound is established by much use.

The disadvantages of this scheme would seem to be as follows:

1 The scheme concentrates on the mechanical aspects of learning to read. It rests with the teacher to see that emphasis is also placed on the importance of reading for meaning. It would be possible to use the scheme and give this aspect very little place. It is perhaps fair to call this a disadvantage, but the danger of forgetting the purpose of learning to read is there. It should be noted, however, that this danger is present with all methods of teaching reading.

2 This scheme starts in a formal way and deals at the outset with sound combinations which are meaningless. The child learning with this scheme in a remedial class is often in a position to see how it leads to reading, for to him printed material is a way of representing speech on paper to which he has not the key. The five-year-old starting to read by this method may not see this. This again seems to throw the onus on the teacher to see that children are learning in a reading environment, where many other aspects of learning to read are evident. I should perhaps add that Dr Gattegno would probably not agree with me here. He would prefer to concentrate on teaching children with the scheme until they could read.

It is extremely difficult to make fair comparisons between methods of teaching reading because they may foster different aspects and abilities and these may not be shown by the tests used for making the comparison. This scheme, for example, fosters the ability to see relationships between words and I know of no test which shows this.

In working with teachers I am continually impressed by the wide variety of successful approaches to the teaching of reading. This is one of a number of highly successful methods which appeals very much to some teachers.

13 What is colour story reading?

J. KENNETH JONES

Journalist, author of
Colour Story Reading

Revised version of a paper presented at Fourth Annual Conference of
UKRA Nottingham 1967, first published in *Reading: Problems and
perspectives*

Colour Story Reading (CSR) is a new approach to the problem of
learning to read.

It is a new medium and also a new method. It is a new medium
because it uses colour to add greater phonetic consistency to the
language. It is a new method, at least as far as reading is concerned,
because it is designed to be learned by discovery techniques.

As a new medium, coloured print has three important advantages.

Firstly, it appeals to young children aesthetically. They like
coloured things, and they prefer words and letters which are in
colour. The coloured print is more enjoyable, and more likely to
arouse their interest and attention.

Secondly, the consistent use of colour makes it easier to distinguish
between different letters and different words. In order to take full
advantage of this visual benefit, letters of similar shape, such as b, d,
and p, have different colours. This visual benefit does not apply to
adults, for they have been thoroughly programmed to respond to
black print. They find coloured print visually confusing at first, not
because it is confusing, but because it is unfamiliar.

The third advantage is phonetic. The words are coloured according to their sounds. When letters change their sounds they change
their colour.

There are fifty-three colour symbols representing forty-two sounds.
Only three colours are used, plus black. Thirty-five of the colour
symbols are individual letters. Red letter 'a' (as in 'acorn') is one
symbol, green letter 'a' (as in 'apple') is another. Letter 'y' is green in
'yes', red in 'try', and blue in 'happy'.

The remaining colour symbols are digraphs and coloured backgrounds. These digraphs are two letters representing the same sound,
and there are nine of them in the code. The first letter of each digraph,

and usually the second letter, is of a different colour from what that letter would be as an individual letter. The green letters 'oi' are a digraph in 'noise', but in a word like 'going' the 'o' would be red (all long vowels are red), and the 'i' would be blue. The nine coloured backgrounds all represent individual sounds, except for the blue circle which represents silent letters. The backgrounds have three shapes (square, circle, triangle) and three colours (red, blue and green). The sounds chosen for the backgrounds are those which have very varied letter representation. The letters 'er', 'ur' and 'ear' would all be written in a red circle in the words 'her', 'hurt' and 'heard'. However bizarre the spelling, if a word contains the sound 'er' it would be written in a red circle, such as 'yr' in 'myrtle', 'olo' in 'colonel' and 'yrrh' in 'myrrh'.

About one word in ten contains a letter or letters which cannot be coded accurately in colour, and these letters are written in black, which is the non-conformist symbol. But most non-conformist letters are regular. Black 'e' almost always represents the sound of short 'i', as in 'pretty' and 'begin'.

It should be noticed that colour does not introduce phonetic cues to the language for the first time. The English language conveys a great deal of phonetic information. The colour coding simply provides more reliable information without altering spelling or introducing new letters.

If *Colour Story Reading* relied solely on a colour code having aesthetic, visual and phonetic benefits, then it would not involve new teaching methods. It could be taught in the way most teachers have tackled reading during the past thirty or forty years—starting with look and say and introducing phonics gradually.

New media do not necessarily require new methods. Gattegno's *Words in Colour*, which uses forty-eight colours on wallcharts, is taught by phonic techniques. Pitman's *Initial Teaching Alphabet* does not involve any new methods.

The new approach in *Colour Story Reading* is not look and say or phonics, or a mixture of the two. The traditional methods involve a great deal of direct instruction, and a great deal of repetition. With look and say the teacher tells the child: 'that word says . . .', and with phonics the teacher teaches the sounds of the letters in the same way.

Colour Story Reading provides nineteen stories which are read or related by the teacher to the children, or played on records. These nineteen stories conceptualize the sounds. There is a green Apple which makes the sound of the short vowel 'a' when he speaks. His friends, Egg, Ink, Orange and Umbrella have adventures. They see the boy next door, Ernest, in a round cloud of red firework smoke. Ernest cannot answer questions and keeps saying 'er . . . er . . . er . . .'.

The children enjoy the nineteen stories purely for their entertainment value and they remember with remarkable accuracy who says which sound. The children's coloured reading books are a series entitled *Mr Nen and his Friends.* They are about the adventures which the children hear from their teacher. The books contain illustrations of Apple with the green letter 'a' coming from his mouth, and a picture of Ernest in his round cloud of red firework smoke. In the coloured text, the name 'Apple' begins with a green 'a', and the first two letters in the name 'Ernest' are printed in a round red background.

The combination of the stories heard and seen permits a departure from the paired-associate learning involved in 'look and say' and in phonics. The stories help ⌣ ᵖrovide a triangular learning situation, which helps the child to help himself to learn to read. This can be expressed diagrammatically as follows:

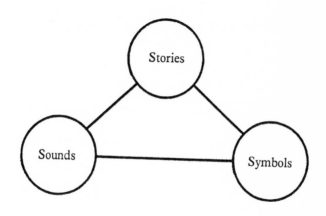

The teacher is advised to present *Colour Story Reading* in three stages.

In the first stage, the teacher presents all the nineteen stories purely for entertainment. Nothing is 'taught'. The children can act episodes, make models of the friends, paint, and so on. Instead of writing in black, the teacher writes the classroom notices in colour. The first stage is concerned with activity and the enjoyment of looking and hearing and doing.

The second stage is visual. This stage takes place when the children are spontaneously drawn to the coloured words in classroom projects or in *Mr Nen and his Friends* and they want to know what the words say. In this stage, the teacher uses visual clues linked with the nineteen stories. She refers to the shape of words, the colours of words, the associations connected with the words from the stories. She does not refer to individual letter sounds. As the coloured reading books are structured, with the gradual introduction of words and colour symbols, it is relatively easy for the children to work out meanings for themselves, for they already know the content of the stories.

In the third stage, the teacher refers to individual sounds, but only because the children do so first. The children's interest in sounds in words is a cue to the teacher that she can follow the children and respond in a like manner, using the stories to help the children answer their own questions for themselves.

The three stages of learning do not supercede one another, they finally coexist side by side, with mutual reinforcement of learning strategies.

This activity with coloured print does not replace black print books, except perhaps in the very beginning. As soon as the children make progress in coloured reading they transfer their skills and confidence to black print. Paradoxically, the more the teacher concentrates on colour, the more the children are able to read in black.

Whether the children write in colour can be left to them. In the early stages they enjoy copying in colour, and later, when they attain fluency, they prefer to write in black because it is quicker. There is some evidence to suggest that the more the children write in colour in the early stages, the better will be the writing and spelling in black later on.

The CSR experiments

Before it was published, *Colour Story Reading* (Jones 1967a) was the subject of many experiments. The aim was to seek answers to the questions of whether children read quicker and easier in CSR; whether these gains transfer to black print reading and spelling; whether the gains are maintained after the children have read the CSR books; whether the gains occur with slower learners and educationally sub-normal children; whether there is any problem about colour blindness and regional accents; and whether adding colour to shape increases the number of things to be learned?

The last question, which is a very common one, is interesting because it is based on a psychological, or linguistic error. It assumes that black print has shape but not colour. It is coloured, and the colour is black. It is a one colour medium just as much as if the colour were red.

Not only do the black letters have a colour, but letters in various colours have just as much 'shape' as any other object. What the question is really asking is whether a one colour code is easier than a code in several colours?

The answer depends on the nature of the objects which the learner or observer has to distinguish. Generally, a multi colour code is much easier than a one colour code. The map of the London Underground is much easier to read in eight colours than in one colour, because each line has its own colour. If all postage stamps were coloured red it would be much more difficult to identify values than with the existing multi-colour code. If all football teams, goalkeepers and referees played in blue, then this one colour code would make it more difficult to read the game.

Playing cards are a useful example of colour coding. The two colour code is better than a one colour code, but a four colour code, one for each suit, would be even more effective. However, a 52-colour code, one for each card in the pack, would be a hindrance in sorting out the suits.

To test the visual aspect of words and letters in CSR colours, compared with a one colour code (black), an experiment was conducted with 110 nursery school children aged between 3½ and 5 years. (Jones 1965a). The letters were those prone to reversal —d, b, p, q, u, n—and English words which had been transcribed into an unfamiliar script, but with similar characteristics. This was to avoid contamination by any previous learning of English words. The idea was to match six items in each test, which was done by pointing to the word or letter which corresponded with the item exposed. The following table shows the number of children who achieved high scores.

Medium	high scores	
	5	6
One colour letters (black)	6	3
CSR colour letters	32	48
One colour words (black)	1	0
CSR colour words	34	24

These results indicate the greater visual difficulty of a one colour medium for young children. In the one colour letter test only 9 of the 110 children had high scores compared with 80 children who scored high on the CSR letters.

The CSR letters had two letters in red, two in blue, and two in green, and it was possible to analyze the scores to see if any children were matching by colour alone which would be indicated by mistakes—matching green 'd' with green 'n' etc. Only one child, a girl aged 3.7 years appeared to be doing this, but the others were obviously paying attention to the whole of what they saw.

Another experiment on the visual appearance of CSR words concerned 5½ and 6½ years olds in a primary school (Jones 1965b). These children were learning to read in black print and had never seen CSR material before. They were given word recognition tests in the two media without explanations. Thus the test was heavily loaded by practice effect in favour of the one colour medium and against the CSR medium as the pupils were not even told the purpose of the colour coding. Two word lists were incorporated. Half the children had Test Y in black and Test Z in CSR, and the other half had Test Y in CSR and Test Z in black.

The experiment resulted in a total of 272 words read in black compared with 286 in CSR, an improvement which, although not statistically significant does not support an adult's first impression that CSR, with its coloured letters and coloured outlines, is visually confusing. In fact, children learning the one colour medium may find black print visually more difficult than their first visual impressions of CSR.

In both experiments the overwhelming majority of children said they preferred the CSR material. The nursery school children gave aesthetic-type reasons: 'Because it is pretty', 'Because I like the colours'. The primary school children gave aesthetic reasons plus visual reasons: 'I can see the word better in colour', 'it is easier to see'.

A third experiment with children who had not seen CSR before was with 8½ to 9½ year olds (Jones 1965b). They were given word recognition tests, but unlike the previous experiment, they were told that the colours and coloured outlines represented sounds, but were not told what the sounds were.

The pupils read more words in CSR than in black, both easy and difficult words. The big difference was with the difficult words, where 57% more words were read in CSR, the result being statistically significant at the 1% level.

Again, the majority expressed a preference for the CSR material, but the reasons given were mainly phonetic—'because it helps me get the sounds', and 'if you have them in black you can't read the words, but in colour they show up. It is easier to see and read'.

These three experiments showed that the one-colour medium was inferior aesthetically, visually and phonetically. Other experiments using hand-produced material of 'Mr Nen and his Friends' indicated that the coloured reading material plus the 19 Stories were very popular. As a result, the Department of Education and Science financed a large scale experiment with printed reading material in CSR which was carried out under rigorous controls by the Reading Research Unit of the University of London Institute of Education (Jones 1967b).

The results suggested the promise of CSR. They showed that *Colour Story Reading* was the most successful reading approach so far subjected to large scale controlled testings.

Gains made by CSR children in (black print) reading and spelling tests compared with control groups in the same schools at the end of the first year

No of schools	Category	Gain in reading	Gain in spelling
14	CSR as a supplementary aid	3 mths	2 mths
5	CSR as the main reading scheme	12 mths	13 mths

Most children read the CSR material within the first year. The pupils were also tested at the end of the second year, and it was found that the gains had been maintained.

Of particular interest was the fact that the lower achievers made gains in roughly the same proportion as the higher achievers, with both reading and spelling.

A further benefit was that many teachers spontaneously commented that CSR helped them to become more aware of the sounds of words and improved their general ability to teach reading.

Regional accents were not shown to be a handicap to the effectiveness of CSR, partly because most differences in regional pronunciation were assimilated unnoticed. For example, the 'u' in 'up' is pronounced differently in the North of England compared with the South. Yet as Umbrella makes this sound in the 19 Stories, and as the pronunciation of the first letter in 'umbrella' also varies according to the region, the blue 'u' can be used without inconsistency within a region. In the North 'up' also has the same sound as that made by 'umbrella' and in the South 'up' also has the same sound as that made by 'umbrella'. Each region attributes its own sound to blue 'u' and uses it without inconsistency.

The problem of colour blind children did not produce any difficulties in the classroom. Despite repeated requests for a special watch to be kept, no teacher reported any reading handicap caused by colour blindness. The reason was probably that the great majority of colour blind people can distinguish between the four colours—red, blue, green and black—even though they do not see them in exactly the same way as people with normal colour vision.

Parallel with the main experiment were a number of pilot studies with slow learners in remedial clinics and in schools for the educationally sub-normal. Unlike the main experiment where only black print tests were used, the children in the pilot studies were tested in CSR as well as in black. The children were usually able to read far more words in CSR than in the one-colour medium, and class records suggested that there was a big improvement in their subsequent ability to read and spell in the one-colour medium.

Another interesting finding was that spelling ability in one colour appeared to improve if the word was displayed in CSR. The children seemed to find it easier to remember the visual impact of the coloured words. This might be due not only to the various colours as such, but also their associations with the 19 Stories. So despite the fact that the children were recalling the words by writing them in black, their performance appeared to be better if the memory of the words was in four colours, rather than if the words had been written in black in the first place.

One school for educationally subnormal children used CSR as the main reading scheme throughout the school with remarkable results. Here are some comments of a class which had been using CSR for two years and were given a Schonell word recognition test in black and also in CSR and asked which they preferred and why.

Only one child, a fluent reader, preferred black, and said 'I think I did more in black'. In fact she, like all the other children, had scored higher in colour. All the other children preferred the words in four colours:

'Because this one is easier.'

'Because the colour helps me. It tells me the word in colour.'

'Because it is easier. You keep getting the silent letters and the red triangles.'

'Because you learn something. You learn the words. Because the colours are better than the black. Because they got things that sound things—squares, triangles and silent letters.'

'Because I like it. Because the colours are nice.'

'It is best. Because you can read in colour.'

'I don't know why I like it best.'

'Because it is helping me, it helps me to read quicker.'

'It is more easier. You know some of the sounds from the colour reading books.'

'Because you can get more words in colour than in black. I like the colours. I can make up words at home with coloured pencils. My mum and dad tick them and say "that's good" and things like that. I tell them all the silents and triangles and things.'

'It is in colour, you sound them all better.'

'Because it was easier, it was in colour.'

These replies show a remarkable consistency considering that they were all given separately in individual testing. It is worth noting that several children commented favourably on the coloured outlines—triangles, squares, circles—presumably because these coloured outlines greatly simplify the learning task. In this school and in others which used CSR as the main scheme, the children's comments had the same theme—it is easier in colour.

Comparisons with other new approaches

The experiments which have been described compare various aspects of Colour Story Reading with traditional teaching in a one-colour medium. But it is also valuable to compare new approaches with each other, and this can be done in various ways.

Phonetic coverage is one measure which can be used. The question is to what extent does a new alphabet, or the existing alphabet, bridge the gap between sounds and symbols. Are the symbols consistent in representing one sound only, or do they represent two or more sounds? The usual way to test the phonetic coverage of a medium is to allocate one sound only to each symbol and then count the number of words which contain symbols which do not have this sound. The greater the phonetic coverage, the easier the task of learning to read.

In theory, Dr Gattegno's *Words in Colour* (1962) has 100% phonetic coverage because each sound has its own colour, and when a letter represents two sounds (i.e. the 'o' on 'one') the top half of the letter is given in one colour, the bottom half in another colour. But in practice the phonetic coverage depends on ability to distinguish between the symbols, and as there are 48 different colours to distinguish, the actual phonetic coverage for most children will be a good deal less than 100% even if they have normal colour vision.

It is much easier to measure the phonetic coverage of i t a and CSR and traditional orthography, and to compare the three media by using identical passages.

In CSR the irregularities are signposted by being in black—the non-conformist symbol, but in i t a and in traditional orthography they are not. Consequently it is easy for the untrained eye (or rather ear) to assume that there are fewer irregularities in i t a or traditional orthography than is the case. Southgate (1970) falls into this error, she alleges that i t a has greater phonetic coverage than CSR. In fact, Southgate's main criticism of CSR is based on her own faulty assessment of its phonetic coverage.

With both easy and difficult passages, CSR has a much greater phonetic coverage than i t a. Here is a comparison using an extract from 'Ernest Owl' taken from Southgate (1970), and 'The little Red Hen' taken from Downing (1967). Daniel Jones' *English Pronouncing Dictionary* has been used for determining the errors.

Phonetic coverage	
Traditional black print	24%
i t a	69%
CSR	93%

In this comparison, each nonconformist symbol in CSR is counted as an error. However, if one were to allocate one sound to each non-conformist symbol (i.e. black 'f' representing the 'v' sound), then the CSR phonetic coverage rises to 97%.

Another way of comparing new reading approaches is to compare results of separate experiments. However, this method of comparison should always be treated with caution because there are often important differences in the design or conditions of individual experiments which produce differences in the results that are not due to the reading approach.

For this reason it is difficult to compare the gains which Dr Gattegno claims for *Words in Colour* with other new approaches. No large scale controlled experiments have been undertaken with *Words in Colour* in this country. However, those results which are obtainable suggest that Dr Gattegno's scheme may produce gains, particularly in remedial situations or with adults. One would like to see *Words in Colour* given the same opportunities as i t a and CSR in rigorous test conditions.

There have been two big i t a experiments in Britain, both carried out by the Reading Research Unit of the University of London Institute of Education and reported by Downing (1967).

The design of the first i t a experiment makes it difficult to compare results with CSR, (or indeed with traditional orthography) because of faulty design.

This first i t a experiment compared schools using i t a with schools not using i t a. As Vernon (1967) pointed out, the experiment 'did not control for variation between schools in method and adequacy of teaching and the time given to teaching reading; nor for such important but intangible factors as the general morale and progressiveness, or otherwise, of the schools'.

As a result of similar criticisms, the Reading Research Unit embarked on a second i t a experiment with more rigorous controls and which dealt with the problems of interschool variability. It was this second i t a experiment which had many similarities with the design of the CSR experiment (Jones 1968).

In both experiments the control and experimental groups were in the same schools, and there was control of the amount of time given to the teaching of reading. The same teachers were used for each group. In neither experiment were there statistically significant differences between groups in respect of age, sex, social class or intelligence.

There were, of course, some differences between the experiments. The CSR experiment covered some 800 pupils (not counting the pilot experiments with backward children) which was twice the size of the i t a experiment. In the i t a experiment there were more tests, as the progress of i t a children was measured in the i t a medium as well as in traditional orthography. The extra testing given to the it a children may have improved their scores compared with their control groups because of the practice effect, but the difference, if any, is not likely to have been significant.

However, there were other differences between the two experiments which favoured the it a scores. Firstly, it a had received a tremendous amount of favourable publicity, and at the time of the second it a experiment it was already being publicized as a success story. If the it a teachers in the second experiment had been neutral on the question, this would not have mattered, but they were not neutral. Most of them, as Downing (1967) pointed out, had already formed the view that it a was 'superior' to t o before the experiment began, and this would obviously affect their confidence and enthusiasm in presenting it a. And as these 'reading teachers' were also teaching reading in t o to the control groups, they must also have thought the control children would not read as well because they had the 'inferior' medium. (It is a common observation that teachers' expectations often influence results.) The opposite situation occurred in the CSR experiment where most teachers classified themselves as 'sceptical' or 'neutral' at the start of the experiment, and changed their minds dramatically to 'keen' or 'very keen' during the first term— but this change was due to experience, not preconceived attitudes.

Another difference favouring it a was that most of the 'reading teachers' in the it a experiment, who were supposed to divide their time equally between the two groups, spent more time with the it a group.

So although the experimental designs were so similar as to permit valid comparisons of the scores in the two experiments, there were some differences which tended to favour it a.

It is also important to note that the comparison is not directly between the scores of it a children and the scores of CSR children. The comparison is between each experimental group in relation to its own control group.

As pointed out earlier, the scores of the CSR children were superior to their control groups both in black print reading and spelling, and with both the high achievers and low achievers. And in schools where CSR was used as the main reading scheme, the gains in both reading and spelling were highly significant. Moreover, the gains were maintained after the children had got beyond the CSR reading books (Jones 1968).

By contrast, the after-transfer results of the it a children were comparatively poor. The results are given by Downing (1967). Ten measures were used in reading and spelling, and in nine of these the non-it a control children came out on top. On the test of silent reading comprehension the difference in favour of the control group was statistically significant at the 5% level.

When a football team loses by nine goals to one not even the supporters claim a victory. So it is somewhat surprising that the first conclusion in Downing's book is that 'i t a as a traditional writing system for beginning reading and writing in English generally produces superior results in t o reading and in t o spelling by the end of the third year of school'.

Some 300 words later he writes 'This first conclusion depends almost entirely for its evidence on the first experiment'.

It was this conclusion which received the publicity and was subsequently quoted to show the success of i t a, thus ignoring the fact that it was based on the faultily designed first experiment and also ignoring the unfavourable evidence of the second i t a experiment.

Another valid comparison between CSR and i t a is the relative success or failure of the lower achievers. If a scheme fails with this group, then there is little to recommend it.

In the first i t a experiment, the scores of each group were divided into ten categories of achievement with the same number of children in each category. It was therefore possible to compare, for example, the scores of the bottom 10% in each group. On most tests in this first experiment the pattern showed two curves which were widest apart (in favour of i t a) in the higher achievers, but which converged and met in the lower tenth, (Downing 1967).

For reasons which are not given, Downing does not use the ten achievement categories for analyzing the results of the second i t a experiment. He uses no categories at all for lower achievers, but he does separate the 'top-third' in each group for comparison purposes. Although he does not give the scores for the 'lower two-thirds' these can be extracted from the figures by subtracting the scores of the 'top-third' from the scores of the whole group.

A comparison of the 'lower two-thirds' shows that, for almost all after-transfer test results the adverse gap is wider for the 'lower two-thirds' than for the 'top third'. For example, in the final spelling test which was given after 3½ years when 96% of the i t a children had been transferred to t o books, the results were as follows:

Experimental category	Relative position
i t a 'top third'	3 months behind
i t a 'lower two-thirds'	6 months behind

If the shape of the 'achievement category' curves was the same as in the first i t a experiment, (and there is no reason to suppose that they were different), then the 'lower tenth' of the i t a children would be more than sixth months behind the 'lower tenth' of the control group.

The marked differences between the results of the two experiments can be seen by comparing the figures just given with those of the 'lower two-thirds' in schools using CSR as the main reading scheme in the early stages. In the final spelling test the CSR 'lower two-thirds' were 8 months ahead of the 'lower two-thirds' in their own control group. In the final reading test they were 10 months ahead.

Conclusions

Two main conclusions can be drawn.
1 The longer children are exposed to i t a as in the case of lower achievers, the worse their eventual reading and spelling ability in traditional orthography.
2 The more a teacher concentrates on CSR in the early stages, the greater the reading and spelling ability in black print, both for higher and lower achievers.

References

DOWNING, J. A. (1967) *Evaluating the Initial Teaching Alphabet* London: Cassell
GATTEGNO, C. (1962) *Words in Colour: Background and Principles* Reading: Educational Explorers
JONES, J. K. (1965a) 'Colour as an aid to visual perception in early reading' *Brit. J. Educ. Psychol.* 35
JONES, J. K. (1965b) 'Research report—phonetic colour' *New Education* Vol. 1, No. 4
JONES, J. K. (1967a) *Colour Story Reading* London: Nelson
JONES, J. K. (1967b) *Research Report on Colour Story Reading* London: Nelson
JONES, J. K. (June 1968) 'Comparing i t a with Colour Story Reading' *Educational Research* 10
SOUTHGATE, V. (1970) *Reading—Which Approach?* University of London Press
VERNON, M. D. (1967) 'Evaluations—11' in: *The i t a Symposium* Slough: National Foundation for Educational Research

14 The use of television with backward readers in the Glasgow area

MARGARET M. CLARK

Senior Lecturer in Psychology,
University of Strathclyde

Paper presented at Third Annual Conference of UKRA Cambridge
1966, first published in *Reading: Current research and practice*

A telerecording of the BBC television experimental series for backward readers in the junior schools was shown at the first meeting of
the West of Scotland Council of UKRA. This was followed by a discussion of the advantages and limitations of such programmes.
Members were asked whether they would be interested in using the
new series *Tom, Pat and Friday,* which was also designed for backward readers in the junior schools, and which was to be transmitted
in February 1966. Interest was expressed, and as a result, eight
schools in the Glasgow area have been involved in this present study
(six in Glasgow and two in Dunbartonshire). A member of the local
council has organized the viewing in all schools involved in the
study.

In four of the schools, the volunteer was the infants' mistress, who
was responsible for selecting the children who were to participate.
The children were drawn from a number of classes, and were
brought together for the broadcasts. In some schools the children
were drawn from as many as four classes. The infants' mistress was
also responsible for the follow-up work, which was done either
immediately after the broadcast or in the following week. In one
school arrangements were made for all the teachers who had children
participating to see at least one of the broadcasts, and they were also
encouraged to assist the follow-up work by providing materials, wall
charts, etc. A complete class—the junior tutorial class—was used as
the group for viewing in one of the schools. This had certain advantages, since the follow-up work could more easily be fitted in at the
teacher's convenience. On the other hand, this group had a very
wide range of reading ability, with a number of non-readers for
whom the programmes were too difficult, and most of the children in
this group were also of low intelligence. The groups in the three
remaining schools were supervised by lecturers from the colleges of

education, who were limited in their choice of children to the classes they used for teaching practice. The follow-up in these cases was done by the lecturers, and had to take place immediately after the transmissions.

Testing

Each child who was selected to view the programmes was tested on the Vernon Test of Word Recognition, either by one of the educational psychologists (for whose co-operation we are extremely grateful) or by one of the lecturers from the colleges. The selection of the group was left to the teacher concerned, and no children were excluded on the basis of their scores on the reading test.

The story of *Tom, Pat and Friday*, which extended over the four programmes, made use of over two hundred different words, which are listed and classified in the teachers' notes. A Word Recognition Test was constructed for this study, using a one-in-five sample of the words in the story, and a rearranged version was prepared for administration after the programmes (this is a similar procedure to that used by Dr Morris in assessing the effectiveness of the experimental series). These tests were administered by the teacher or lecturer organizing the group, and were given immediately before the commencement of the series and in the week following its completion.

Finally, I tested each child on the English Picture Vocabulary, Test II, to secure some idea of the level of oral vocabulary possessed by the children in the study. In this test, the child has only to respond by pointing, or by saying a number, indicating which of four pictures most appropriately represents the word said by the tester. This test could be used with the whole group, as there are norms for children from age 7 to 11 years 11 months.

It should be stressed that this is not a controlled experiment—no selection of schools was made in an attempt to secure a representative sample—all schools taking part were volunteers, and no test was used to determine which children should be permitted to take part. Finally, no direction was given to the teachers as to the amount and type of follow-up activities they should do. The main value of the study lies in the fact that it brought together in a co-operative venture members of the newly formed local council—teachers, lecturers and educational psychologists, together with representatives of the BBC television staff. A certain amount of factual data on test scores has been accumulated, and in addition, those who have taken part in the project have sent reports to the BBC. A meeting was also held at Broadcasting House, where we submitted our views and put forward suggestions for future programmes.

The report which follows is based on the results of the tests, on

Margaret M. Clark

my own observations based on visits to the schools during the actual transmissions, and on discussions with those who took part.

Administrative considerations

The use of any television programme involves a certain amount of inconvenience in a school setting; while the use of one designed—as in *Tom, Pat and Friday* —for a limited group of children, involves even greater difficulties. Not only do the children have to be taken at the appropriate time to a room where a television set is available, but also the children have to be assembled from different classes, a teacher has to be available for supervision during the transmission, and someone has to be available to undertake the follow-up work. The schools which participated in this study did not find this a great difficulty. It should be borne in mind, however, in considering the extension of use of such a series, that these were volunteers (and enthusiasts), who agreed to take the programmes knowing that the conditions in their schools made this possible. If it were not possible (*a*) to provide a separate room in which the selected group could view the programmes on its own; (*b*) to release a teacher for the period of the transmission to supervise; and (*c*) to ensure that adequate follow-up work was possible, supervised at least by the teacher who supervised the viewing, then, in my opinion it is not worth while taking such programmes. One further point in this connection is the question of what provision is made for absentees, although there is always the possibility that they *might* view the programme at home. This is an important point, since the absentee rate is likely to be high in a group such as this—particularly if the length of the series is extended.

Size and Constitution of the Groups

These two aspects are interdependent, since the more homogeneous the group, the larger it can be and still form a unit. In this study, the largest group had twenty-three children (the tutorial class) and the smallest group had nine. It would seem that the upper limit for such groups is perhaps about fifteen, unless the children are very similar in ability; in which case the viewing group might be larger, provided that the follow-up work is done with smaller units.

In determining the optimum size of group, the following points should be borne in mind:

1 *Absolute Size.* This is influenced by such factors as size of the television screen. It is essential, particularly in this type of programme, that viewing conditions be such that the children can see the print on the screen clearly and without strain. Some attempt was

164

made in this series to encourage all children to make responses, and to prevent groups from being dominated by a few individuals.

2 *Age Range.* Here the question of interest level of the stories comes in. The story in this series was aimed at the 8–9 age-group, and did seem to be effective in its appeal, as the children, sophisticated viewers though they be, remained interested in the story throughout the four episodes. There seems no harm in including slightly older children provided that they are immature enough to accept stories of the interest level in such programmes. In one of our schools, several boys were included who were in the 10–11 year age-group, boys who were particularly poor in reading, and they did profit from inclusion in the group.

3 *Intelligence Range.* Again, it is important not to have too wide a range of intelligence, unless the children are very similar in reading ability.

4 *Range of Reading Ability.* If this is too great, then those with the superior level will dominate the group. This type of programme was not designed for all levels of ability and would not be successful if so used—for example, the rate of presentation of the print on the screen would be slow for fluent readers.

The programmes were devised for children who, though backward in reading, had begun to read, though not with sufficient fluency. The stimulus of the motion picture and auditory presentation helped to give the story more interest than would have been possible with the limitations of vocabulary necessarily imposed by the children's reading level. Children who, after two or three years at school, are only just beginning to master the technique of puzzling out each single word, are likely to proceed too slowly to get meaning from print, or enjoyment from their reading books. This is where the form of this series acted as a stimulus to these children, giving them enjoyment from the print which was still on a simple enough level to be within their powers. We felt that the programmes were suitable not only in interest level, but also in the level of vocabulary which they utilized. They were not suitable for children who had not started to recognize words out of context. As a rough guide, I would suggest that only children who can read some of the words on a test of word recognition should be included. In our groups we had some children who made no score on such a test. Children who have reached their third year or more at school and are in this state require more individual treatment than this approach provides. They enjoyed the break from routine, but they did not really participate. Children with reading ages as low as 5 year 6 months made a marked improvement, but none below this level. (Thirty-nine children in this study had reading ages below 5 years 6 months, and they could read few of the words in the programmes. After the series they were in the same state, while children with a reading age of 5 years 6 months could read about half the words before the series.) Some of these children made a striking improvement in level of word recognition, and in attitude to reading. One has to consider, of course, to what these changes should be attributed—the stimulus of being selected, the follow-up by the teachers or some other factor. Children with reading ages above 7 years 6 months are likely to be able to recognize almost all the words in a programme such as this. If, however, they are still reading with hesitation and little enjoyment, then a series such as this may well act as the stimulus they require. For example, it may be of use with children who lack fluency because of repeated absence in their first two years.

Summary of our comments on the series and suggestions for future programmes

1 We felt that the story aspect was well planned and that interest in the pictorial presentation was sustained throughout the series. If future programmes are aimed at this age and ability group we suggest that the length of the series be extended, but that a single theme should not be carried over more than four or so presentations. Mystery stories seem to be popular with the children. Several of the teachers commented that they felt some stories should use city settings which would utilize experiences and vocabulary which were more familiar to the children.

2 The story book which accompanied the series was acceptable to the teachers, who felt that the print was clear and of reasonable size. They also approved of the lack of pictures, and reliance on the experience of the film to provide the necessary images. It was felt that the children should not have access to the whole story in their books from the beginning, since they were to be discouraged from continuing to read the book so that they did not spoil the following episodes. This made follow-up work more difficult to organize, as the teacher had to ensure that each child was reading only the appropriate passage. It was suggested that, in future, the children should be issued with only the appropriate section of the story for a particular programme, and that they should have the fun of assembling their own story books, using the printed material and their own illustrations.

3 The teachers felt that more detailed teachers' notes should be provided, as this would enable them to make better use of the programmes. They felt that it would be a mistake for teachers to do any preparatory work which would detract from the novelty of the

programmes, but they did wish to know what rules would be covered in each programme, and to have some idea of the general scheme.

4 There was general approval of the techniques used to introduce the rules. It was felt that children such as these who had failed to make progress on first presentation of the rules would be helped by the devices employed on the screen. These teachers were very critical of the kind of 'gimmick' which was used in the experimental series.

5 The speed of presentation of the continuous reading material seemed suitable for the level of child for whom the programmes were devised. The only technical difficulty which I observed was that on several occasions a part of some of the words on the left-hand side of the screen was not visible.

6 On a number of occasions, the presenter called on the teacher to select children to give the responses. The teachers were not prepared for this. Though I feel that it is a good idea to involve the teachers in the programme to some extent, this requires adequate prior briefing of the teachers. It also means that the teacher must sit in such a position that she can speak to the children without distracting their attention from the screen. I do not feel that the programmes should depend too much on the teacher's participation. Children who are likely to be in such groups are likely to be more than normally distractable, and it is therefore important to maintain their active concentration on the task in hand. Variety in the programme seems to me a more successful way of achieving this than teacher intervention during the programme.

7 The teachers all felt that the most such programmes could be was a stimulus and introduction to the work, and that an essential part of the course must be follow-up work. They therefore felt that the programmes should not be longer than twenty minutes, and that once a week was sufficiently frequent, especially in view of the organizational difficulties in using such a series. Activities could, however, be suggested which would reinforce the ideas presented in each programme.

The general feeling among the schools who took part in this project was that it had proved a worthwhile experience, and that they would consider using any future series aimed at the same age and reading level. The pictorial aspect which such a series provides is, I think, particularly valuable for such children, who, when they turn to the printed page, may still have the images of the film before them. The importance for such children of widening their experience and their understanding vocabulary is brought out by their results on the Picture Vocabulary Test; all but three of the group tested were below average and the majority were well below average. In short, these children have a limited understanding of words which are known to the rest of their age-group. Certainly their failure to learn to read will have widened this gulf. Illustrations in a reading book will not help much with children whose linguistic experiences are limited. Visual stimulation, such as the film provides may, however, be of assistance.

It should be borne in mind that many of the children who would be likely to be of the reading level for such programmes are likely to have poor memories for visually presented material, and they will therefore require many repetitions of material before they will learn it. Presentations is perhaps a better choice of word, as this implies the need for repetition with sufficient variety for interest to be sustained. In this way, the novelty of these programmes may act as an incentive to children who, after two years at school, for whatever reasons, are slow and stumbling in their reading.

One has to weigh up the gains from making use of a series such as this in the way we did in this study. It is certainly true that the children were interested in the programmes; that they did pay attention during the programmes; that a number of them knew words which were used in the programmes better at the end of the series than they did at the beginning; and that there was a striking change in attitude to reading in some instances. What we cannot separate out in such a study is the extent to which this is the result of the programmes, or the extra individual attention that the follow-up work involved in some of the schools. Even less can we say the extent to which any change in attitude was the result of the fact that, perhaps for the first time for some of these children, they had been singled out for attention; they viewed a special programme which their classmates did not see, the infants' mistress and headmaster were interested in the programmes and visitors came to see them. In short, all the problems which are present in any assessment of any new approach to reading are present here. This was certainly a Reading Drive. As an educationist I am delighted to see anything which does lead to a reading drive, especially when it concerns children in this age-group who have been slow in acquiring the mechanics of reading. A drive at this stage before the problem is aggravated by the reading backwardness affecting all their school work, and also affecting their attitude to school, is an important achievement. Though I would be the first one to point out the limitations of television as an educational medium, I do feel that the stimulus it can provide for children of this age-group is such that it has a useful place as *one* of the approaches to helping the slow-starters achieve fluency in reading and enjoyment from the printed page.

Editor's note

Response to the experimental series from various parts of the United Kingdom was generally favourable. Consequently, the BBC has since continued to produce programmes for backward readers with the series title *Look and Read* and, more recently, a series for infants call *Words and Pictures*.

At the annual study conference in Durham (1970), the BBC series were the subject of a symposium called 'The TV Medium'. The papers of the three main speakers are published in the conference proceedings, *Reading and the Curriculum* London: Ward Lock Educational (1971).

15 The SRA Reading Laboratories: review of a programmed course in reading

JOHN E. MERRITT
Professor of Educational Studies,
Open University

Paper presented at Third Annual Conference of UKRA Cambridge
1966, first published in *Reading: Current research and practice*

There is a growing tendency for teachers to rebel against the use of highly structured reading programmes in which the child is very much dominated by the material. They see the child as being called upon to behave like a well-trained circus animal—leaping through the appropriate hoops when called upon to do so instead of being encouraged to select, to explore and to reflect. Programmed instruction, for all its obvious advantages, is seen as the apotheosis of the former approach. The reaction is seen in the increasing interest in what has come to be called the language-experience approach to reading (Carrillo 1965) and the individualized reading programme (Frazier 1961).

The advantage of the commerically produced reading programmes, or at least the best of these, is that they hold out the prospect of developing reading skills in a systematic and orderly fashion—with plenty of revision built in to the programme. As against this, or so it is argued by those whose approach is more child-centred, there is a serious disadvantage inherent in failing to work from the start from the child's interests. If the child is to apply his reading skills effectively in later years, he must acquire them in a context in which the skills are needed to satisfy his own immediate purposes—not just the teacher's or the purpose specified by the programmes—and these purposes should be significantly related to purposes which will become important in later years. Failure to ensure this brings the danger that skills laboriously acquired will fall into disuse because there is no motivation to achieve transfer, i.e. to make use of the skills in other contexts.

The difficulties inherent in the child-centred approach are, of course, obvious. First, there is the loss of control over the learning sequence. This can only be accepted if the teacher can spend sufficient time with each individual child to ensure that essential skills are being adequately developed. Next, the teacher cannot be expected to know in precise detail the content of every book so that day-to-day diagnostic problems are magnified and overall assessment is blurred. Furthermore, all teachers are not reading specialists. Their ability to supervise the full development of reading skills is limited by their inadequate understanding of what is involved. For such teachers, it may be argued, a well-designed reading programme is a very useful, and perhaps even essential, tool. Clearly, compromises have to be made and one very interesting form of compromise is that represented by the Reading Laboratories produced by the North American firm, Science Research Associates.

The SRA Laboratories provide what is basically a fairly orthodox reading programme for every age-group from admission-class to college level and includes material that is largely factual rather than imaginative. I do not use the term orthodox in any critical sense here, for the best of the orthodox programmes on the market today are research-based and carefully tested constructions, with many years of practical application and frequent modification behind them. The SRA Laboratories, however, differ from other reading programmes in that they have been designed to take advantage of some of the features of what is now known as programmed instruction. The SRA Laboratories do not, however, slavishly follow the frame-by-frame presentation characteristic of the teaching machine or the programmed text — neither can they be strictly categorized as either linear or branching in type — although they have more in common with the latter than the former. The underlying principles of programmed instruction are, of course, general principles of learning. The outstanding feature peculiar to programmed instruction is the extent to which systematic and rigorous application of these principles is achieved and exploited through the development of sub-principles and specialized techniques. The teacher certainly cannot match these achievements unless he spends all his time with one pupil, and that, you will agree, has both advantages and disadvantages.

What then, are the general principles and considerations involved in programmed instruction which have influenced the design of the SRA Laboratories.

Individual Variation

No teacher needs to be told that however carefully he selects, streams or groups his pupils they will still vary in their level of thinking, their problem-solving styles, their specific attainment levels and their attitudes to work in different situations. However closely we may try to match any two children they will still differ from each other in innumerable different and important ways. The child also varies within himself, however — from year to year, from day to day,

John E. Merritt

and even from minute to minute. A series of tasks of uniform difficulty will find one child struggling at the beginning and finding it easier later, whilst another child, after making a flying start, may fail later as he gradually loses impetus and interest. Programmed instruction aims to provide for this individual variation by providing materials which enable the child to work at his own pace.

The SRA Laboratories seek to provide for individual variation by means of what they describe as a muli-level approach. The reading materials are designed to cover the whole range of difficulty required for an unstreamed class. At each difficulty level there is a range of material so that the children may have sufficient reading experience to enable them to achieve mastery of the skills practised at that level. Once they have achieved mastery they may progress to the next level. The levels are indicated by colours so that there is no confusion—a child simply selects a card of the same colour as the completed card or moves on to the next colour level. Some children, therefore, may work through the levels very rapidly, working on few cards at the early levels and on more cards at each subsequent level. Others may work slowly through the lower levels only but enjoy the feeling of doing the same sort of work as the more able. The fluctuating child can skip through some levels here and there, but spend time working through extra cards when, for a variety of reasons, he finds the going hard.

Now it is of importance to emphasize that although each child works at his own pace, and has some freedom of choice within any level, all the children are able to work at the same sort of task at the same time. This means that administration problems are greatly simplified. Indeed, after the first moderately chaotic week, the administration is so simple that the children handle it themselves. To some extent, therefore, we get the best of both worlds—an individual approach but with the administrative convenience of an ordinary class lesson. There is an additional advantage in this approach, however: as the teacher has materials available to cover the whole ability range, there is no need for either streaming or grouping. There is no labelling of the children and no tendency towards the development of stereotyped B or C stream attitudes. No heart-searching decisions are required as to whether a child needs to be moved up from one stream or group to another. The system is entirely flexible and when a child makes progress rapidly he moves up automatically to a higher level without disrupting any relationships he may enjoy within the class. Diagnosis is built into the programme so that no pupil is held back or allowed to press on too quickly before mastery is achieved. And, not least important, habits of not-learning are not built up by successive increments of boredom or frustration. Thus, there is no idle capacity, if one may borrow a term from industry. Progress is continuous—and comfortable, because it is essentially child-determined.

The Learning Process

Every learning sequence should be accompanied or followed by knowledge of results if learning is to be effective—that is, if the right things are to be learned. Correction of last week's errors is of little avail if these same errors have been rehearsed repeatedly in the meantime. If we follow Skinner (1959) we shall try to reinforce every single bit of approved behaviour by confirming its correctness the moment it is elicited or emitted. Now this is possible in the case of some of the subsidiary skills, but in continuous reading it is more difficult. It is essential, therefore, that errors should be kept to a minimum and detected as soon as possible when they do occur. Errors may be largely avoided by providing sufficient preparation prior to a continuous reading sequence. Thus, if the reading sequences can be kept short, clarification and correction will be reasonably prompt. This is largely achieved.

Errors may also be avoided by ensuring that new responses are well cued, then elicited in different contexts with cues successively reduced—the process known as fading—until the response is well established and needs no prompting of any kind. In the early stages of learning to read, for example, colour cues may be used initially and gradually withdrawn—although this particular technique is not used in the SRA programme. Again, in vocabulary development, new words may be placed in contexts which clearly reveal their meaning. Subsequently, they may occur in contexts in which there is less and less lexical support so that recall of the meaning gained in earlier contexts is essential to the understanding of the passage. This process of cueing and fading, is, of course, part of the technique of any accomplished teacher. In programmed instruction, however, the techniques are extremely highly developed—they are not simply *ad hoc* procedures resorted to from time to time under the influence of the occasional burst of inspiration. The materials used in the SRA Reading Laboratories do not readily lend themselves to the straightforward and rigorous exploitation of cueing and fading techniques found in typical programmed learning devices. It is clear, nevertheless, that the principles have been deliberately borrowed and applied—although we may not agree with the methods used in every case.

With regard to the process of reinforcement, there is now a great deal of evidence which indicates that the precise timing of reinforcement of learning sequence, and the regularity of the reinforcement, makes a considerable difference to the general level of motivation. Very high levels of motivation can be developed and sustained. From

John E. Merritt

subjective observations of children using the SRA Laboratories there appears to be a similar degree of motivation generated in working through these programmes, with their regular reinforcement provisions. Teachers who have been using the SRA Laboratories confirm this observation—again, on a basis of subjective judgment. Now there can be no certainty that there is a precise, or even an important degree of relationship between experimental work on reinforcement schedules and level of motivation sustained by children using programmed instruction materials. And, of course, the control over reinforcement in the SRA Reading Laboratories is far from being so rigorous as that to be found in typical programmed instructional materials. Nevertheless, it does look as though the movement towards more systematic control over reinforcement may be at least partially responsible for the increased motivation—even if the reinforcement is delayed beyond the point of close association with the individual response.

Certainly, morale must be appreciably improved when a child suddenly finds himself consistently achieving over 90% success rates! It is difficult for the teacher to provide for this sort of achievement, however intensively he works on his materials and techniques.

The Development of Reading Skills

At this point, perhaps we could look again at the SRA material and consider what skills are being developed.

1 *Listening skills*
First, there is a continuous programme for the development of listening skills running through the laboratories for all grades. There is material for encouraging general language-development and for the systematic expansion of vocabulary. There is systematic training to establish habits of attending to auditory material, the habit of active listening, i.e. listening for answers to question, habits of review and habits of recall. This is comparable with the SQR technique, i.e. 'Survey, Questions and Read' developed in the reading programme itself, and the SQ3R technique (Robinson 1960) from which this is derived.

2 *Word-attack skills*
Parallel with the early laboratories there is a separate laboratory for the systematic development of phonic and structural word-attack skills. In the early material there is a most unfortunate grouping of initial letters and of voiced and unvoiced phonemes. 't', 'd', 'b' and 'p', for example, all appear on one envelope when the child is making his first attempts to match initial sounds and letters. It is difficult to conceive a situation more calculated to create confusion—both in letter recognition and in sound-symbol association. There is also a

recommendation that phonemes should be sounded separately—'Say the first sound you hear in the word "pie".' (SRA Teacher's Handbook 1961). The intelligent teacher will not, of course, follow the instructions rigidly, but will depart from these as reason and training dictate in the relatively few instances where this seems necessary.

In the reading programme itself, attention is paid to both power and rate, i.e. word meaning and word analysis, as well as reading speed. In both, the reading-thinking skills of getting main ideas, noting details, discovering cause-effect sequences, inferences, classifications, etc., are all developed. Some of the laboratories cover a very restricted range of material, however, and extensive supplementation is essential. This is not really a criticism of the laboratories, of course. The laboratories help to define and practise the skills. It is up to the teacher to develop these skills as part of his normal work in the subject areas, and in recreative reading, at a level comparable with that reached in the reading laboratory. The pupil administration involved in the programme may be regarded as a worthwhile additional activity in its own right.

Finally, there is one aspect common to all activities. The children correct their own work and keep their own records. Diagnosis is thus continuous and thorough with self-assessment supported by teacher guidance. There is no incentive to cheat, for the student is merely competing against himself—not against his fellows. In the rare instances where cheating does occur, this becomes evident when the teacher sees the child individually, and cheating is in itself an additional diagnostic indicator.

Experimentation in English Schools

Mr Chroston, Headmaster, Breconbeds Primary School (Chroston 1965) adopted an SRA Laboratory for a three-month trial period for children whose ages ranged from 8 years 10 months to 11 years 7 months. Using the Neale Analysis of Reading Ability, he found that Accuracy scores, i.e. word recognition, held steady. The children gained 3.2 months of reading age in the three-months' period. In Reading Rate, however, there was a gain of 11.4 months, whilst in Reading Comprehension there was a gain of 7.7 months.

A more extensive enquiry has been conducted by R. H. Pont (1966) on behalf of the Midlothian Education Committee. In this investigation, children in three different schools using the SRA Laboratory gained 9.5, 12.95 and 15.1 points respectively after three months. They were tested on Schonell R.4—a test of reading comprehension. The reading-age scores were converted into reading quotients. In two of these schools, where there were matched control groups, the relative gains in the experimental group were 4.9 points and 6.3

John E. Merritt

points respectively. On retest, seven months later, however, these gains were lost, and the difference between the groups were not significant.

Pont posits the old ceiling of attainment idea to account for the apparent failure of the experimental group to sustain their lead. Whilst no one would dispute that such ceilings exist, it is unduly complacent, surely, to adduce this concept on this evidence. One wonders, for example, to what extent there was an attempt to transfer the reading skills developed by use of the laboratories to reading in the subject areas and other reading. One also wonders whether reading skills were systematically rehearsed in both groups during the seven months following completion of the laboratory programme. If not, it is scarcely to be wondered that the skills declined. Moreover, as the same test was apparently used on all three occasions it seems not unlikely that the ceiling effect in this case was due to maximising of specific practice-effects in all three groups. The Schonell R.4, it must be noted, is extremely limited in its examination of comprehension skills.

In the Breconbeds Study, parallel tests were used—a much more defensible procedure. In addition, however, it is essential to use tests which sample the whole array of reading skills. What is now required is a longer-term study in which the laboratories are used over a number of years—with emphasis placed upon the transfer of skills to reading in the subject areas over the whole period—together with an adequate diagnostic testing programme.

Pont concludes that the laboratories are capable of raising the reading level quickly. This is fair comment—but it is surely up to the teacher to exploit these gains. Pont also expresses the view that the laboratories may be particularly useful for retarded readers. E. G. de Havigue (1966) has, in fact, used them with small groups of retarded readers in Secondary Schools in the former Borough of Wood Green. Although he does not provide statistical evidence he concludes that the results are sufficiently positive to justify continued use of the laboratories.

Conclusions

I am personally convinced that the most effective learning is that which is generated by students seeking to learn more about themselves, their fellows and their environment by direct investigation. I further believe that reading skills can by systematically developed and practised as part of such a programme (Merritt 1966). In the meantime, whilst relatively formal instruction in the subject-areas continues, and whilst higher-order reading skills are left to develop with little or no assistance, there is a very great deal to be said for the adoption of programmes such as those I have discussed. They have a great deal to offer the experienced reading teacher who has not yet conceptualized the reading skills as thoroughly as she might. They have a very great deal to offer to all those teachers who have had no special training and who are required to function as reading teachers. They help to create an environment in which the continuous and systematic development of reading-thinking skills is regarded as an essential part of the curriculum. They will help, I hope, to provide a higher starting point for further development. And, whilst not essentially child-directed, the SRA Laboratories provide a certain degree of freedom for pupils to exercise choice and judgment as well as opportunities for the development of responsible attitudes. In spite of my expressed reservations, therefore, I should like to see these Laboratories, or other comparable programmes, used on an increasing scale in the next few years—not just in one class in each school but throughout the whole school wherever they are used.

Editor's note

Since Professor Merritt's review of the SRA *Reading Laboratories* there have been several developments in the field. Gordon Shiach (1971), The effectiveness of SRA Reading Laboratory 2a with boys of below average ability *Educational Research* 13.3 reports a small study of the effectiveness of the approach in a remedial situation while the report of a larger survey undertaken by the Inner London Education Authority's Research and Statistics Group involving 27 schools is available from the ILEA.

Early criticisms of the American nature of the material have been met to some extent by the introduction of international editions of the various laboratories starting with the 2a in 1971. In addition Ward Lock Educational have produced *Reading Workshop 6–10* (1971) and *Reading Workshop 9–13* (1969) which operate on broadly similar lines.

References

CARRILLO, L. W. (1965) The Language-Experience Approach to the Teaching of Reading *The Second International Reading Symposium, London, 1965*, Eds. J. Downing and A. L. Brown. London: Cassell

CHROSTON, R. C. (unpublished 1965) Report on the working of the SRA Reading Laboratory at Breconbeds Primary School

FRAZIER, A. (1961) The Individualised Reading Programme in Controversial Issues in Reading and Promising Solutions *Supplementary Educational Monographs*, No. 91, Ed. Helen M. Robinson. University of Chicago Press

M

John E. Merritt

DE HAVIGUE, E. G. (1966) The SRA Reading Laboratory *Remedial Education* 1

MERRITT, J. E. (1966) Developing competence in reading comprehension in *Reading Instruction: An International Forum* Newark, Delaware: International Reading Association

PONT, R. H. (1966) An Investigation into the use of the SRA Reading Laboratory in the Midlothian schools *Educational Research* VIII, 3

ROBINSON, F. P. (1960) *Effective Study* New York: Harper & Bros

SKINNER, B. F. (1959) *Cumulative Record* New York: Appleton-Century-Crofts

SRA Reading Laboratory 1a Teacher's Handbook Chicago: Science Research Associates 1961

REMEDIAL READING

16 The comprehension difficulties of the deprived reader

CONSTANCE M. McCULLOUGH

Professor of Education, San Francisco
State College, California

Paper presented at Fifth Annual Conference of UKRA Edinburgh
1968, first published in *Reading: Influence on progress*

Deprivation is a slippery term. Because three McCullough brothers left Scotland in 1736, I was deprived of a Scottish accent. Because your ancestors did not go with them, you were deprived of my Indiana nasal twang, plus other characteristics which can either annoy or amuse. My early teachers spoke very much as I spoke, in a dialect of English close enough to what I like to call book English to give me a privileged rather than deprived status in learning to read.

I was fortunate in having parents who liked to read aloud and who felt a genuine responsibility for the education of their children. My father read King Arthur stories to me because he liked them and probably was less disgusted when the next night he had to retrace some of the passages which I had slept through. My mother read me stories from the Bible. My sisters and brother enjoyed reciting poetry and writing poetry of their own. It would have been very hard for me to escape literacy.

Deprivation is a term which many people feel is derogatory; yet intrinsically it is not. It is, rather, a term of relativity. Equipped with the experiences and skills which your environment and ability have made possible, you may be highly adequate in one situation but deprived in another. It depends on the task you are set. A deprived reader is unready in one or more ways for the task of reading whatever he is required to read.

Before I went to India in 1963 to join a reading project sponsored by the Indian Government and the U.S. Government through a contrat with Columbia University, I was a deprived specialist in reading, in at least two respects. I did not know enough about linguistics to diagnose the language needs of children of varied backgrounds in my own country. And I had swallowed whole the idea that if the children knew the words by sight or sound or context, and knew what they meant, they could answer comprehension questions on

Constance M. McCullough

the content. I was no worse or better than most reading specialists in my country at that time. Happily, we are all improving now. But it is with some embarrassment that I confess to having specialized in the teaching of reading for many years with so little forward movement in the areas of cognitive and linguistic deprivation.

In 1960 I had developed a schema of cognition from observation of the kinds of thought patterns I had found in expository material in school textbooks. Of course, Guilford, the psychologist, had been doing much better things behind my back, with his cubic structure of the intellect. But I, being a simpler soul, find fifteen behaviours easier to handle and remember than fifty-five. One cannot expect all of one's ignorance to be dispelled at one time.

The thinking of the schema is this: The English speaker receives sensory impressions of objects and living organisms in patterns of events and situations, with thought and feeling predispositions and reactions. In observing and reflecting on these things he becomes aware of certain relationships; whole-part, cause-effect, sequential comparison-contrast, subordinate-co-ordinate. These observations of relationship lead to the development of theories, laws and principles, generalizations, definitions, classifications, procedures. And these products of the mind are supported by examples, elaboration, or application.

I had had the happy thought that I would find dependable patterns of thought in certain kinds of material. Instead, I found that the reader cannot depend upon the occurrence of any set pattern in reading material. Whatever the author's composition teacher may have imposed upon him at a tender age is lost as the author struggles with ideas. And while he may have certain habits of mind that recur in his writing, the behaviour of each writer is highly individual. We cannot in good conscience teach children to expect patterns. We must teach them to detect them. What kind of thought is the author presenting, and what is the relationship of that thought to those which precede and follow?

Now, what has this to do with deprivation? India educated me in deprivation. While the country offers a broad spectrum of conditions, poverty is very much in evidence. In the United States and Europe, poverty is less visible. It is not only less extreme but it is hidden in special parts of a city or special parts of the countryside. There are many children in India whose parents provide a language-rich environment, but there are many more children who are spoken to very little as they are growing to school age. Their parents treat them with a silent language—a language of picking up and taking and putting and pushing and patting and pulling. While parents work, their children who are too young for the work stand and watch or sit and stare vacantly.

These children know a physical cause-and-effect. It is the *language*

180

medium of cause-and-effect of which they are deprived. They know their hut from other huts; yet they could not express its appearance or location in words. They could point if they understood your question, which is language, too. They are familiar with whole-part relationships, such as that of the cart with the missing wheel or the buffalo with the missing horn, but have never learned how to state those relationships. They are increasingly aware of hierarchies—social, political, economic—as they encounter barriers.

In story-rich India they have never been told a story. They have never touched a book. The best of India's cultural achievements are not their heritage.

They may know the many uses of the neem tree, but chances are that they could not tell you its name or classify its uses, or generalize in words the great value of the tree to Indian people.

Now, if a child does not know the names of the objects and events in his life, that loss, great as it is, can be readily rectified. But to express ideas about these objects and events is an additional task which requires ear and speech training in the variety of ways ideas can be expressed in the language concerned.

Have you ever taken a simple statement apart, to see how many different ways it might have been presented, and how many challenges it throws to the listener? Take a sentence a child might hear very often. It is all rolled up in one word: 'don't!' It is so general and so brief that the cautious child will stop breathing. 'Stop what you are doing' or 'stop that' may take more words but is just as vague. Language-deprived children grow up in situations in which adults address them in very few words. Sentence fragments, commands to action or inaction without explanation of cause or effect or the limitations of the command, are the diet. Meanings are derived more from the situation than from the wording. It is no wonder that many teachers find it difficult to reach such children.

A child in a verbal family may be told, 'don't climb the railing, or you may hurt yourself,' or 'if you climb the railing, you may hurt yourself,' or 'stay away from that railing because you can hurt yourself,' or 'keep off the railing. 'You'll fall.' The child learns from such exposure that a 'don't this, or that may happen' is a stop signal for his own safety. So is 'if this, that may happen.' 'Stay away from that railing' is a positive way of demanding cessation of action. The 'because' clearly suggests consequence. The last example is interesting because it is in two sentences unconnected by 'if' or 'because' 'Keep off the railing. You'll fall.' The child has to infer the relationship. 'You'll fall' goes further than the other statements, for it is a prediction of a specific way of injuring oneself rather than a statement of general possibility: 'you *may hurt* yourself.' There are lots of ways to hurt oneself with a railing, and one of them is to fall. Of course, there are many ways of falling, too.

Constance M. McCullough

Imagine the mother saying to the child, 'don't climb the railing or you may hurt yourself. Then you'll be sorry.' Notice that in the first of these two sentences we have a statement of cause and effect. The second sentence follows with an effect of the effect. Three events threaten to come in sequence: climb the railing. Get hurt. Be sorry. 'Hurt yourself' is a generalization of injury. The mother is not specific, and the smart child will wonder what the hurt will be. 'You'll be sorry,' is also general, for a particular kind and intensity and duration of sorrow would accompany a particular kind and degree of injury. Notice, too, that the word 'or' is used in a special way. It is not the 'or' of choice between climbing and being hurt, as one would have a choice between having candy or a soft drink. That 'or' really means 'because'. The expression 'may hurt yourself' instead of 'will hurt yourself' is another expression to watch. 'May' is suggesting possibility, not permission. How does the child know it is not permission? Is it that his mother would not ordinarily give him permission to hurt himself? Is it that permissible alternatives are usually both positively stated?

Actually, the trouble between mother and child is that the child does not see climbing a railing as a cause of anything except pleasure. It is a positive expression of power, to him; not a sure path to a broken neck. Mother gave up climbing railings a long time ago. Part of the child's problem in understanding her order is that he has not learned to fear what he has not yet experienced. It is an attitude difference.

I think it significant that some children miss the opportunity for tremendous sophistication in grasping language meanings, while others are exposed to language which, even in the sample of two sentences which I have given, may reflect the compounding of sequence, generalization, cause, effect, and other cognitive relationships. Language-deprived children have missed a very basic listening and speaking background for reading book English.

The relationships which I have pointed out here are the essential architectural features of the author's idea. As in a Japanese painting, the unexpressed is as important as the expressed: 'you'll be sorry if you hurt yourself on that railing.' Here is a mother who does not give the child the comfort of the sure limit, 'don't.' She makes a simple prediction, raising the possibility of injury on the railing. It is up to the child to decide what to do about the railing. He can feel the loneliness of one who must judge for himself, even though he may know perfectly well what his mother wants him to do. And he can feel the flattery of being offered an opportunity to use his own head. Whether the intent of the remark is threatening, malicious, or gently remindful, the child can know only by reading his mother now as well as he may some day read books.

The comprehension difficulties of the language deprived reader stem from many deficiencies. Linguists know them well, but as yet have been less interested in comprehension problems than in descriptions of language. We have to use what they know to get what we need for diagnosis and for teaching. We have a long way to go.

In India the Reading Project developed tests to determine the ability of Hindi-speaking children to discriminate the sounds of their language. Some of those children could well have been from families of generally non-verbal habit. Mr D. S. Rawat, who designed and arranged for the administration of these tests, found in a pilot study of fewer than two hundred cases what was confirmed later for near ly five thousand children in Delhi: the greatest difficulty they had was in discrimination of vowel sounds. Next was the discrimination of a spirated versus unspirated sounds. Sounds whose production could not be distinguished in the position of the lips were a problem. Obviously, since language depends upon sound distinctions for differences in meaning, these children are heading for trouble in comprehension.

In the United States recently a great deal of effort has been made to meet the reading problems of so called disadvantaged children. A characteristic of some children is a terminal fading which essentially produces a language of consonant-vowel structure in most words. This characteristic may be the product of generations of poor models and little need for accuracy in the concrete situation. It may also stem from the language which the ancestors used— possibly a language made of consonant-vowel syllables. In any case, this terminal fading—which for the children is not fading at all, but complete absence of final consonant sound—creates havoc in the English language. There are enough homonyms in English as it is, to make us all wary and at times misunderstood, but the problem is now multiplied. A certain Harlem dialect, studied by William Labov in New York City, is such that 'bear', 'bed', 'bell', 'bet', 'beg', 'Ben— are all pronounced the same. Worse, vowels in that dialect tend to be sounded alike—monophthongized—so that words beginning with a 'b' and continuing with any vowel plus t, d, g, k, l, r, s, z, may sound alike. In words ending in m and n, m and n are nasalized. Just for curiosity, I analyzed the Dolch sight vocabulary list to see what that dialect would do with those words. Out of 220 words, 158 were altered.

Now, you may think that I am off the subject. These children have a dialect, and it is dialect interference that is the case, not strictly language-deprivation. But my point is that a child who is not accustomed to listening for sound distinctions in English utterances because English is not being uttered at all or very little in his home, is going to have trouble distinguishing words and therefore meanings.

Furthermore, think what sound distinctions do for the role of words in sentences. The Harlem dialect Labov studied practically eliminates future and past tenses, possessives, number, the verb to be. The one feature that remains strong in the dialect is the order of English sentences. When Joe eats the tiger, it is the tiger, not Joe, that disappears. But a child who had been deprived of language in his early years would not have even this advantage. He has to learn the order of the language, and the relationships of words and phrases within the terminable units.

So what does language deprivation mean for comprehension difficulties? It means that the child will have comprehension difficulties in listening even before he learns to read. If we wish to give him a fair chance with other children, we should reach him as early as possible. Follow the ambulance! But at least do not make him feel inferior to other children by delaying help until the competition in learning to read is begun. The reading readiness programme in Hindi includes the usual charts for identification of objects and development of concepts. But the use of those charts includes expressing relationships among objects, with concern for the kinds of thought pattern I have mentioned. Songs and stories give experience in hearing and speaking the patterns in the language and learning what they mean and what delight they can be.

What does language deprivation mean for comprehension when the child faces the printed page? Suddenly the crutch of the concrete situation, which in oral face-to-face situations has taken the major burden for meaning, is removed. The symbols of the spoken word are on the page to be decoded. Now, we admit that written English is not exactly representative of spoken English. Bernard Shaw and others have thought they could do better. But the language deprived child will see whole words and part of words whose sounds he has never noticed, unless we have prepared him well in school. In the United States we are now asking how we can effect some of this learning before the child is five or six years old. We have long talked about the importance of those early years. Now we have even more reason to believe in it. And we know too well that the price of delay is wasted lives.

17 Reading difficulties and what else ?

A. T. RAVENETTE
Senior Educational Psychologist,
London Borough of Newham

Paper presented at Sixth Annual Conference of UKRA Nottingham 1969, first published in *Reading skills: Theory and practice*

Problems in the scientific approach

The scientific study of reading difficulties has a long history but has apparently contributed little to the understanding of those teachers who have the job of contending with problems in the classroom. The classic comment at the end of each study is that more research is needed. Some of the many variables discovered by research have been discussed elsewhere (Ravenette 1968) and these will only be named in this paper: intelligence, social background, perceptual difficulties, neurological (real or imaginary) anomalies, family factors and so forth. There are however a number of underlying issues in this scientific approach which are not fully debated, and these may be the very issues which need to be challenged in order that workers may have a better understanding of the reading difficulties of the individual child.

The classic approach used in the study of reading difficulties involves the selection of a specified group of children labelled retarded and a control group in which children are normal. Tests thought to be related to the learning of reading are given to each group, and the verification of hypotheses rests on establishing significant differences between the two groups. If differences are demonstrated a variable defining retardates is said to be established. The development of computers has enabled this style of research to become more sophisticated in that more tests, and hence more variables, can be introduced. The scores on tests can be intercorrelated and so called factors can be deduced whereby children in the different groups can be further defined.

One recent study (Lovell and Gorton 1968) calls for some comment because of its comparative sophistication, and also because of its unfinished conclusions. The investigators used a number of tests which were thought to indicate impaired cortical functioning. To the investigators' surprise, they found that the spread of scores on each test were no different for the retarded children than for the non retarded. The sophistication of the study was shown when the investigators asked if the *patterns* of scores for children in the two groups were different. By correlating the scores in the two groups, they found two different patterns, one for each group. On the basis of this they deduced that some 2% of the retarded children showed a pattern of test scores which was consistent with the notion of cortical impairment (specific development dyslexia). The unstated, and perhaps unrecognized, further conclusion should have been that a comparable number of children had a pattern of scores that were completely inconsistent with this notion. These children were still retarded in reading, and the research data gave no answers as to why they were retarded.

Why are such complex and detailed studies of so little help in understanding the individual child?

According to Siu (1957), the aim of science and scientific investigation is the development of concepts. The more these concepts match up with reality, the more useful they are, but there is no necessary truth value in the results of research. Frequently the value of concepts arrived at in this way becomes apparent only in the far future, sometimes never. The scientific investigation of reading retardation, therefore, can be reputable without the teacher deriving any practical help. The seeming irrelevance of such research stems from other factors.

Individuals, unlike objects in the physical world, are complex and unique. In consequence, the research strategies devised for investigating people are aimed at discovering concepts derived from groups of individuals rather than from single individuals. But the group is not comparable to the individual, and concepts relevant to the whole group are not necessarily relevant to the individual in that group. Thus if, on average, a group of retarded readers shows lower scores on, for example, a test of visual perception than a comparable group of normal readers, this does not mean that every child in the retarded group is inferior to every child in the normal group. In fact the overlap is usually very great, and the statistical significance of research findings need have no psychological significance.

Findings from the study of groups have actuarial, as opposed to individual, value. If it is known from such studies that, for example, working class children tend to be more retarded than middle class children, then special provision should be provided for schools in working class areas in order to meet this difficulty. But within such a school there will be retarded children for whom a different understanding may need to be invented and for whom other resources may be needed. In this context the research finding has value at a planning and administrative level, but not at the level of the individual child.

A further problem which group studies highlight is the fact that, even if a single variable is isolated, there is no one to one correspondence between performance on that variable and performance on the criterion (e.g. reading). Although many children who are retarded in reading may show difficulties in right/left discrimination, there are many children with the same difficulty who read perfectly well. In other words, the child's retardation is not explained away by this handicap. It might be thought possible to attempt a description of the child in terms of all the possible handicaps which are thought to lead to reading retardation, but in practice this would be quite impractical, even if all the possible variables had been discovered.

However, the most basic assumption underlying the study of groups is at a different level and is far more important. For scientific study the individual is treated as if he were an object, not an individual. If an object lacked this supposed deficit, the object would perform equally well in comparison with other objects which did not have this deficit. The therapeutic task is to remove the deficit. But the individual is a living, breathing, evaluating, thinking, feeling, acting organism. He chooses, decides, acts upon his wishes and grows. What he achieves will be related to all of these attributes. At the simplest level, when invited to undertake an activity, he can either do it with delight, see it as irrelevant, or consider it a waste of time. He can view it with active distaste or be frightened of its implications. Scientific study has not yet come to terms with the object as subject. But in real life, in the classroom, in front of the teacher, the child is indeed fully a subject, and he approaches the tasks he is expected to master with well developed cognitive, reflective and cognitive attitudes. The results of scientific enquiry lead to description, not to explanation, nor to understanding. Their certainties are probabilities, not absolute truths, general not personal. If, then, traditional research strategies are of little value at the individual level, what should be done?

Towards a different point of view

Koestler (1967), in connection with the development of literature, art and science, makes the following comment: 'Cumulative progress within a given 'school' and technique end inevitably in stagnation, mannerism or decadence, until the crisis is resolved by a revolutionary shift in sensibility, emphasis, style.' It may not be too far removed from the present to suggest that a new sensibility is needed in the understanding of children with reading difficulties. Koestler quotes L. L. White: 'I ask the reader to remember that what is most obvious may be most worthy of analysis. Fertile vistas may open out when commonplace facts are examined from a fresh point of view.' In the case of children with reading difficulties, perhaps the most obvious fact is that the child is an individual with hopes and fears, expectations and disappointments, abilities and loyalties. He brings all of these to school and to learning as a statement of himself as an individual. Is it possible to make this a new starting point for the understanding of reading difficulties?

It is unfortunately the case that theories which are developed amongst the few seldom become disseminated amongst the many. The acquisition of new ideas seems to be at best fortuitous, and at worst discouraged by the conservative inertia of existing ideas. Two basic assumptions about the nature of the individual have led to two comparatively new theoretical points of view. Kelly (1955) has suggested that the individual is basically a scientist—although not necessarily a good one—and faces the onrush of life by developing bases for making and testing hypotheses. In the light of the outcomes of his ventures he modifies his theoretical assumptions.

From a different, but related, point of view Watzlawick et al (1967) suggest that an individual is always presenting a statement of himself in everything he says or does. More generally: 'Life is a partner whom we accept or reject, and by whom we feel ourselves accepted or rejected, supported or betrayed. To this existential partner man proposes his definition of himself and then finds it confirmed or disconfirmed.'

Behaviour is itself a communication, a confirmation or disconfirmation of others' views of us, or a request for confirmation or disconfirmation. Learning and non learning are each aspects of behaviour and as such may be seen as communications.

Both views, behaviour as communication and behaviour as experiment, imply the presence of other individuals. On the one hand, it is people who confirm or disconfirm, and on the other hand a person's behavioural experiments involve the anticipation of what others do. Thus, people (parents, teachers, siblings, peers) become important factors when the individual is seen as either experimenter or communicator, and when learning and not learning are seen as experiments or communications. The adoption of these views may provide starting points for that new sensibility which is needed in the understanding of reading difficulties.

Every theoretical framework leads to the development of appropriate techniques, and if this way of thinking about children and their learning difficulties is to be taken seriously, appropriate investigation procedures must be devised. The child's behavioural questions and his behavioural experiments take place in an area of life in which significant people provide the validators, i.e. those who confirm of disconfirm. It is necessary therefore to invent questioning techniques which encourage the child to give his views of himself and those people who are important for him—parents, teachers, siblings, peers. Moreover, the simple answer to the simple question needs further explanation from the child. At the same time, the child must be asked questions to embrace as wide a range of validators as possible. The interview therefore is comparable to a Piaget style interview, in which reasons become important. Perhaps it is even more important for the child to be invited to indicate his wishes for things to be different and his views on the implications of change. This style of investigation is inevitably of a different order from that of the psychometrician. There is no normative data. Comparisons are not made with others. There are no specific diagnostic signs. Instead the child is invited and encouraged, in a structured way, to describe his view of life as mediated through people who are important for him.

The case of John

John is aged seven and was referred by the headteacher because, although he seemed to be of above average ability, he had made no start in reading. This made him abnormal in the class because the one or two other nonreaders were children of limited ability.

Investigation of his intelligence indicated that his ability was well above average, although some of his responses indicated a certain immaturity and a Piagetian egocentricism. On performance tests he worked imaginatively and efficiently. Thus there is no reason to believe that failure to learn to read stemmed from either lack of intelligence or from deficits in specific abilities.

What happens if he is asked to describe himself in the context of his parents? He says he is not like either parent 'because we're not the same'. He would like to 'be like P.M.' (a boy in the junior school). If he had done something he was pleased about he would not tell his parents, he would tell his mates 'because I usually go out with mum and dad. It's no use telling mum and dad, they already know, so I tell my mates'. He would like it different: 'I like to go out on my own'. If he wanted to attempt something new he would tell his parents first 'because they just tell me off if I try to do it first'. 'I wish I could just walk out and do it'. He feels that neither parent understands him 'because they don't listen to me'. He would like it different: 'I wish they knew'.

When he is asked to elaborate his complaints about other people, he says that boys like playing with dirt because 'it's gooder'. They should 'go swimming instead', then 'they would be clean instead of dirty. My mate P.M. always says Let's go and play in the dirt.' Brothers and sisters 'like going to work'. It would be a good thing if 'they could not go to work' then 'I could play with my brothers and sisters'. Fathers 'won't let you do things' because 'they are angry'. Mothers 'are always saying 'shush, I'm doing the dinner'. He wished 'someone else could do the dinner, then she could play with me'.

When John is presented with a picture of a boy sitting at a desk with a book and someone standing, he can recognize what the situation is, but is unwilling to tell a story about it.

This was the evidence from one interview with the boy. Evidence about the family was provided by the headteacher. John is the youngest of six children. The next older is eleven years old and is likely to go to a residential grammar school (the family is working class). Whereas the older children all came to school on their own, mother always brings John. Perhaps mother has been overprotective in the past. Mother has been co-operative and helpful to the school in practical ways, but she may have pushed John too much with reading.

In the light of John's own testimony and the headteacher's observations, what is his view of himself? of his parents? his family? and his peer group? He feels an odd man out in his family, his parents don't understand him, nor do they validate his enterprises. His mother and sisters go their own way and he seeks confirmation of himself through one friend—unfortunately he has mixed views about what his friend thinks is good fun. He feels that his parents are forcing his dependence on them and that, in any case, they know everything he does but without understanding him.

Learning to read can now be seen as a refusal to experiment in one of the areas where apparently his mother is making heavy demands on him. He would seem to be rejecting their view of him and, in the process, rejecting the development of a skill, which is important in his own development. He has no allies in this because the school is demanding the same thing as his parents. To opt out of the situation is the easiest solution. He may also be saying 'if you treat me as a baby still, I will be like a baby because babies can't read.'

This formulation is of no value unless it has implications for action, and the implication here is straightforward. Learning to read must be seen by the boy as unrelated to his parents, but positively related to himself and to school. The evidence and the formulation were worked out with the headteacher, who agreed to advise the mother to desist completely from any concern about John's learning in school. The headteacher also made herself responsible for John's reading in her own remedial group. The mother accepted this dictum, and within nine months John was reading at his age level and was even prepared to read to his mother. In retrospect, his action can be seen to answer some of the implicit questions which his behaviour was suggesting. His lack of independence from his mother was rectified in part by allowing his schooling to be the concern of himself and the teachers. This inevitably changed the nature of the mother-child interaction and communication patterns. The full extent of the change is not known, but it is possible that the mother might now tolerate even greater independence in John.

The case of Steven

A second case is Steven. He was referred at the age of eleven years because of failure to make reasonable school progress. The head-teacher thought he might be ESN. He had been attending a remedial reading centre for some time, but he had not been able to benefit from this. He was found to have dull average ability, but his scores on different tests showed a range from an IQ equivalent of 70 (mental arithmetic) to one of 105 (two performance tests). In Piaget type experiments his development was better than his IQ of 82 would have indicated. Moreover, he was able to give adequate verbaliza-tion of conservation of number, length and area.

In unstructured situations he was anxious and ineffectual, but when he was given a model to work from he could cope in a rather restricted way. Likewise, in school, he is reported to be unable to initiate activity on his own until he has seen someone else do the activity.

Steven's view of himself in the context of his parents is interesting. He is more like mum and dad 'because mum says so, nan says so. Dad says I look like him'. If he had done something he was pleased about he would tell mum, dad and friends because 'I just like it'. If he wanted to do something new he would tell his parents first and his reason was 'not to do it again'. He would be more likely to make mum cross than dad, and would rather be found out by both parents, but in neither case does he know why. He thinks mum and dad both understand him because 'mum says so, dad says so'. On no occasion was Steven prepared to say that he would like things to be different.

When asked to elaborate his attitudes to parents and siblings, he could only refer to ideas of listening and not listening. Listening seemed to be related to being understood on the one hand, and having to keep silent on the other. To listen to what his parents said seemed to be in the nature of a moral imperative.

A picture of a boy sitting at a desk with an open book and a person standing behind him was quickly drawn. Steven was invited to make up first one story, then a different one, and then a third story, to this picture.

Story 1 A teacher came up and said open the book and he said 'no', and then he has to go up to the headmaster. The headmaster said 'don't you say that again, go back and open the book and read the story'. (The boy said 'no' because he wanted go.)

Story 2 There was a teacher standing there. There was a boy. He read the book. The teacher said 'well done' and then he told him to sit down and he wouldn't. Then the teacher went to the headmaster and the boy got the cane.

Story 3 Once upon a time there was this boy running about and then the headmaster told him to sit down. He said 'no'. He went to hit him but his mum came in and then he had to go to the dentist. He had a loose tooth. That's why he said 'no', because his mum was coming in.

The cumulative effect of this evidence points to Steven's reluctance to experiment and in the stories activity seems to be followed by negative outcomes. At the same time his behaviour in the stories is tantamount to a refusal to learn. The defensive responses to questions about himself and his parents suggest that the basis for these attitudes stem from interactions within the family which cause him concern. Consequently, he was referred to the child guidance clinic.

The impression the mother and boy conveyed to the psychiatrist is described in the following way: 'mother was extremely dominating, non-stop talking, pushing, shoving, pressurizing the boy, plucking words out of Steven's mouth and almost preventing him from speaking. She uses verbal behaviour as a punishing technique either by nagging or by keeping silent. In her own words the boy "just refuses to read".' At a subsequent interview the father was present. He is a docker and is also dominating. Surprisingly, he reads a great deal and the mother holds this against him. She nags the boy for not reading and the father for reading.

Nonreading in this case can be seen as stemming in part from the crushing by the mother of the boy's experimenting. This attitude of the mother was developed when Steven was a premature baby, and she had overprotected him consistently all his life. Reading itself must be seen as problematical by Steven in view of the mother's attitude to father's reading. More generally, how could this boy view the prospect of growing up and being a man? Perhaps the low verbal IQ itself was more a function of the unsatifactory verbal communication in the family than of genuinely limited ability.

Three family interviews in which these interactions were discussed were sufficient to allow the boy to start reading—and get pleasure from a developing skill. The family interactions changed completely to everyone's satisfaction, and no further appointments were made.

Conclusions and implications

These two cases illustrate the practical application of a way of thinking about child development in general, and learning disorders in particular. This way of thinking recognizes the experimental and communicational implications of behaviour and relates these to tasks in the school, and to interactions between the child and other important people.

There are clear implications for the teacher in the classroom. Is it possible for the teacher to deduce the underlying questions which a child is posing? Is it possible to deduce what learning to read means to the child in terms of what is happening between the child and others? Can the teacher be sufficiently powerful validator for the child so that his involvement with the child will enable him to learn?

At the simplest level it is important that the child likes the teacher and the teacher values the child. Such statements are usually accepted as obvious, but the obvious is seldom taken seriously. At a second level, the teacher needs to know the family and be prepared to ask questions about what happens in the family. The habitual family interactions may provide a clue to what the child's non-learning means. At all levels the teacher needs to pose new questions, both verbally and behaviourally, and to be sensitive to the child's questions, both verbal and behavioural.

Learning comes out of positive interactions, non-learning out of negative interactions. Whatever factors are associated with reading difficulties, reading difficulties themselves are also a reflection of the child's behavioural questions, his behavioural experiments and the interactions with life that each of these implies. Teachers are a part of a child's life.

References

KELLY, G. (1955) *The Psychology of Personal Constructs* Norton

KOESTLER, A. (1967) *The Ghost in the Machine* Hutchinson

LOVELL, K. and GORDON, A. (1968) A study at some differences between backward readers of average intelligence as assessed by a non-verbal test *British Journal of Educational Psychology* 38

RAVENETTE, A. T. (1968) *Dimensions of Reading Difficulty* Pergamon

SIU, R. G. H. (1957) *The Tao of Science* MIT

WATZLAWICK, P., BEAVIN, J. H. and JACKSON, D. (1957) *Pragmatics of Human Communication* Norton

N

18 Criteria for a remedial reading programme

DONALD MOYLE

Senior Lecturer in Education, Tutor to the in-service course leading to the Diploma in the Teaching of Reading, Edge Hill College of Education

Revised version of a paper presented to the Workshop following the Sixth Annual Conference of UKRA Nottingham 1969, first published in *Reading skills: Theory and practice*

Schools in our culture are based upon literacy and the increasing use of discovery methods has placed more, not less, importance upon reading. Thus there is really no satisfactory education available in normal schools for the child who doesn't gain some mastery of the reading process. Not only does school become a largely boring experience for the non-reader, but try as we might to discourage competition and anxiety, such a child inevitably has a growing feeling of inadequacy and failure. This leads to a generalized feeling of being very much a second class citizen and an unsatisfactory self image. Tansley (1967) has stated that a satisfactory self image is gained mainly through a sense of success and suggests that there is evidence that some of this feeling of sucess must originate from work in the basic skills. Even in the supposed progressive child centred schools teachers seem to add to the child's difficulties, for John's piece of creative writing draws, albeit unconsciously, more praise than Bob's creative art work. The schoolchild without reading attainment, therefore, draws little satisfaction, success and enjoyment from his tasks and is in great danger of having a crippled personality added to his existing difficulty.

In adult life, the nonreader is a social outcast and often develops a large chip on his shoulder, feeling that all the plums of life are being denied to him. He misses of course the enjoyment which can be gained from reading and the stimulation reading can give to emotional stability and development of personality. In the intellectual sphere he is also denied access to a good deal of the store of human knowledge and cannot go to the printed word to help in the evaluation of his personal experience. Further he is far more at the mercy of the propagandist and the mass media than one who has some mastery of reading skill.

194

I would suggest, therefore, that we endeavour to achieve the objectives set out below for our children:

1 To give them sufficient skill to ensure that reading is not an arduous task when they are called upon to undertake it. This means that we must enable them to gain independence in reading.

2 That they become able to evaluate what is read. At this moment in time the only confident prophecy we can make about the life which lies ahead of our children is that it will be one of continuous change. The ability to evaluate will ensure that the decisions and value judgments which they will constantly be called upon to make will not cause over much anxiety. There is a good body of evidence to suggest that evaluative skills are best learned on the printed word where there are no limitations of speed, stress and intonation. There is no doubt in my own mind that a reasonable level of insight can be generated even among quite dull children.

3 That the child will enjoy reading. Obviously few people will read if they find the process difficult. To enjoy reading means that it is so mastered that the skills involved are subconscious and automatic. Many achieve this level of skill, but it brings little enjoyment. We cannot hope that all people will become avid readers—some prefer bridge, or other abstruse pursuits, but I am convinced that the numbers could be raised very much above the thirty or so per cent of people who regularly enjoy reading at the moment.

In order to achieve these three aims for our reluctant or failing readers we must ensure:

1 That an efficient diagnosis has been made in order to reveal the nature of the child—his strengths and weaknesses, his needs and desires. This will include as full a knowledge of the child as it is possible to obtain so that we can view him as a person, know his attitudes, his opinion of himself as a learner, and something of his history and environment. I will return in a moment to the diagnosis of specific reading skills, but would stress here that often with the more difficult children help may be needed from the psychological, medical and welfare services in order that the work undertaken can achieve maximum effect.

2 At all times we must keep in view our ultimate objectives and ensure that any activity undertaken at the moment does not forbid achievement of these, e.g. overemphasis on mechanics may limit the child's fluency and ability to comprehend.

3 Activities designed for the child must bring success, especially in the early stages when we are endeavouring to overcome his own sense of failure and inadequacy.

4 Whatever the difficulties or weaknesses, we must start from where the child is and, more important, what he is, and not press too

quickly for vast improvements in either reading or behaviour patterns, or the child's resistance may increase.

5 Work in the area of the child's strengths if at all possible, until progress is made.

6 The instruction given and materials presented should not only be in accordance with his reading and intellectual standard, but also with his physical and emotional maturity.

7 Work at all times should be meaningful, realistic and seen by the child as vital to his needs. Furthermore it should also be enjoyable.

8 The work must be tied as far as possible to all his other work in school for if it is done in isolation the child is unlikely to see its relevance and transfer the new skills learned to the generality of reading elsewhere. Reading is one section of the language arts and if treated in isolation from speaking, listening and writing, will result in imbalance. One of the most common features of the slow reader is poor linguistic development, and unless the child is helped his knowledge of vocabulary and language structures he will not get very far in the reading process.

9 A carefully planned developmental programme must be employed based on knowledge of the steps in the development of reading skill on the one hand and the child's strengths and difficulties on the other. Progress made and continuing difficulties observed must be recorded so that the needs of the child—which will no doubt vary from time to time—can be catered for. This approach might well be seen in Ruth Strang's (1970) term 'diagnostic teaching'.

Diagnostic procedures

Let us return now to examine diagnostic procedures. We could start off by giving every child who is observed to be having difficulty in learning to read an extensive battery of diagnostic and attainment tests. This would give us a tremendous amount of data—a good deal of it useless and meaningless. To do this would only increase a tendency to concentrate instruction in the area of the child's weaknesses and to treat symptoms rather than causes. At its worst, such a procedure results in teaching discrete skills rather than children.

The most helpful document would be a history of the child; unfortunately these are rarely available in sufficient detail to make a significant contribution to our understanding of him.

We need first of all to establish a knowledge of the child's reading level and here a whole range of tests are available most of which can also give us a considerable amount of information concerning the child's difficulties.

If the child is a nonreader or virtually so, a quick run down of the contributory skills in reading can be helpful. Daniels and Diack's diagnostic materials in The Standard Reading Tests could be used, but much of the work can be undertaken informally by observations in the general class situation if the teacher is clear in his/her mind what is being looked for.

More sophisticated diagnostic work is best employed later as a result of observations over a period of time for many errors made in a test interview are not consistent with the child's everyday work.

I would like to suggest now two ideas for the structuring of materials and instruction which may stimulate individuals into devising systems for their own situation.

The first is based on a division of the types of children evincing reading difficulty. The aim here is to divide the resources of materials and methods and to use them where they would seem to be most effective.

Some 80% of children in the first two years of the junior school who have made little or no start upon reading and a smaller percentage of secondary children whose reading is somewhat below their capabilities can make considerable progress if simply given intensive and sympathetic teaching. The younger children have usually never had anyone who could give them some interest in reading and the secondary children, usually boys, have been so busy polishing up their football abilities that reading has not been given the necessary practice.

1 For the primary school nonreader:
Taped introductory work e.g.
Pre-Reading tapes (Remedial Supply Company)
Racing to read (E. J. Arnold)
Oxford Colour Books (OUP)
Griffin and Dragon Books (E.J. Arnold)
Programmed schemes e.g. Programmed Reading (McGraw-Hill)
For the secondary school:
Reading Laboratories (SRA)
Reading Workshops (Ward Lock Educational)
2 English Colour Code Reading Programme (NSMHC)
Phonic Tapes (Remedial Supply Company)
Programmed Reading Kit (Holmes McDougall)
Sound Sense Books (E. J. Arnold)
3 Colour systems e.g. Colour Story Reading (Nelson) Language-experience approaches
Audio-visual materials

The second group of children might be said to need supplementary teaching. This can take many forms but perhaps two examples will serve to illustrate:

The primary child with poor language development which prevents satisfactory progress. If we had the time we could give the child a rich experience and develop his language in relation to this, but if we are to help him to catch up we must select experiences which are most fruitful in gaining language growth. For this purpose the use of a language development kit such as the Peabody can be most helpful.

In the secondary school many children have a plateau in their reading development round the eight to nine year reading stage. At this stage in order to proceed a vast increase in reading vocabulary is necessary and this cannot be achieved unless the child has developed some method of word attack. Help can be gained here from:

Remedial Supply Co Phonic Tapes
Stott's Programmed Reading Kit
Moxon's apparatus

The third group might be termed as needing remedial education for a cure has to be found. These children will have emotional problems, be frustrated by failure and generally uncooperative in the reading situation. Many of these may need psychiatric help and/or speech therapy.

Colour systems
Language experience
Visual/Verbal—Webster
Moxon's machine
Audio-visual methods (Talking Page)

The final group presents a far more difficult problem but fortunately is the smallest in size. These are the children who have gross specific disabilities which are not improved by normal direct approaches. These would seem to need a compensatory approach, i.e. to use other channels to achieve the purpose of the one which is under functioning. Most of these children fail in the sequencing section of the ITPA test, but many can make reasonable scores on the parts dealing with the reception and transmission of language.

The approach to such difficulties is perhaps best illustrated by Tansley's 'haptic' approach.

A complementary idea for increasing structure in our teaching can be represented diagrammatically as:

1 Skills	2 Interest	3 Books
Perceptual Word attack Fluency (inter- mediate) Comprehension Speed Study	Language experience work Links with other work elsewhere in the curriculum Use of simple reference books, e.g. Ladybird Our World Macdonald Starters	All readers, graded so that the child feels the book to be a reward. Therefore they must normally be at a less challenging level than work in the skills column

Priority must always be given at the commencement of any remedial programme to giving the child a feeling of success. To start with work in the area of the child's weaknesses or difficulties can tend to reinforce failure.

A further general principle should be to ensure that wherever possible the skills of the reading process are learned in a highly motivating situation where the child can see the uses and enjoyment of reading.

Careful diagnosis and the selection of the most appropriate materials is very necessary but much more important to the child's progress will be the enthusiasm of the teacher and his/her knowledge of the process of learning to read.

MOYLE, D. (1969) Materials for remedial work in the secondary school *Remedial Education*

MOYLE, D. (1970) Diagnosis of Reading Difficulty *Special Education*

MOYLE, D. and L. M. (1971) *Modern Innovations in the Teaching of Reading* ULP

STRANG, R. (1970). *The Diagnostic Teaching of Reading* McGraw-Hill

TANSLEY, A. E. (1967) *Reading and Remedial Reading* Routledge and Kegan Paul

19 Backward readers — research on auditory-visual integration

ASHER CASHDAN
Senior Lecturer in Educational Studies,
Open University

Paper presented at Sixth Annual Conference of UKRA Nottingham 1969, first published in *Reading skills: Theory and practice*

Teaching backward readers

The number of children in our junior schools who do not reach a satisfactory standard in reading is still distressingly large. One cannot measure this purely in terms of how much their reading ages lag behind their chronological age. For one thing, two years of retardation is clearly more significant in an eight year old than in an eleven year old. For another, the important issue is not the normative one —how children compare with each other or with the average for a particular age—but rather, the effective level of literacy they eventually reach. Nevertheless, as Joyce Morris's researches have shown, children who fall seriously behind at primary school level do not often become competent readers later on. So, to use the reading age terminology, if a reading level of eleven years is considered a minimum for anything approaching real literacy in adult life, then we must be quite concerned about any child who leaves the junior school with a reading age of less than nine. And far too many still do so—in fact the educational standards attained by at least 10% of school children are sufficiently low to give us good cause for concern.

The organizational problems of remedial provision are outside the scope of this paper. But it is important to note that follow up studies of the more typical arrangements have tended to produce discouraging results: in the long run much of our effort seems to prove abortive. It seems timely, therefore, to look at the main orientations in remedial work and to see what suggestions can be made.

It has long seemed to me that there are two main approaches to helping the child who has reading difficulties. Some teachers concentrate on seeing the child in his total context. Thus they focus their attention on his emotional and social life, his interests and his motivational problems. Very often they will spend some time working with the child semi therapeutically or providing him with general cultural enrichment and language practice before doing any work in reading at all. And their reading work, too, tends to be informal, to focus on interests and meaning rather than upon specific skills. Other teachers approach the whole task from the point of view of the learning programmer. They work systematically through the basic reading skills, with the expressed aim of progressively advancing the pupil's mastery of the elements involved in translating the spoken into the written code, followed by their integration into the complex skills of efficient reading.

Of course, most backward children need both kinds of help, but not many teachers function equally well in both spheres. Hopefully, the child who gets personal and background help will soon have the confidence and motivation to teach himself; while the experience of success in mastering some of the technical skills will help the general adjustment of those children who encounter the other type of teacher. My concern is not to support the one or the other approach. Clearly the ideal is a real synthesis of both of them. At the same time I cannot help feeling that the cognitivie analysis—exploring what it is that the poor reader cannot do—is one that needs particular attention. And it is with one small aspect of this that this paper will now be concerned.

Intersensory skills in reading

Birch and Lefford (1963) suggest that one of the major ways in which human beings are superior to lower animals is in their ability to translate incoming messages in one sensory channel into those presented through another. For example, if you put your hand behind your back and I put a pencil into it you will know what it is immediately, although you normally recognize such an object visually. In other words, you can integrate tactile with visual information. Birch and Lefford have studied the development of such skills in primary age children using simple geometrical forms and the three modes of vision, touch and kinaesthesis (moving the hand round the object). They show that infants have not yet acquired the ability to perform such tasks competently and that it is only in the later junior school years that children can manage such tasks with ease. They go further and suggest that 'the development of intersensory functioning follows a general law of growth' and that 'the emergence of such functioning is developmental'. In other words, they are implying that, like the components of Piaget's stages, this type of skill develops relatively independently of specific environmental factors, that it unfolds as it were naturally and that it would not be easy to hasten artificially. We shall return to this argument later.

Birch has applied this work in various fields. In particular (Birch and Belmont 1964) he has shown that backward readers perform less well than comparable normal children at an intersensory task. In fact, learning to read obviously draws heavily on such skills. The child has to learn to integrate auditory and visual messages. He has to appreciate how a heard sequence of sounds is represented by a seen sequence of symbols. Birch and Belmont's auditory-visual integration task consists of sets of rhythmic taps which the child listens to and then has to identify from a choice of visual patterns. A typical item is as follows:

Auditory Taps   Visual Stimuli

  . . . .

The child hears the auditory taps and then has to say which of the three visual stimuli (shown to him on a card) is the same as the one he heard. It is quite a reasonable inference that if backward readers have particular difficulty with this task by comparison with those who are good readers, this is in part what is holding them up; though in such matters it is never easy to say with certainty which difficulty is the chicken and which the egg! Birch clearly thinks that the retarded reader will often be suffering from a developmental lag in this type of skill, even if his general intelligence is relatively good.

The nature of this deficiency does, however, bear further consideration. Blank and Bridger (1966) think that the important problem may lie, not in the cross-sensory integration, but rather in the backward reader's reluctance to use verbal coding. What happens is that the child fails to translate the stimuli because he falls down in the mediating aspect. If he said to himself, in effect. 'that was two and then a pause and then another two' the problem is solved. By using flashing lights instead of auditory stimuli, Blank and Bridger were able to show that the difficulty still existed, although the whole task was now in a single mode (that is, both parts were visual). Furthermore, children who were good at verbal labelling—that is, naming the stimuli in the way just suggested—found the task much easier than those who did not seem to do this, even though both groups of children clearly had the requisite vocabulary at their command. One way of putting this, as these researchers say, is by suggesting that the backward readers do not attend as well and fail to adopt strategies that would help them.

Whether one adopts the Birch analysis or that of Blank does make a practical difference. In the one case, one might be inclined to spend time helping the child to translate messages from one mode to another, perhaps devising special exercises to facilitate this. In the other, the focus would need to be on language and on isolating the features to which attention must be paid. Furthermore, the Birch approach, with its stress on 'developmental emergence' is less encouraging to the teacher than one which points to a more obviously remediable deficit.

The investigation

One of my advanced students (Fearn 1968) has recently carried out a small investigation which we hope makes the position a fraction clearer. Our aim was twofold: to confirm the Birch and Belmont findings in a group of retarded readers; and then to see how far the difference between our normal and retarded readers could be lessened by a modification in the test procedure. As this modification consisted of offering the children language labels we hoped at the same time to be able to support Blank's suggestion that this is where the main difficulty lies.

TABLE 1   *The Groups*

	Good readers (N)	*Backward readers* (R)
Uninstructed (U)	Group UN (7 boys, 4 girls)	Group UR (7 boys, 4 girls)
Instructed (I)	Group IN (7 boys, 4 girls)	Group IR (7 boys, 4 girls)

We took a group of twenty-two 9 year olds, whose average Burt reading ages were 6.5 years and matched them for age, sex, socio-economic group and non verbal intelligence (Raven's Matrices) with a similar number of good readers—Burt mean 10 years. Each group was subdivided at random into two sub-groups of eleven children. In each group one sub-group was given the instructed version of the test, and the other the uninstructed version (Table 1).

In both versions the identical test material was used. After three demonstration examples each child was given a twenty item auditory-visual test of the type explained above. After items 5, 10 and 15 an extra example was given—different each time. Whenever any example was given the experimenter pointed to the correct selection and said, irrespective of the child's choice, 'it is this one'. In the instructed version the same tasks were presented in the same way except that, with every example, the examiner gave a verbal description of the taps made, before he exposed the visual pattern. For instance, with the example given earlier, he would have said, 'that was two taps and then two taps'—that is, he indicated the number and position of taps and pauses.

Asher Cashdan

The purpose of the instructed condition was to see if the retarded group would show better performance when the idea of verbal labelling was presented to them than when they were left to devise their own strategies (if any). The intervention was a mild one in that no suggestion was made to the child that he should code in this way—he was simply exposed to the fact that the experimenter did this with the examples. In the case of the normal children, no differences were expected between the instructed and uninstructed groups, on the grounds that these children would probably spontaneously be making use of verbal labels.

TABLE 2   *Task Scores* (Maximum 20)

| Group | Mean Number Correct | |
	Task 1	Task 2
UN	16.0	15.17
UR	9.82	5.64
IN	16.45	15.27
IR	13.51	9.73

As a further check, each child was then given a second task. He was presented with twenty further items but this time he was merely required, after listening, to explain verbally what he had heard.

Results
After appropriate analysis of variance and 't' tests had been applied, it was seen that the experimental hypotheses were amply confirmed. Both groups of good readers scored better than the backward ones. The instructed retarded readers performed better than the uninstructed group, but there were no differences between the two groups of good readers. The findings were virtually identical for both tasks. Mean scores are given in Table 2.

Comments on the results
Looking first at the uninstructed, or natural, condition it seems clear that the good readers can manage an auditory-visual task better than backward readers, even when they are of similar non verbal intelligence. On reflection, we should probably have matched them on verbal ability too, but this would have been harder to do and it

seems fairly safe to say that the verbal abilities of the poor readers were well up to the demands of the task—their inferiority was more in their ability to use a verbal strategy without it being suggested to them.

In the instructed condition Group IR scored significantly better than the other poor readers (Group UR) though they were still significantly poorer than the good readers. But they had closed the gap somewhat (in Task 1 Group UN performed significantly better than Group UR at the .001 level, whereas the difference between Groups IN and IR was only significant at the .05 level). These results seem to suggest that although auditory-visual integration tasks are not performed as well by backward readers as by more competent ones, the differences lie more in their willingness to attend and plan to label spontaneously, rather than in a major and relatively irremediable failure in integrational ability, whether due to maturational lag or minor neuropathology. If such a study were repeated with the addition of a deliberate training programme, I would expect to see the poor readers close the gap entirely.

In the same vein, another of my students (Mrs O. S. Gregory 1968) looked at the possibility of training backward children to perform the kind of word analysis skills which Bruce (1964) found quite difficult for normal children before the middle of the junior school age range. In essence, the experimenter presents the child with a word such as 'table' or 'pin' and asks him what would remain if the 't' or 'p' respectively were removed. Mrs Gregory found that after a relatively short training period her group of eight year old retarded readers could perform this task quite well. Again, an apparently developmental function begins to look relatively teachable.

Some conclusions

In the light of these admittedly rather small studies what kind of conclusions can we reasonably draw? Clearly, we need to decide to what extent specific skills, such as the ability to integrate auditory and visual messages, are crucial in learning to read and how far we can help children who are slow to acquire them. We must admit that we are not yet in a position to give definite answers; but we have confirmed that retarded readers are poor at this kind of task, and reading does involve, at least in part, the ability to translate heard sequences of phonemes into a visual code (and vice versa). But Blank's work (1966), as well as our own, certainly suggests that strengthening children's verbal labelling skills gives them specific help in this kind of task and quite possibly in the reading situation also. The more general question of the validity of Birch's analysis (1963) is one that will have to wait on much further study. It would be interesting to know at how young an age one could train children to perform well on intersensory tasks—and it may well be that what proves relatively easy to do with a retarded nine year old may be well beyond the powers of a normal five year old.

Finally, what is the relevance of this kind of research for the practising teacher—particularly in remedial work? Three points seem to be worth making. First, the value of relatively abstract research must seem problematical at times to those who are engaged wholly in the day to day work in the classroom. But there is enormous potential in such studies, even when there is no immediate pay-off. With but a little imagination we can see the investment value of any hard work that we put into understanding the development of children's skills—and their deficiencies—even when we are working at one remove from the classroom. As in the physical sciences, all fundamental study proves of value in the end—some immediately and some in the longer term. We do pitifully little basic research in child development in this country and we need both the courage and the support to do far more.

My second and third points are more immediate. The one is that we must continue to take the mystique out of learning difficulties. If, as some neurologists have seemed to argue (Critchley 1964), we were to stop at the point where all our tests yield negative results and say simply that the child has a maturational lag and cannot yet manage complex higher order skills, such as reading, we would be doing a pretty incomplete job. What we must do is to find out what it is that the child cannot do which makes reading progress difficult for him—in other words we need to continue to work towards a satisfactory model of both the components and the totality of reading ability.

The remaining point is simply that, even in our present state of knowledge in this field, we can certainly draw out some useful guide lines for the remedial practitioner. We can suggest that the child might usefully be briefed on the nature of the auditory-visual translations he is being asked to accomplish. Rather than assuming that the child has the mental sets of the established reader we must help him to achieve these, quite often by offering him appropriate vocabulary. J. F. Reid (1967) has pointed out how often normal five year olds are unaware of the precise significance of terms such as 'letter' or 'word', as well as how quickly they can learn these. Further analysis of the kind I have been discussing in this paper could provide us with a better appreciation of how reading skills develop in normal children as well as with suggestive ideas about what we might already do for those who show difficulties.

References

BIRCH, H. G. and BELMONT, L. (1964) Auditory-visual integration in normal and retarded readers *American Journal of Orthopsychiatry* 34

BIRCH, H. G. and LEFFORD, A. (1963) Intersensory development in children *Monograph of the Society for research in child development* 28, 5

BLANK, M. and BRIDGER, W. H. (1966) Deficiencies in verbal labelling in retarded readers *American Journal of Orthopsychiatry* 36

BRUCE, D. J. (1964) The analysis of word sounds by young children *British Journal of Educational Psychology* 34

CRITCHLEY, M. (1964) *Developmental dyslexia* Heinemann

FEARN, D. (1968) Do children differ in auditory-visual integration tasks even when given verbal labels? Dissertation Manchester University

GREGORY, O. S. (1968) Phonic analysis in young children Dissertation Manchester University

REID, J. F. (1967) Talking, thinking and learning *Reading* 1

RESEARCH

20 A critical appraisal of *Standards and Progress in Reading*

MAURICE CHAZAN

Reader in Education,
University College of Swansea

Paper presented at Fourth Annual Conference of UKRA Nottingham 1967, first published in *Reading: Problems and perspectives*

I have been asked to assess the significance of Dr Joyce Morris's second and final report on her research work in Kent which began in 1953, and I have been given instructions to be completely un-inhibited in my appraisal. The scope and complexities of the research studies undertaken make it difficult for anyone to sit fairly in judgment upon them. As any research worker knows, there is often a wide gap between the ideal, fantasy world of the research plan and what can actually be done when considerations of money, per-sonnel, and cooperation from others have to be taken into account, so that it is far too easy for the armchair critic to find fault with a research report. Nevertheless, the critic should have his say, and it is important that such reports should be subject to free and open examination and discussion. I hope, therefore, that any criticisms which I may make will be accepted in the right spirit.

Let me, however, begin with well-deserved words of praise. This report is a solid piece of work, outstanding for its cool, objective approach to matters which often arouse emotions. As reviewers have said, the report gives us many conclusions about 'matters which have hitherto been the subject of unsupported opinion'; and it is 'the most detailed and comprehensive British, and in many respects inter-national, look' at the topics dealt with. The extensive or cross-sectional approach is combined with intensive, longitudinal studies of smaller sub-samples, and we are given pictures of individual children as well as detailed statistical analyses. Reading ability has been assessed not only by tests but in terms of the books which the children can read at different stages.

The particular merit of the report derives from the attention given to the actualities of the school and classroom situation. Many of us have suspected for a long time that not a few children, who are backward in reading, or even labelled 'dyslexic', are in this situation

208

partially or, in some cases, wholly, because they have not been taught—or to put it in more modern terms—because they have not been exposed to appropriate learning situations. The important variables of the quality and quantity of teaching available to the child have received little more than a casual mention in most previous research on backwardness in reading, and we are indebted to Dr Morris for her detailed investigations of these factors. I felt while studying the book that her heart lay in the investigation of school conditions more than anywhere else, and in her emphasis on this aspect I would very much go along with her. We still need detailed studies of the factors related to reading disability which lie in the individual child or his family background, but when all these have been examined, the child must be placed in a flexible and appropriate teaching situation, and it is in developing facilities for dealing with reading difficulties at the earliest possible stage within the ordinary school that, in my opinion, the solution to the reading problem lies.

After this preamble, let me now turn to consider the report itself. Every page is so packed with detail, all of it relevant, that I can do this only inadequately, and it is necessary to use up a good deal of my limited space in outlining the main findings of the enquiry. The report can be divided into three main sections:

1 The *extensive* study of over 2,000 pupils born in 1946 from fifty-one schools, which involved:
(*a*) comparing their attainments in their last year of the primary school, at age 10+, with available national norms (1957);
(*b*) a study of these pupils in the years 1955, 1956 and 1957 (C.A.s 8+, 9+ and 10+) to examine certain factors in relation to the reading standards and progress of juniors (especially methods of teaching the beginnings of reading, types of school organization and non-verbal ability).
2 The *intensive* study of ten selected schools, with a sample of 714 children, which involved, mainly:
(*a*) finding out why the reading test results of the ten schools deviated markedly from the total Kent sample in the initial enquiry;
(*b*) the study of the associations between the specific characteristics of children's schooling in 2nd, 3rd and 4th-year junior classes and their reading achievements;
(*c*) studying groups of good readers and poor readers to compare their basic reading skills, individual attributes, home circumstances and school conditions.
3 *Follow-up* studies of good and poor readers (as classified in the junior school), to ascertain their secondary school and occupational status.

I shall discuss the report under these main headings. For the present purposes, I have had to omit a great deal, for which I apologize to Dr Morris, but I have tried not to distort any of her results.

Extensive study

1 *A comparison of the reading attainment of Kent children with National Standards*

Method
In March, 1957, the Watts-Vernon Reading Test (Sentence-Reading Test 2) and the NFER National Survey Reading Test (NS6) were taken by 2,253 children born in 1946 and with an average age of ten years seven months. Both tests are of the incomplete-sentence type.

Main Findings
(*a*) The Kent mean was significantly higher than the national mean on the Watts-Vernon Reading Test (this was confirmed by the NFER NS6 test).

(*b*) The mean score in 1957 on the Watts-Vernon Test was significantly higher than in 1954, confirming the picture painted by the DES's *Progress in Reading* of a definite rise in standards of reading in recent years.

(*c*) On this test, 0.8% of the Kent boys and 0.5% of the girls were in category E (semi-literate and illiterate) as compared with 1.5% of the boys and 1% of the girls in the 1954 testing—a decrease, though not statistically significant.

(*d*) No significant differences between the mean scores of boys and girls were found (though the further study of these pupils revealed that there was a greater number of male poor readers).

One might, at first glance, question the validity of the comparison of the Kent children with norms obtained in a completely different survey, in different conditions and in different years. Furthermore, the Kent children were 5.2 months younger, on average, when tested than those in the national sample. However, all these factors were taken into account and appropriate statistical adjustments were made, so that I think that we can accept these findings, and derive satisfaction from further evidence of general progress in raising the standards of reading.

2 *Sequential Study of 1946 age-group in 52 Schools (at 8+, 9+, and 10+)*

Method
Data on 1,848 pupils born in 1946 was obtained for 1955, 1956 and 1957 to throw light on three questions:

(*a*) Phonic versus whole-word methods for teaching beginning reading;

(*b*) The effect of a junior with/without infants type of organization;

(*c*) The association between non-verbal ability and reading standards.

The Watts Sentence Reading Test 1 and the NFER Non-Verbal Test 5 were given in 1955 and 1956; the same reading test and a different non-verbal test (Jenkins NV1) were given in 1957.

Main Findings

(a) Phonic v. whole-word methods for teaching beginning reading

The sample of 1,848 children was divided into two groups:
1 Those who had been in phonic infant schools;
2 Those who had been in whole-word infant schools;

The results showed no statistically significant differences in reading performance between schools using phonic or whole-word methods for beginning reading in each of the three years from 1955 to 1957.

(b) The type of school organization: junior with v. without infants.
A comparison of standards in the two types of school showed that pupils attending separate junior schools had significantly higher mean scores on test SR1 in each of the three years of the inquiry. The greater achievement of pupils attending separate junior schools appears to be related mainly to their several material advantages, such as size and location.

(c) Reading and non verbal ability
Statistical analysis disclosed no significant association between non verbal ability in 1955 and improvement in reading from 1955 to 1957. It is concluded that it is a doubtful procedure to base classroom practice and the initial selection of children for remedial treatment on the results of a single group test of non verbal ability; nor can any decisions about methods of teaching children be based on the results of a non verbal test.

Problem of backwardness

Finally, as we are concerned with establishing whether there is a reading problem, it should be pointed out that in 1957, 254 out of the 1,848 pupils (i.e. nearly 14%) were classified as poor readers, i.e., with standardized scores of eighty-five and below on the SR1 (Watts). The rating of these children was confirmed by a book criterion, and, furthermore, not one of the children classified as poor readers in their second junior year was subsequently awarded a place in a grammar school. I would very much endorse Dr Morris's plea that 'all lower juniors whose reading attainment falls below average should be carefully studied, and that every effort should be made to help them improve their reading standards without delay.'

Maurice Chazan

Dr Morris has given us valuable objective evidence about three vital questions. The actual method of beginning reading does not seem all-important, non verbal test results must be treated cautiously, and it is best to start one's schooling in infant and junior schools which are separate from one another. We should not, however, draw the wrong conclusion from the last finding and assume that the liaison between infant school and junior school is not extremely important.

There is, of course, a lot missing from this part of the study, and, in an ideal situation, one would have liked to see data derived from tests of verbal ability and language development as well as from non verbal tests, and to know something about the relationship between such test results and reading performance. However, this is a lot to ask for in one project.

Intensive study

In this part of the study, ten out of the fifty-two schools involved in the original March 1954 survey of over 7,000 children (7–11) were studied to find out why they deviated markedly from the total Kent sample. Of the ten schools:

Three had markedly superior attainments in reading (good);
Three had markedly inferior attainments (bad);
Two showed a markedly good rate of progress over the four years of the junior course (improvers);
Two showed a markedly poor rate of progress over these four years (deterioraters).

The schools were studied by means of various observation and assessment schedules which were well-designed, and the appendices which give these in detail are worth looking at carefully.

Main Findings
(a) In the study of the general environment, the most important factor to remember was effective leadership, i.e. the heads of the good schools were very good at both the infant and junior stage. They were able administrators, they organized smaller classes for backward children, and they were good teachers themselves. The heads of the unsuccessful schools, on the whole, did not have these qualities. Good heads meant a capable staff who tended to stay in the school. The unsuccessful schools were handicapped by staffing difficulties. Thus, in the good schools we find a combination of good material conditions plus an advantaged child population plus a good head plus a good staff; in the bad schools, there is a combination of poorer material conditions plus disadvantaged children plus a not-so-good head and staff.

(*b*) Next, the following classroom conditions of the 714 children were closely studied during the last three years of the junior school:

(i) size of class;
(ii) material classroom conditions;
(iii) reading environment.

To sum up the findings here, children with the higher reading standards tended to be found in classes which were relatively large and homogeneous with regard to age and ability. Their material classroom conditions and reading environments (e.g. libraries) also tended to be superior to those of the poorer readers.

Dr Morris rightly stresses that these findings must be interpreted carefully. For example, the superior children were often put in larger classes to give greater opportunities for individual attention to the backward. Furthermore, all the heads believed firmly in streaming, though few were able to translate their beliefs completely into practice.

The details of the pupils' school and classroom conditions are most valuable, and it is impossible to do justice to them in a brief appraisal. I cannot help feeling, however, that it would be valuable to have the results of a similar study of a representative sample of schools, including some average ones, rather than this very mixed bag of schools alone. I am a little doubtful about the *general* validity of correlations derived from the sample of 714 children from these ten deviant schools. Dr Morris says that these 714 children were, in fact, representative of the whole sample in spite of the deviant nature of the ten schools, but this seems like having it both ways!

(*c*) Quite a substantial portion of the book is devoted to a comparison between 101 poor readers (55 boys; 46 girls) and 98 good readers (51 boys; 47 girls). The children were selected in the 2nd junior year (1955) on the basis of a test score of 85 or below on Sentence Reading Test I for categorization as poor and 119 or more for placement in the good category. These children made up 28% of the total sample of 714 in the ten deviant schools.

These children were studied in respect of:

(i) Basic reading skills.
(ii) Individual attributes.
(iii) Home circumstances.
(iv) School conditions.

(i) *Basic Reading Skills*
Schonell Diagnostic Tests were given, and the conclusion was reached that poor readers lack the ability to attend carefully to details, an ability which Dr Morris believes can be developed by systematic training and practice in word analysis and synthesis.

Maurice Chazan

(ii) *Individual attributes*
These were studied under the following headings:
(a) mental; (b) physical; (c) emotional; (d) attendance.
(e) changes of school.

(a) *Mental attributes*

(i) *Non verbal ability*
This was measured by group non verbal tests, which showed a marked difference between the two samples. There was, however, some degree of overlap, which showed that *some* poor readers are not handicapped by lack of non verbal ability, and that some good readers are not over endowed with this commodity (whatever it may be!).

(ii) *Arithmetic attainment*
Again, good readers tend to be better at arithmetic than poor readers, but there is some overlap, so that it does not follow that poor readers are necessarily poor at mechanical arithmetic or that good readers are necessarily good at this subject.

(b) *Physical attributes*
Information about physical condition and defects was obtained mainly from the children's medical records. These records do not seem to be a particularly reliable source of information for research purposes, for which one really needs a specific examination and a full recording of the results. This criticism is, in fact, supported in the case of the study of hearing defects, where the data suggested that poor hearing is more closely associated with superior rather than inferior reading ability—a conclusion that most people would find hard to swallow. And, indeed, we are then told that about 38% of the good readers had a proper audiometric examination, which was not given to as many of the poor group. I think that this illustrates the difference between routine medical examinations and full diagnostic investigation. A further point is that, in view of the recent evidence concerning neurological impairment and severe reading disability, a study of the physical condition of poor readers is incomplete without information about possible brain damage. And finally, little information was available about minor ailments—which can be of importance in the aetiology of backwardness in reading, as, for example, when a child has a series of coughs, colds, etc., in the infant school which may not be very serious in themselves, but which may prevent him from settling down.

To sum up the results, there was no significant difference in the numbers of poor and good readers with a fair or good physical condition, or with particular types of body build, or in the incidence and type of eye defects. Speech defects and unsatisfactory language development were, however, associated with poor reading ability— though again these were not thoroughly investigated. No relationship between handedness and reading ability was established in this study.

(c) *Emotional attributes*

We are given a detailed account of the social adjustment of the children based on the Bristol Social Adjustment Guides. An association was found between reading ability and social adjustment. On the whole, the good readers adapted themselves to the school situation significantly better than the poor readers, who showed many more signs of maladjustment and unsettledness in their last two years of the primary course. There was a greater incidence of both inhibited and aggressive characteristics among the poor readers and these findings lend further support to other work showing that a considerable proportion of educationally backward children are maladjusted in some way. It is interesting to note that the adjustment of the poor readers was better in the 4th year than in the 3rd year—there does seem to be some sort of spontaneous improvement in behaviour after about nine or ten.

(d) *Attendance*

The differences between the average attendance of children in the two samples were not statistically significant at the infant stage, but in the junior school, the good readers had a significantly better record of attendance than the poor readers. The finding that there is no definite link between the amount of infant schooling received and later reading ability is somewhat surprising, as in clinical work one often finds that children referred for reading difficulty have a history of missed school at the ages of six and seven, and it should be noted that the infant school data were, in fact, incomplete.

(e) *Changes of school*

On the whole, changes of school between the ages of five and nine do not appear to be directly linked with the reading ability of juniors.

To summarize the differences so far between the poor and good readers: the poor readers tended to be inferior to the good readers in non verbal ability and attainment in arithmetic, to have a less favourable attitude to reading, to show more signs of maladjustment in school, to have more speech defects, and to attend less well in the junior school. In other words, the attributes which differentiated between the two groups were intellectual and emotional rather than physical—but, as I have pointed out, the intellectual and emotional aspects were much more systematically studied than the physical. When the combination of attributes was looked at, it was found that poor readers tended to have a much greater number of unfavourable individual attributes than good readers, but it was also the case that some of the failures had no more unfavourable attributes than some of the successes.

(iii) *Home Circumstances*

The children's home circumstances were studied with reference to:

(a) Socio-economic status;

(b) Cultural standard;

(c) Stability of home circumstances;

(d) Size of family;

(e) Parental help and encouragement;

(f) Children's leisure reading;

(g) Other out of school acivities.

Information was obtained from teachers, the children themselves and from available records. Again, I would venture to say that some of the important variables looked at here cannot be adequately studied without visiting the home and interviewing the parents. Even a single home visit is usually inadequate; how much more so are assessments of the home without seeing the parents themselves. I do not wish to be over critical, but I would venture to suggest that we have now gone past the stages of crude assessments of home conditions. If research is to contribute more knowledge, we must refine our methods of approach and make as deep a study as possible of the variables concerned.

I have space only to give a brief summary of the findings relating to the home circumstances. These were clearly superior in the case of the good group in these respects:

(i) Most of the father's occupations were of higher socio-economic status;

(ii) A smaller proportion of the mothers had full-time jobs outside the home;

(iii) The parents did much more reading themselves;

(iv) The parents were more encouraging to the children;

(v) Family size was smaller.

There was no statistically significant difference between the two groups as regards the number of children whose home circumstances were classified as difficult, but I would suggest that a much deeper investigation of this aspect is needed.

(iv) *School Conditions*

The school conditions of the children were studied in respect of:

(a) Organization (e.g. size of classes, staff changes);

(b) Material class environment (e.g. accommodation, equipment);

(c) Reading environment (e.g. libraries, availability of books);

(d) Reading materials (e.g. suitability of books);

(e) Reading methods (e.g. types of instruction);

(f) Contributions of teachers.

The findings here tend to reiterate those listed in the section on the school and classroom conditions of the 714 children in the ten deviant schools. The good readers tended to be less handicapped by staff changes, to be in more homogeneous classes, to have superior material classroom conditions and reading environments, and to be taught by better teachers.

The poor readers were better off in two respects: they had fewer teachers at the infant stage and were taught in smaller classes throughout their primary school course.

This aspect has been thoroughly explored, and in this section one finds much interesting material not hitherto available.

(d) *Factors related to reading standards at the end of the primary school course*

Here, we learn that the ten schools did not significantly change the numbers of poor readers in 1957 as compared with 1955, though the overall number of good readers increased; and that the fifteen children who attended part-time remedial classes achieved higher reading scores than the remaining children in the poor group.

Follow-up studies to school-leaving

In the case of the poor group, the main question asked was: how many of them managed to achieve satisfactory reading standards by the age of fifteen? The children were retested in March 1961, and although there was a statistically significant general rise in mean standardized score, the reading standards of a high proportion of children in sample P on the national survey tests were still very poor when their average age was fourteen years seven months. On the Watts-Vernon test, forty-seven of the children were backward and eight semi literate, according to the DES classification. In functional terms, fifty out of the ninety-eight pupils read in a halting fashion and barked at print. Only 13% reached the norm for their age.

Dr Morris can be commended for looking at the question of the permanence of backwardness in reading by means of follow-up studies. We have surprisingly few studies of children which relate their progress and adjustment at various stages of schooling to their standards at school leaving age and to their post school lives.

Conclusion

In conclusion, I should like to summarize the findings that particularly relate to the problem of backwardness in reading.

1 15.5% of the total sample could be classified as poor readers at the age of eight.

2 At best, 'the chances of 2nd year juniors with a reading problem eventually achieving average or normal competence is about one in eight, and at least half of them will remain very poor readers to the end of their schooldays.' There is definitely a reading problem.

3 Nearly all these children need teachers with some knowledge of beginning reading, but few junior school teachers are equipped with this expertize.

4 Joyce Morris states that 'the study as a whole lends little support to the idea that specific developmental dyslexia is an identifiable syndrome distinct from reading backwardness', i.e. the poorest readers were not a neurological problem. She bases her observations on the fact that even the twelve worst readers did respond to teaching without clinical diagnosis and treatment. I am no fanatical supporter of a concept of dyslexia, and, as I have said, I agree wholeheartedly with Dr Morris's emphasis on poor school conditions as a neglected cause of reading backwardness. I would say, indeed, that our over preoccupation with dyslexia has helped to distract attention from the role played by poor teaching and poor reading materials. However, I think that it is fair to say that Joyce Morris's study provides no real evidence for or against the concept of dyslexia, as a thorough clinical examination of the very backward readers was not carried out.

5 The backward readers tend to have speech defects, to be socially and emotionally maladjusted and to be poorly motivated. They not only come from relatively under privileged homes, but they are also the pupils who get the poorest teachers, the most unsuitable, battered and oldest books, and the worst classroom conditions (though not the largest classes). Dr Morris emphasizes that one of the major factors in the persistence of reading difficulties is the poor selection and supply of materials for backward readers.

6 Good heads and good teachers seem to be more important than particular methods of teaching (i.e. phonic v. look-and-say). I would suggest that we ought to do more about producing good heads and making average heads good, by arranging more courses specifically for them, and by making it easier for heads to attend courses.

7 Little diagnostic work is carried out in the classroom and little systematic teaching is given to the backward. But the evidence suggests that part-time remedial classes for all backward readers in junior schools would be well worthwhile.

8 An important finding is that few teachers use any apparatus other than books for the teaching of reading, that is, there is little emphasis on reading *activities*.

There has been, then, an improvement in the general standard of reading, but the problem of reading backwardness in the junior school is still a serious one. It can and should, we are told, be tackled directly by better teaching and better materials and equipment. With this I concur, and would only add, firstly, that parents must be brought fully into the programme for tackling backwardness in the junior school and, secondly, that tackling the problem might well begin at the nursery and infant school stages, through providing appropriate compensatory experiences and language stimulation for children in need of help.

To try to sum up the significance of this report, I would say that it tells us a great deal about the schools and the teachers which has not previously been documented; it tells us about the permanence of the state of backwardness for most children, not all of whom need to be permanently backward; and it tells us a lot about the general standards of reading. I do not, however, think that it tells us enough about the children themselves and their backgrounds, and there are some questions like that about the efficacy of streaming which require further investigation. Perhaps too much was attempted with too scanty resources. But the book deserves to be on the shelves of every one concerned with reading standards and progress.

21 An evaluation of the research report on the British experiment with i t a

JOHN E. MERRITT
Professor of Educational Studies,
Open University

Paper presented at Fourth Annual Conference of UKRA Nottingham
1967, first published in *Reading: Problems and perspectives*

Introduction

As long ago as 1644, Richard Hodges (cf Downing 1964) took the
trouble to produce what he described as 'the easiest and speediest
way, both for the true spelling and reading of English, as also for the
true writing thereof, that ever was publicly known to this day'.
He added a quotation: 'If the trumpet give an uncertain sound,
who shall prepare himself to the battle?' (Cor. 14.8.). This was by no
means the first expression of concern at the irregularity of English
spelling—neither was it the first expression of concern at the effect
of irregular spelling upon reading. Three centuries later, however,
Richard F. Hodges (not, I think, any relation), together with E. Hugh
Rudorf (1965) claimed that our much abused traditional orthography
(t o) is more regular in spelling than is generally recognized. Under
the direction of Dr Paul R. Hanna (United States Office of Education,
1966), these authors conducted a monumental research into the structure of the American-English orthography. Taking into account such
variables as phoneme position in the syllable, syllabic stress, and
characteristic letter sequences, they produced rules which permitted
the correct spelling of 8,346 of the 17,000 words fed into a computer
—a 50% success rate. It is unlikely, perhaps, that this finding would
have satisfied the earlier Mr Hodges—and there is little doubt that
the argument over the need for spelling reform will continue un-
abated.

During the last hundred years or so, the advocates of spelling
reform have had much of their thunder stolen by those who advocate
the use of a regular alphabet merely for beginning reading—a
development which is largely due to the work of the 19th century
philologist, A. J. Ellis, and, of course, the Pitman dynasty.

The most significant recent contribution in this field has been made by Sir James Pitman who devised the orthography now widely known as i t a—the initial teaching alphabet. As a result of his initiative the National Foundation for Educational Research (NFER) and the University of London Institute of Education agreed to sponsor a major field experiment to assess the importance of a regular orthography in beginning reading and the long term effects of using a simplified initial teaching medium. A Reading Research Unit was established in 1960 to conduct this experiment and Mr (now Dr) John Downing was appointed as Director. The Director was responsible to a Committee comprised as follows: Sir Cyril Burt, H. L. Elvin, D. B. Fry, J. M. Morris, W. R. Niblett, I. J. (later Sir James) Pitman, P. E. Vernon and W. D. Wall. The investigation was launched with the blessing of Sir Ronald Gould, Secretary of the National Union of Teachers and Sir William Alexander, Secretary of the Association of Education Committees. The interest and goodwill of the (then) Minister of Education (Parliamentary Debates [Hansard] May 7, 1953, London, H.M.S.O.) had been vouchsafed in 1953 in response to a request for a statement of policy towards an investigation of this nature by Dr Mont Follick.

An initial grant was provided by the firm of Pitman and Sons and a personal financial guarantee was given by Sir James Pitman. It was made quite clear by Sir James, however (Pitman 1960), that any publisher was free to publish material in the i t a script—'the copyright in the characters has been made free to all'. Most of the funds were provided by the Ford Foundation but other grants were received from the Ministry of Education (as it was then styled), the Grant Foundation, the Fund for the Advancement of Education and the Nuffield Foundation.

The experiment was begun in September, 1961, with 400 children in twenty English primary schools learning to read by means of what was then called the Augmented Roman Alphabet. Later, this sample was increased to include some 2,000 children.

Clearly the experiment could not have been more powerfully sponsored nor supported by more responsible authorites. The resources available, although less than desired, were certainly substantial, and the scale of the experiment was not a limiting factor.

In view of the vast amount of energy which has been devoted to investigating and debating the precise role of the orthography in learning to read and in fluent reading, it must be agreed, I think, that a rigorous investigation comparing t o and a reasonably regular orthography was much overdue.

The aims, methodology and design of the experiment

Downing set out to answer the following questions:

Question 1: Can children learn to read more easily with i t a than they can with the traditional orthography?

John E. Merritt

Question 2: Can pupils transfer their training in reading i t a to reading t o?

Question 3: After the whole process of beginning with i t a and transferring to t o, are reading attainments in t o superior to what they would have been without the intervention of i t a?

Question 4: Will children's written composition be more fluent with the simpler i t a code for speech? (i.e. will the gap between their spoken and written vocabularies be narrowed?).

Question 5: How will children's later attainment in t o spelling be influenced by their earlier experiences of reading and writing the different spellings of i t a?

As the answers to these questions were likely to have a direct affect on teaching practice, Downing decided in favour of a field experiment, i.e. an experiment conducted under normal classroom conditions. This, as Burt (Eval. 2) points out, '... entailed sacrificing some of the more rigorous requirements of an ideal experimental and statistical research, but,' he continues, 'in dealing with a practical problem of this type, it was, in my view, the correct policy to follow. Before time, trouble and money could be spent on a more refined and carefully controlled investigation, the first essential was to secure concrete and detailed evidence to show whether or not there was at least a *prima facie* case that the advantages expected... might be fulfilled'.

What, we must now ask, were the 'rigorous requirements of an ideal experimental and statistical research' which were sacrificed perforce in the field experiment?

Matching of children and of schools:
Children were matched on age, sex, social class (by father's occupation) and I.Q. The school variables checked were urban/rural location, type of organization (infant, or junior & infant combined), size, pupil-teacher ratio, and certain amenities of the school building (Morris' scale).

The matching procedure, in the circumstances of the experiment, could not have been more meticulous. Nevertheless, Downing found that some significant differences did emerge on the matched variables on successive occasions when the children were tested. The differences observed generally favoured the control group. (But see Marsh, 1966, for a discussion of the age variable.)

When matching for experimental purposes it is always preferable for member pairs to be assigned randomly to experimental and control conditions in order to ensure that sources of variation which cannot be controlled are dispersed as evenly as possible between the experimental and control groups. Although this was not possible it does not seem very likely that bias attributable to pupil variables or school variables seriously affected the results.

Matching of teaching and of method:
The matching of the teachers gives rather more cause for concern. The decision whether or not to participate in the experiment lay with the headteachers. And it was they who decided, after consultation with their class teachers, whether to volunteer for the i t a experimental or t o control group. But a consequence of this voluntary procedure is that it might well introduce a number of differences between the teachers in the two groups.

Such possible differences might relate, to some extent, to age, length of service, attitudes to teaching, training in teaching reading, experience in teaching reading, etc. Now, although the voluntary principle was unavoidable, some evidence concerning its effects should surely have been offered.

With regard to method, we are told only that both groups were representative of normal practice in Britain. But is normal practice in Britain with t o the best possible practice when using a more regular orthography? I very much doubt it. One could have wished, in this experiment, not only for more precise evaluation of method, but for a statistical design which permitted assessment of interaction between method and medium. In fairness, however, one must recognize that the difficulties in gaining cooperation were already sufficiently serious without adding this further complication.

Downing, was, of course, all too aware of these problems and, in a second experiment (Downing and Jones 1966), has tried to control for teacher and method variables by having all teachers divide their time equally between experimental and control groups. This also ensures control of the school variables. The difficulty with this expedient, as Downing and Jones indicate, is that there can be no guarantee that teachers are equally competent in handling teaching problems in both orthographies, that they are constant in their method, in the two different situations, or that they approach both groups with equal enthusiasm. Nevertheless, as perfect conditions are, by the nature of things, impossible to achieve, this variation in design is welcome for the additional insights it may yet provide.

The Hawthorne Effect:
In almost any investigation in which the adoption of a new teaching method is reported, the change in method appears to improve the performance of pupils. This effect is widely described as the 'Hawthorne Effect'—by loose analogy with the effects observed in the Hawthorne Works in Chicago between 1927 and 1933 where adult factory workers were studied under a variety of working conditions. In educational experiments it is argued that the improvements are due, at least in part, to such factors as novelty of material, teacher enthusiasm, the interest shown by observers, and so on. Downing

John E. Merritt

made every effort to produce this effect in the control group, but these efforts were not demonstrably successful.

The novelty of the i t a script and the new materials, it is argued, may have benefited the experimental group. In addition, Southgate (1965) suggests that what she called a reading drive was more evident in the i t a classes. Certainly, it is hard to believe that teachers in the experimental group did not feel more challenged than those in the control group. But, if this told in favour of the experimental group, it must also be added, for example, that this group was often short of reading material and that many of the books were of the unattractive paste-in variety. Again, the teachers were no doubt subject to anxiety about how to proceed both with initial teaching and with transition, in spite of the help they received.

The statistical analysis:

Following Downing's interim report, his application of the Kolmogorov-Smirnov test for the significance of differences on background variables was strongly criticized by Marsh (1966). Marsh objected to the use of this test on the grounds that Downing neglected significant differences in his matching data as a consequence of grouping the data too coarsely. This charge does not appear in the evaluations of the final report. Downing is criticized, however, for using the technique at all. Burt (Eval. 2), Vernon, M.D. (Eval. 11) and Holmes (Eval. 6) would have preferred a multivariate analysis— but Holmes concedes that the use of the Kolmogorov-Smirnov technique was acceptable. As Wall points out in his summary, 'a factorial design would have been less open to criticism; but its exigencies would have clashed with those imposed by the voluntary nature of participation'.

Given the inevitable difficulties of the field experiment and the extent to which Downing was able to reduce their influences, are the residual defects so serious as to render the results completely invalid? The majority of the contributors to the i t a symposium do not think so. Wall points out that the findings are remarkably consistent and his considered view is that the results may be accepted with reservations, rather than rejected. It must also be recognized that, until additional evidence is forthcoming, the figures may be regarded as being as likely to be biased in favour of either group—and not necessarily one or the other.

Results

Question 1: Can children learn to read more easily with i t a than they can with t o?

The answer provided by the experiment is that children in the control groups, learning to read in t o, made much slower progress through their series of readers than children who were learning in i t a. They obtained lower scores on all tests of reading, especially, as would be expected, on tests of word recognition and accuracy.

Among all the criticisms levelled at the various aspects of the i t a experiment by contributors to the i t a symposium, not one challenges this finding. For Artley (Eval.1) the evidence that t o is a deterrent to learning to read is a definitive finding. The degree of superiority was less marked in the second experiment, however, and Downing proposed that possible reasons for this should be investigated.

In view of the number of published studies supporting the finding that t o impedes learning to read to an appreciable degree very powerful arguments would need to be adduced to support a contrary conclusion. Such arguments would also need to be powerful insofar as they conflict with common sense. Indeed, few of those who would produce well reasoned arguments against the general adoption of an initial teaching alphabet would subscribe to the view that t o is not more difficult than i t a for the child who is ready to begin learning to read.

Question 2: Can pupils transfer their training in i t a to reading in t o?

Pupils who learned to read in i t a certainly did read competently in t o so the answer yes could be given to this question. Downing set a more stringent criterion, however, and asked whether achievements among fluent readers would be sustained without loss after transfer. To this question the general answer is no. The children lost ground appreciably, except in reading speed.

Downing analyzed errors made by children in the reading tests used at this time. Naturally enough, he found fewest errors among those words which most closely resembled their counterparts in i t a. Conspicuous configuration and upper coast-line differences characterized many of the words which produced the greatest relative number of errors.

This kind of analysis, however, is extremely superficial. Investigations similar to that conducted by Wilson (1964) were required in order to provide any real indication of the nature of the variables affecting fluent reading before, during and after transition. Wilson studied the effect of method, type, position and size of letter deletion on syallabic redundancy in written English words. His subjects were university students but the technique used could readily be adapted for testing children.

There would be as many implications for method, in the case of such an investigation, as there would be for the orthography itself. If we know the cues on which children are placing greatest reliance then, clearly, we can help them to use these cues more efficiently. As ease of transition is the pivot on which the whole argument for an initial teaching medium turns, it is a pity that it was the subject of such a limited analysis.

The main conclusions to be drawn concerning this part of the investigation are that children can transfer, as predicted, but that they lose more ground than was anticipated during the transition period. On the other hand, the losses may perhaps be unnecessarily severe owing to defects in method and/or medium.

Question 3: After the whole process of beginning with i t a and transferring to t o, are reading attainments in t o superior to what they would have been without the intervention of i t a?

After three years children taught in i t a were significantly ahead of t o children on the Neale Reading Test in speed, accuracy and comprehension, in spite of the set back during transition. On a test of silent reading comprehension (Standing N.S. 45: NFER unpublished) the t o children scored slightly higher after two years but the positions were reversed after three years. These differences in silent reading, however, were not statistically significant.

In view of the zeal for library books so often reported of i t a children it might seem surprising that their superior scores on a silent reading test should not achieve statistical significance. The direction of the differences is consistent with the results obtained on the other tests, however, and it would appear that Question 3 should be answered in the affirmative.

Some critics have pointed out that gains which are statistically significant may still not be sufficiently large to be of educational significance. A superiority of the order of five months in three years does, however, seem reasonably substantial, and this was the gain in reading accuracy. If the gain of two months in comprehension is less impressive this may simply indicate that this aspect of reading receives far too little attention. In this connection we may note that Ruddell (1965), using a cloze procedure, showed that reading comprehension is '... a function of the similarity of patterns of language structure in the reading material to the oral patterns of language structure used by children'. If this is so then, as word recognition skills are progressively mastered by the t o group, and their progress is increasingly determined by linguistic competence, they must, presumably, begin to gain ground in the i t a group, for linguistic competence must be the same in both groups if they are properly matched. In addition, insofar as the development of the reading-thinking skills is left largely to the child's natural intelligence, and not expressly nurtured by suitable procedures, the gap may be expected to close further, for intelligence too should be comparable in both groups. Only if education in linguistic skills and reading-thinking skills forms a major part of a development programme would one expect the initial gains of i t a children to be maintained over a long period. In the meantime, gains in one area should not be discounted merely because we have not yet sufficiently developed our educational techniques in related areas.

Question 4: Will the children's written composition be more fluent with the simpler i t a code for speech? (*i.e. will the gap between their spoken and written vocabularies be narrowed?*).

Even after the majority of children in the experimental group had transferred to t o their written work appeared to be superior to that of the control group in terms of total number of words used, and numbers of more advanced words used. As Downing himself points out, such differences could arise as a result of factors not controlled, e.g. choice of topic. He reports, however, that syntactic analyses and analyses of content confirm the overall impression that i t a children were genuinely superior in their written work.

Question 5: How will children's later attainments in t o spelling be influenced by their earlier experiences of reading and writing the different spellings in i t a?

In the fourth school year the scores for the experimental group were higher than those for the control group, albeit, at the 5% level of significance.

It could well be that the initial classification of phonemes in terms of a fairly consistent sound-symbol representation provided a more precise framework within which to learn spelling rules. Some pro-active inhibition occurs, of course—misspellings with i t a symbols persist for some time—but on balance facilitation appears to be dominant.

This suggestion receives some support, I think, from a study by Peters (1967a). In this investigation, Peters compared spelling mistakes made by children whose initial learning had been in i t a with mistakes made by children who had been taught in t o. She concluded (Peters, 1967b) that '... children needing remedial teaching in spelling possess a more receptive base for spelling conventions if they exercise the skeletal spelling found in children taught by i t a than children taught in traditional orthography'.

The conclusions:

These may best be summarized in Downing's own words: 'The unequivocal conclusion from the results of these experiments is that the traditional orthography of English is an important cause of difficulty in teaching and learning reading and writing in English-speaking countries. So long as t o is used for beginning reading and writing one must reckon that children are more likely to become

John E. Merritt

confused about the tasks of reading and writing than they would be with a more simple and regular system for English'.

Since the beginning of the i t a experiment Downing has shown in a variety of publications that he was all too conscious of the difficulties presented by the investigation—many of which permitted no practical solution. In spite of these difficulties, and all the provisos, he nevertheless draws this particular conclusion quite firmly and decisively. Among the ten evaluations of the experiment which appear in *The i t a Symposium,* only one, that of MacKinnon (Eval. 7) contains views which indicate that the writer would dispute that the above conclusion has been satisfactorily established. Mackinnon's position is ambiguous, however, for he states: '...we are left still with the problems of simplification and the difficulties of traditional orthography'. Whilst dissatisfied with the evidence, therefore, he apparently accepts the conclusion!

Many people who are extremely reluctant to accept the above conclusion are no doubt concerned that in doing so they concede the case for i t a. This does not, of course, follow. Among the evident alternatives to i t a are the following:

1 The linguistic approach: this is an approach owing much to work of Bloomfield and Barnhart (1961) and Fries (1963) in the United States. In this country, the phonic word approach of Daniels and Diack may perhaps be classed in the linguistic category. The principle adopted is that of strict regularity of phoneme/grapheme relationship in the early stages of reading. Irregular spellings are introduced gradually. The American reading schemes in this category owe much to studies in the field of programmed learning. This distinguishes them from the old-fashioned phonic readers in that progressions such as 'Can Dan fan Nan?', 'Nan can fan Dan', etc, replace 'The cat sat on the mat'! The reading scheme associated with the names of Daniels and Diack produces much more acceptable language—but the first stage is unexciting. It is in this first stage—the most crucial stage—that the linguistic approach is at such a disadvantage for the phonic constraints make it impossible to produce patterns of language structure resembling those used by children.

2 The use of phonic cues: the most commonly advocated cues are colour, and diacritical marks.

In recent years the use of colour has become associated with the names of Gattegno (1964) and Jones (1965), although a very much simpler, if less well known, colour cueing technique has been devised by S. Harrison and developed by E. Joynton (cited in Morris, 1963).

No advantage was shown for diacritical marks over i t a in an experiment conducted by Fry (1966). In view of the reported teacher differences (the i t a teachers had substantially more teaching experience) the negative findings for diacritical markings should not be too readily accepted. It should also be noted that the experiment only ran for 140 days, only 40% of the i t a children had transferred when tested, and all children were tested on reading tests printed in t o.

3 A modified initial teaching alphabet: for the teacher who adopts a language-experience approach to the teaching of reading there is no doubt that a regular orthography is particularly advantageous. Children are free to write whatever words they wish with a minimum of assistance from the teacher. In reading, they can go more rapidly to meaning without having to struggle through the phonic complexities. At transition, a suitably modified form of i t a might well permit a smoother transfer.

As to transition in spelling the best practices of the informal teacher may be exploited. As the child, encouraged by the teacher, seizes with delight on a fascinating idiosyncracy of spelling— ' "i-g-h" for "ie" '—the whole class can, if the situation is right, join in the search for other words in the same family. In so doing, there will be a higher proportion of children capable of making a contribution, because this point arrives when all are more mature, and more able, consequently, to profit from phonic instruction.

Some further thoughts on the orthography

1 *The effect on the learner:* in considering the traditional orthography, we might well think that at least our problem is not as bad as that of the Chinese. When a class of Chinese children were told that their orthography was to be simplified, Chou en Lai (1958) reports that 'the children were so delighted that they clapped and cheered'. The simplification permitted them to write 515 characters with an average of 8.16 strokes instead of 544 characters with an average of 16.08 strokes. (Wu Yu-chang (1965), Director of the Committee for Reforming the Chinese Written Language, complained bitterly of 'vicious attacks' by 'rightists' who alleged that the simplification was a failure. The level of debate in China was evidently no higher than it is in the west.)

Whilst it in no way compares in difficulty with Chinese, the learning load problem in t o may still be a serious cause of learning difficulty. I suspect, however, that there is a much more serious aspect to this problem than the load *per se* and that is the effect on the learner of ambiguity in initial learning situations. This argument was advanced regularly in the earlier days of the i t a controversy, but it was supported, largely on grounds of logic and commonsense—not very powerful weapons against ingrained habit and tradition. Downing (1964) asks, for example, 'does the irrationality of conventional English spelling cause some children to lose confidence in and reject the whole parent-teacher-school complex of authority?'

John E. Merritt

It seems to me that more specific effects may be envisaged, and, in the absence of direct evidence, one must go to the literature for studies which give some indication of what may be the precise psychological effects of introducing ambiguity in learning situations. Most of these studies, unfortunately, have been conducted with animals—but perhaps this is as well in view of the nature of some of the effects.

The earliest observations to which we may refer are those of Pavlov, who noticed that dogs subjected to too difficult or prolonged conditioning developed chronic emotional disturbances. He called these states experimental neuroses. When a dog was confused about whether a signal, or stimulus, meant food or no food it exhibited symptoms equivalent to what would in humans be described as a nervous breakdown. This condition was elicited most readily when the dog was called upon to distinguish between a circle and an ellipse. The dog was first trained to anticipate food after the appearance of the circle and not to anticipate food after the appearance of an ellipse. When these anticipations were established the ellipse was made more and more like a circle on successive occasions. Pavlov's intention was to find out how small a difference a dog could recognize. The dog responded well at first, but as the differences became very small, the previously placid dog reacted violently. It fought the restraint of the harness in which it was confined, howled, and resisted being brought to the laboratory. When it was induced to go there, it was discovered that it had lost all its previous responses and could no longer discriminate between a circle and the grossest elliptical shape.

Consider now the case of the child who has formed an association between the 'a' sound in e.g. 'at', 'an', 'as', etc., and the letter 'a'. Here is the equivalent of responding appropriately to the circle. But now the child encounters the words any (eny), able (æbl), all (aull), are (ɑr), etc.* This is equivalent to the dog's being presented with an ellipse which is, to the dog, quite indistinguishable from the circle—for at the level of the single letter, the stimulus for each of the diffierent phonemic responses is identical in each case.

It may now be objected that children do not learn to respond to single letters, or indeed to letter combinations, but to whole words in meaningful contexts. If this is so, it may be thought that the situation for the child learning to read does not closely resemble the experimental neurosis situation.

But the above argument, whilst it provides an important corrective to over-molecular thinking, rejects the response sub-structures instead of incorporating them—rather as if one were to argue that a school building, being a place of learning, does not need bricks.

* The spellings in brackets are printed in i t a.

In this connection, Gibson, *et al* (1963) showed, in an experiment using pronounceable and unpronounceable trigrams, that 'a child in the early stages of reading skill... has already generalized certain predictions of phoneme-graphene correspondence, so that units which fit these simple " rules" are more easily read'. They continue thus: 'even though a child is presented with "whole words" and encouraged to associate the printed word as a whole with the spoken word, he still begins to perceive some regularities of corespondence between the printed and written terms and transfers these to the reading of unfamiliar items. This generalizing process undoubtedly promotes reading efficiency. . . .' (For an excellent review of the research leading up to the investigation quoted above see Gibson, et al (1962).)

Whatever else the child may be doing, therefore, in the reading context—seeking ideas, facts, context clues, or whatever—he is responding simultaneously to phoneme-grapheme relationships from the outset, and these, according to Gibson, *et al* (1962), form the critical unit of language for the reading process.

There is, however, a further complication. In responding to a series of regularities, and there is a high percentage of these, the child is presumably forming what Harlow (1949) would describe as a learning set—in this case, a tendency to respond as if all spellings are regular. Thus, at a higher level of generalization we also find the circle-ellipse conflict—a general tendency to impose regularity conflicting with tendencies to make unique responses. The teacher himself will ask the child who is having difficulties with a word 'now, can you think of any other words that begin like that?'. And in the next instant, the child applies the same technique to another word with the same beginning—and finds that rules don't work. Thus, whether the responses are induced at a sub-conscious level or at the conscious and verbal level, the incompatibilities are as they are in the experimental analogue.

The dog's response, it will be remembered, was to struggle to escape, to howl, to resist being returned to the same situation, and to show a complete loss of previous learning. With little amendment this might be taken as a description of the responses of many children who fail in reading.

Liddell (1954), when inducing experimental neurosis in sheep, showed that the presence of the parent was remarkably effective in ameliorating the effects of his treatment. The kindly teacher no doubt has a similar effect. It could only be predicted, however, that whilst the presence of the teacher may reduce the degree of general anxiety, the conditions for the breakdown in the efficiency of the learning process would still seem to be present. And, of course, the teacher typically has too large a class to be able to give a sufficient amount of attention to every child to ensure that anxiety is reduced.

The term reading neurosis is often used to indicate a generalized emotional disturbance which owes its origin to failure in reading, and Downing (1964) cites studies by Gates (1941) and Vernon (1957) which indicate that reading failure may be a cause of maladjustment in some cases. Downing argues that the nature of the learning task '. . . may produce reactions in the learner which are transferred to other schools and out-of-school situations'. What I am proposing, however, is that the effects may remain situation-specific—as in the typical case of experimental neurosis. Initial success in other subjects, exciting programmes, a pleasant teacher, etc., may well limit the spread of generalization—and make the presence of specific disturbance more likely to remain unrecognized.

The implications of this proposal are:

(a) That many so-called word-blind children may owe the greater part of their learning difficulty to specific reading neurosis rather than to neurological deficit.
(b) That over the whole range of intelligence there is a greater or lesser degree of reading impairment due to specific reading neurosis.

In the case of the first hypothesis, it would be interesting to know what proportion of children in the i t a and t o groups might be diagnosed as word-blind. A very small difference between the two groups would cast serious doubt on the hypotheses, whilst a larger difference would leave the question open for further investigation.

In the case of the second hypothesis, it would be interesting to know whether under-achievement was less in the i t a group than in the t o group. This is a much more complicated question than it looks, but an examination of the relationship between IQ and attainment in the two groups might throw some light on this problem and indicate further lines for investigation. If the second hypothesis is true, it is almost certainly true that some children suffer more than others. Children who tend to be rigid in their learning, rather than flexible, would presumably be most affected. (cf. summary of research in Broadhurst, 1960). From this point of view it would be interesting to know whether there were marked differences in personality patterns between under-achievers in the two groups. The data is still available and it seems incredible that this cannot be followed up, owing to lack of funds.

2 *The immediate problem*: The initial teaching alphabet of Sir James Pitman was not the product of any sudden burst of inspiration. It was designed as a result of the careful evaluations of the advantages and disadvantages of other alphabets, particularly those which have been produced in the last hundred years for a similar purpose. Its immediate ancestors, 'Phonotopy' and 'Nue spelling' were both used for initial teaching, and highly successful results were reported. i t a

has also been used with great success, as we have seen. Should we therefore use it?

There are, I think, two major points to consider at this stage.

First, may i t a be regarded as the final form for a satisfactory teaching alphabet? Burt (1962) and Downing (1964) both indicate that i t a is by no means perfect and that a series of experiments in the psychological laboratory should now be conducted to produce a more satisfactory medium for initial teaching and for transition. There is, I think, sufficient evidence to justify expenditure on further research of this kind.

Second, does i t a offer a sufficient advantage over t o to justify its use, even if improvement can be envisaged?

It has been argued above that i t a as it stands has produced worthwhile gains, all things considered. Furthermore, it is extremely doubtful whether funds will in fact be found for the sort of programme required to produce an improved version. If funds are found it is unlikely, in my view, that any new version would be available within a decade. The teacher who uses a formal approach to teaching reading may be prepared to wait. For the teacher who adopts a language-experience approach to teaching reading, particularly with five-year-old beginners as in this country, the advantages of using a regular orthography for the first two years are obvious— whilst there are no demonstrable disadvantages. In my view, the question is no longer why should I use it, but, why not?

But in this matter, each must make his own decision. And if you have read through as far as this, then you have no doubt read contrary views also, and as a result of this, your decision either way will assuredly be the wiser.

References

BLOOMFIELD, L. and BARNHART, C. L. (1961) *Let's Read* Detroit: Wayne State University Press

BROADHURST, P. L. (1960) Abnormal animal behaviour in: Eysenck, H. J. (ed) *Handbook of Abnormal Psychology* London: Pitman Medical Publishing Co

BURT, C. (1962) Preface to Downing, J. A. (1962) tꚙ bεε *or not to be.* Later—The Initial Teaching Alphabet. Explained and illustrated. London: Cassell.

CHOU EN LAI (1958) Current tasks of reforming the written language in: Chou en Lai, Wu Yu-Chang and Li Chin-Hsi (1958) *Reform of the Chinese Written Language* Peking: Foreign Language Press

DANIELS, J. C. and DIACK, H. (1960) *Progress in Reading in the Infant School* Nottingham: University Press

DOWNING, J. A. (1964) *The Initial Teaching Alphabet* London: Cassell

John E. Merritt

DOWNING, J. A. and JONES, B. (1966) Some Problems of evaluating i t a A second experiment *Educational Research* 8

DOWNING, J. A. (1967) *The i t a Symposium* Slough: NFER
Evaluations:
Eval. 1: ARTLEY A. S.
Eval. 2: BURT, SIR C.
Eval. 3: DIACK, H.
Eval. 4: GULLIFORD, R.
Eval. 5: HEMMINGS, J.
Eval. 6: HOLMES, J. A.
Eval. 7: MACKINNON, A. R.
Eval. 8: MORGAN, A. H. and PROCTOR, M.
Eval. 9: NEALE, M. D.
Eval. 10: REID, J. F.
Eval. 11: VERNON, M. D.
The Evaluations: A Summary. WALL, W. D.

FRIES, C. C. (1963) *Linguistics and Reading* New York: Holt, Rinehart and Winston

FRY, E. B. (1966) Comparing the diacritical marking system, i t a, and a basal reading series *Elementary English* XLIII

GATES, A. I. (1941) The role of personality maladjustment in reading disability *J. Genet. Psychol.* 59

GATTEGNO, C. (1962) *Words in Colour: Background and Principles* Reading: Educational Explorers

GIBSON, E. J., PICK, A., OSSER, H. and HAMMOND, M. (1962) The role of grapheme-phoneme correspondence in the perception of words *Amer. J. Psychol.* 75

GIBSON, E. J., OSSER, H. and PICK, D. (1963) A study of the development of grapheme-phoneme correspondences *J. Learn. verbal Behav.* 2

HODGES, R. F. and RUDORF, E. H. (1965) Searching linguistics for cues for the teaching of spelling *Elementary English* 42

JONES, J. K. (1965) Colour as an aid to visual perception in early reading *Brit. J. Educ. Psychol.* 35

LIDDELL, H. S. (1954) Conditioning and emotions *Sci. Amer.* 190

MARSH, R. W. (1966) Some cautionary notes on the London i t a experiment *Reading Research Quarterly* 11

PETERS, M. (1967a) The influence of reading methods on spelling *Brit. J. Educ. Psychol.* 37

PETERS, M. (1967b) Learning to spell *New Education*

PITMAN, I. J. (1961) Learning to read: an experiment *Journal of Royal Society of Arts* 109

RUDDELL, R. B. (1965) The effect of the similarity of oral and written patterns of language structure on reading comprehension *Elementary English* 42

234

SOUTHGATE, V. (1963) Approach i t a results with caution *Educational Research* 7

UNITED STATES OFFICE OF EDUCATION (1966) *Phoneme-grapheme correspondence as cues to spelling inprovement* Project director: P. R. Hanna. Washington D.C.: Government Printing Office, OE-32008

VERNON, M. D. (1957) *Backwardness in Reading* Cambridge University Press

WILSON, W. T. (1964) The effect of method, type, position and size of letter deletion on syllabic redundancy in written English words University of Georgia in: *Abstracts of Dissertations, Linguistics* 16 The complete dissertation is available from University Microfilms Inc, 313 North First Street, Ann Arbor, Michigan, U.S.A.

WU YU-CHANG (1958) Report on the current tasks of reforming the written language and the draft scheme for a Chinese phonetic alphabet in: Chou en Lai,, Wu Yu-Chang and Li Chin-Hsi (1958) *Reform of the Chinese Written Language* Peking: Foreign Language Press

Editor's note

Attention is drawn to the following report which was published after Professor Merritt had delivered his paper:

WARBURTON, F. W. and SOUTHGATE, V. (1969) *i t a: an independent evaluation.* The Report of a study carried out for the Schools Council. Edinburgh and London: W. & R. Chambers and John Murray.

22   Evaluation of prereading skills

SHIRLEY C. FELDMANN
Associate Professor of Education,
City University, New York

Paper presented at Fifth Annual Conference of UKRA Edinburgh
1968, first published in *Reading: Influences on progress*

One of the most serious problems facing educators concerned with urban education is the failure of large numbers of disadvantaged children to learn to read adequately. Reading is instrumental to school achievement not only because it is the basis for instruction in the upper grade levels. Equally important, early reading achievement for the disadvantaged child often facilitates his acceptance of the school's values, and ultimately of the culture's values. Thus failure in early reading not only seems to preclude success in school, but often lessens chances of success in the mainstream of the culture. This means in concrete terms that there may be little hope of holding a job in our increasingly technological culture.

In the last decade the problem of reading failure has become more pressing as the number of disadvantaged children has increased in the urban schools. In New York City we now estimate that almost half of the million children in the public schools are disadvantaged and have some difficulties with reading. Remedial work for such a large number of children is an almost impossible task and much too expensive a way to try to get children through school.

A more hopeful way to tackle the problem is through preventive means, that is, to diagnose early problems in learning to read before they happen so that there will be no failure. This is not a new approach, of course, since it has existed as long as there has been measurement of reading skills. Those concerned are familiar with many studies and reading readiness tests which attempt to assess the readiness or prereading skills of young children, in order to indicate when beginning reading instruction should be undertaken. All such tests are based on the assumption that there are certain skills which are related to beginning reading, and that possessing such prereading skills will facilitate learning to read. This assumption is a good one, I think, and one which has served us well in the past. However, in work with disadvantaged children we have found that it has not been sufficiently spelled out in existing tests to make those tests useful predictors for these particular children.

We have found that existing reading readiness tests were not meaningful for disadvantaged children because the majority of such children received very low scores on any given test. Using the norms and tables given in the test manuals the prediction was almost always the same: the child was not ready to read. Such a prediction seemed of little value since this was usually known to the teacher already through her classroom experience with the child before the test was given. What the test did not indicate was the specific skill level of the child and what the teacher could do in order to prepare the child to learn to read.

In examining the existing tests it seemed to us that they were constructed for another group of children, middle-class children, who brought different skills and experiences to the test situation. The tests were not appropriate in many ways for disadvantaged children. Specifically, we found three major weaknesses in existing tests.

First, the tests measured only high-level prereading skills, such as one would expect to find in a child on the threshold of learning to read. It was seldom that the tests measured skills found in younger or less mature children. Therefore disadvantaged children tended to score very low or not at all on existing tests. Very little information was thus available to the teacher from the test. She knew only that the child did not know the skills tested and that he was not a very good risk for learning to read. No knowledge was given her about what skills the child did know, or any indication that he might have lower-level skills which could be developed.

Second, existing tests were found to be biased towards middle-class children in format, content, and methods of testing. They presumed fairly sophisticated test taking skills on the part of the child, which of course the disadvantaged child does not have. For example, a test might ask the child to keep two directions in mind while answering items or to write numbers to show knowledge of another skill, both of which are high level skills by themselves. We found that a disadvantaged child might put a line over or put an X under the answer when the directions called for a line under the answer. The child's answer was considered incorrect even though he had indicated the correct choice, although by an incorrect means.

In other cases we found that a child got incorrect answers because he was not familiar with the content of the question; when tested on the same skill with familiar content he got the answer correct. We found that tests often contained words, concepts, or experiences outside the disadvantaged child's life. Knowledge of country birds, seaside resorts or the workings of a locomotive are all foreign to the urban New York child; yet such items are in readiness tests.

Such features of the tests were seen to be distractors for valid measurement of prereading skills. They hid true measurement through ambiguous and confusing format. It was hard to know what the child did know when he had been misled by the format of the test.

A third weakness of existing tests was similar to the second weakness in obscuring the skills to be measured. Often there seemed to be three or four skills mixed together in one test, although it was labelled as measuring only one skill. We found for example that a test of visual perception might also be assessing labelling of alphabet letters, or short term memory. A language test was found to require unusual auditory attention or ability to discriminate visual forms. Many tests seemed to be mixing measurement of skills to such a degree that the failure of the child on the test items told very little of his knowledge or lack of knowledge of that skill. Thus it was impossible to know what should be done in the classroom. We felt that a good test should delineate specific skills so as to provide a clear-cut base for teaching purposes.

An attempt to remedy some of the deficits in existing readiness tests through my participation in the Beginning Reading Project, a United States Office of Education project, sponsored by the Centre for Urban Education in New York, and directed by Professor Miriam Goldberg, of Teachers' College, Columbia University. We were asked to construct a battery of prereading tests to be given to about 6,000 disadvantaged children, five years of age, who were to be taught by a variety of reading programmes in their kindergarten, first and second grade years.

Our aim was to construct tests which would give prereading skill information about every child in the programme, information giving a valid picture of the child's skill status before reading instruction was initiated. In addition, it was hoped that the tests would also be useful in planning curriculum if skills deficits were found.

The tests were to be based on the assumption, already stated, that certain prereading skills were related to reading achievement. Those skills were identified as language, visual perception, and auditory perception. A more detailed description of the skills will also be given shortly. A second assumption was also made, that developmental skill levels in those three areas could also be identified and measured.

For example, there is some evidence to show that in the language area a child can recognize names for objects before he can say those names. He can say those names before he can describe the objects. Likewise, it is known that a child can see gross differences between a chair and a dog before he can discern differences between a metal and a wooden chair otherwise similar.

We reasoned that if the child did not have the skill levels most closely related to reading then perhaps his skills were at a lower developmental level. If tests could be given that successively measured levels of skills, then at some point, however primitive, a skill level could be established which would indicate how much the child needed to learn before reading teaching would be successful.

Therefore it was planned to construct the tests with more low level skill tests than usually found in existing tests. Because of the wide range of skills expected to be found among disadvantaged children, it was decided to test the same skill at varying levels of complexity, so that every child could be placed on the same scale for a particular skill as knowing more or less about that skill area. Instead of including a variety of levels in one test several tests were to be constructed in the same skill area.

Clearly a large number of tests was needed if every desired skill was to be tested in depth. Indeed, we finally assembled twenty-seven tests in our battery to get at the skills we thought important to beginning reading. But to maintain the sanity of both the tester and the child some compromise was needed to avoid giving all twenty-seven tests at once.

A testing scheme similar to that used in the Stanford-Binet Intelligence Scale was used to short cut administration time. In each skill area the middle level test was given first, which in most cases was a group administered test. Cut off scores were established for each test to indicate whether or not the child had passed the test. Then, depending on the child's score on the middle level test, he was given either a higher level test or a lower level test. The third round of tests depended on the child's score on the second test. If he continued to test poorly he got an even simpler test. If he had tested well he got a higher level test. So in no case did the child take all of the tests in an area; he received just as few tests as needed to establish his skill levels in all areas took about thirty minutes per child to give.

A brief description of the tests is in order. The three major areas, already mentioned, were language, visual perception, and auditory perception. Also to be mentioned was a fourth area, beginning reading skills, which contained reading tests used to identify children already learning to read before receiving formal instruction; however this area will not be included in the discussion. Within each of the three major areas there were several sub areas, each to be described briefly.

In the language area were included three sub areas which seemed related to reading. First was the child's knowledge of labels or definitions for objects or ideas. We called the sub area meaning vocabulary. It is well known that such a skill is highly related to reading achievement, in that the child who has knowledge of his language to the extent that he can express common meanings for things is likely to begin to read rather quickly. It is likely that such a child understands that reading is an extension of his oral language. We wanted

Shirley C. Feldmann

to know whether the child not only knew such definitions but whether he could express them in language acceptable to adults.

It seemed that asking disadvantaged children for definitions of words would yield little information about their language skills. In another study completed several years ago I found that from a list of fifteen words commonly known to young children the average number that disadvantaged children could define was three to four, whereas the middle class child could define seven to eight words. Thus lower level tests were needed in the meaning vocabulary sub area.

Without going into much detail, five sub tests were constructed, each dealing with labels or meanings of words. The highest level test required definition of words presented orally. The easier sub tests had pictures as stimuli to give the child more clues, and the very easiest tests had objects for the child to view. The child's response ranged from a verbal response in the harder tests to making a picture, and to pointing with a finger on the easiest test.

The second of the language sub areas was auditory comprehension. Here we were interested to see whether the child could take in language and show in some way that he understood what had been said. Competent language intake seemed necessary in order that the child make some sense out of the words and sentences he was to decode. In this sub area the child was told simple stories with subjects and situations similar to those in his own environment. Then he was asked factual material about the stories; complex inference or sequential questions were not used. In various levels of the tests the child could respond by verbal answers, by marking pictures, or if that was difficult, by pointing to objects.

The third sub area of the language area was visual comprehension. It attempted to measure skills similar to those in auditory comprehension but with visual stimuli. The tests were constructed to see whether the child could take in symbolic material visually and show that he understood what he perceived. The test task was similar to that already described. Stories were presented through pictures, and simple questions were asked about the stories. Various modes of response were required, ranging from description of the pictures to making a picture corresponding to the correct answer.

The second major area was visual perception. Three sub areas were included in it: discrimination; knowledge of reading from left to right, and memory.

The discrimination sub tests were concerned with the child's ability to differentiate symbols, a major task in the reading act. All of the tests had the same tasks, in that the child was asked to find the one different symbol in a group of otherwise identical symbols. Stimuli ranged from objects in the easiest test to pictures, letters and finally words.

The test of knowledge of reading from left to right required that the child name pictures of familiar things presented to him in two rows. His direction for proceeding, not his ability to label, was under scrutiny, in order to see whether he would use the acceptable left to right order required in reading.

The memory sub area measured short term memory, a skill needed to fix symbols for later use in reading. Objects, then pictures, letters, and then words were used in the easiest to hardest tests. The child responded in recognizing the stimuli by pointing or marking his answers so that no expressive language was involved.

The last of the three major areas was auditory perception. As far as possible the sub areas in it paralleled those in visual perception. Discrimination tasks dealt with differentiation of initial consonants in spoken words, with the child responding by pointing to an object or by marking a picture. With higher level tests the sound discriminations became increasingly difficult.

In the memory area a single test was constructed which asked for repetition of a series of words given orally.

To summarize, three areas, language visual perception and auditory perception, each contained sub areas of skills thought to contribute to beginning reading achievement. For each of those sub areas, tests measuring varying levels of skills were constructed so that a wide range of skill levels could be assessed.

A major question about the tests is whether they are able to meet the objectives set for them and prove themselves to be better tests for disadvantaged children than existing tests. At present, the study for which the tests were constructed is still underway so there are no definite findings to give regarding either their validity or usefulness.

However, a smaller study can be reported briefly which does show some value for the tests. This study was a field study, exploratory rather than experimental. It came about because one of the public elementary schools affiliated with my college, the City College of New York, asked the college staff to help them improve their beginning reading programme.

The school is in a disadvantaged neighbourhood, near Harlem, having about half Negro and half Puerto-Rican children, about 180 first grade children in all. The school staff had observed that from a third to a half of their children did not learn to read during their first year, despite concentrated staff efforts. It was felt that perhaps better evaluation and an improved prereading programme might assist their efforts.

Because of the intensified effort on the part of the central administration to improve instruction, there were to be two teachers assigned to every classroom of thirty children during that school year. Therefore it was possible to have considerable flexibility in method and grouping, a factor which simplified planning considerably.

The college staff talked with the teachers, supervisors and the principal, and finally decided on a three part programme. First the children's existent prereading skills would be evaluated in September. Next, based on the test results, special instruction would be given to those children whose skills were not at the level needed for reading instruction. Third, the children would be tested at the end of the year to see what they had learned.

For the first part of the programme all the children were given the middle level prereading tests, which were group tests, in each of the various sub areas. Any child whose score fell below the predetermined cut off score in any area was given the easier level tests in that area. Children whose scores were higher than the cut off scores were not retested because the school staff felt that they could manage the instruction for those children without further testing. The major effort was focused on the low scoring children. For those children a score was established at some point in each area by use of the easier tests. Thus information was available for each child about skill levels.

On the basis of the test results, the children judged to need extra skill instruction in a particular area were given small group instruction in their classrooms by a college staff member. For example, four to five children from a particular classroom who needed extra instruction in auditory comprehension were seen about forty-five minutes each week for extra instruction. In addition, the college staff member planned with the classroom teacher what additional activities could be given the children in the classroom at other times.

Instruction was geared to the particular deficits of the group of children involved. Generally it consisted of practice on activities, ordered in difficulty, that would lead the children closer to the skills needed to learn to read. No one method or set of materials was used; rather, materials were gathered or constructed as the need arose. In some cases reading instruction was postponed for a few months for the lowest-scoring children. In most cases reading was taught as a parallel activity. These compensatory programmes were continued throughout the school year, or until it was judged that the children no longer needed practice in the skills.

In May and June the low scoring children were retested on some of the prereading tests, and it was found that they scored considerably higher than previously. Thus some small evidence was given that the children were able to learn the skills that the tests had indicated were needed.

The study was not set up to give evidence of whether learning those prereading skills did contribute to learning to read, since there were no control groups involved. However, the teachers and supervisors did feel that the prereading instruction had helped the low scoring children markedly in learning their reading skills. There was enthusiasm for the programme and plans to use it another year. Clearly, another year will be needed to see whether enthusiasm for a new programme or the programme itself might facilitate reading learning.

But to us, this small study demonstrated that in a practical situation the tests were of considerable value in evaluating prereading skills and in planning compensatory programmes for low scoring children. The tests seemed to give the teachers more information than they had had available to them previously, as well as suggesting means of helping children within the classroom setting. Statistical studies now under way will give more evidence as to the validity of the tests, but we think that they have already been useful in our work with disadvantaged children.

Author's note

In 1971, the tests of the preading skills battery were revised so that they could be group administered in the classroom by the teacher. The tests were then tried out with 900 urban kindergarten children, representing Black, Spanish-speaking and other groups as well as the two level of socio-economic status to obtain further data on their functioning. As a result, the experimental edition of the battery, now consisting of 13 tests is being prepared for publication.

23   Research to improve the teaching of reading

RUTH STRANG
Peter Standford Visiting Professor of Education,
Ontario Institute for Studies in Education

Paper presented at Fifth Annual Conference of UKRA Edinburgh
1968, first published in *Reading: Influences on progress*

I should like to describe briefly seven types of investigations designed
to improve the teaching of reading and related language arts.

Close study of the child and his reading development

First and most practical is the child study that is an intrinsic part of
teaching. By observing children's responses to instruction throughout
the school day teachers can assess children's reading strengths and
weaknesses. By asking the children to describe the process they are
using, the teacher can gain understanding of their successful methods
and their difficulties. With a little practice enforced by the teacher's
appreciation of their effort children can acquire skill in analysing
their own reading processes. Jessie Reid in Scotland and A. R. Mc-
Kinnon in Toronto reported significant research of this type approximately ten years ago.

When I asked successful readers 'how did you learn to read so
well?' some said 'I don't know; I just did.' Others spoke of sounding
out the word by letters or by syllables. Still others remembered that
their mother had taught them words printed on cards. Quite a few
learned by asking someone to tell them words that they saw on
labels, streets signs, and in books. Many mentioned hearing someone read aloud to them while they looked on at the print on each
page. Each seemed to be learning by a method appropriate or
appealing to him.

When a teacher of beginning readers, Mrs Pamela Hoecker, asked
the children to describe their methods of pronouncing unfamiliar
words, she found they they, too, were using many different methods
such as the following:
'singing': 'I knew "sing" and "ing" and I put them together.'
'bring': 'I knew "sing" and put the "br" sound in place of "s".'

244

'seem': 'I knew that word by the two "es" together.'
'bark': 'I sounded the "b" and it was with "a" and "r" and ends in "k".'
'pail': 'It has two vowels together so the "a" is long and the "i" is silent.'
Oswald (a name in the title of a story they were reading): 'I saw it in the newspaper. He killed the President.'

Included in the repertory of this single class were variations of structural analysis, phonics, letter naming, consonant substitutions, recognition of unique visual configurations, application of phonic rules or generalizations, and recognition of the word as a whole.

An example of a more formal study using pupils' retrospective reports as the main source of data was an investigation of how twelve- and thirteen-year-olds acquire the meanings of certain words. It was made by William Elfred, the principal of a large elementary school, with the cooperation of his sixth grade teachers. He first gave a test of the vocabulary words usually taught at these ages to ascertain which words the pupils did not know. He then asked the teachers to use any methods they preferred to teach these words. At the end of six weeks he gave a retest. It was at this point that the most important part of the study began. He interviewed each of these pupils to find out how they had acquired the correct meanings and what had misled them when they made errors.

Among the associations by which they had attached meaning to these words were out of school experiences; dramatization of word meanings, teachers' explanations; associations with people, e.g. 'pessimist' was associated with one boy's grandmother. 'My grand-mother,' he said, 'is a pessimist; she has the habit of saying every-thing bad is going to happen.' Others associated words with things, e.g. 'tranquil' with the too familiar tranquillizers. Some gained mean-ing from auditory and visual similarities and contrasts, and in many other diverse and roundabout ways. Such reports give insight into the child's thinking, his ability to express his thoughts, and his under-standing of the spoken or written words of others.

Introspective-retrospective verbalization may also show the inter-action of thinking and feeling, and the role of personal relationships in successful reading. In their reading autobiographies pupils above the fourth grade seldom recalled any specific instruction in reading that the teacher had given them. From this we may infer that the teacher had actually given them little help in learning how to read, or that they were unaware of it.

Retrospective-introspective verbalization has also been employed in Ph.D. dissertations at the University of Chicago and at the University of Arizona. The general design is to select a group of students below average in reading and another group above average; give them a short story, a poem, or an article to read, and ask them to analyse their reading process. For example, in a study of adolescents' methods of reading a short story Charlotte Rogers (unpublished dissertation at the University of Arizona) first invited the subjects to describe freely and spontaneously their reading process. In the second stage of the interview, somewhat after the manner of Piaget, she asked for explanation or elaboration of certain points that they had made. Finally she tested the limits by asking point blank a series of statements based on methods that students might employ. A similar method was used by Harold Cafone in his study of a group of severely retarded readers.

Observation and introspective-retrospective reports, uninfluenced by leading questions or suggestive checklist statements, give teachers a glimpse into students' diverse and often devious reading processes. This kind of information is useful in curriculum planning, in teaching, in appraising the effect of any sequence of instruction, and in giving teachers a more concrete, effective basis for instruction.

Research basic in test construction

A second type of research is more common; it is the research necessary in constructing reading tests. For example, the Wepman Test of Auditory Discrimination has a deceptive simplicity. Actually Dr Wepman incorporated scientific linguistic information in his choice of word pairs and made thorough studies of the test reliability and validity.

Still more elaborate and continuing research is being done to perfect the Illinois Test of Psycholinguistic Abilities which identifies strengths and weaknesses in the reading communication process from intake (seeing the printed words) to output (making a verbal or motor response to the selection).

	Conceptualization	
	integration	integration
visual and	sequencing	and
auditory	memory	organization in
receptivity	discrimination	larger thought
	perception	patterns
	Intake	*Output*

Diagnostic tests of this kind enable the teacher to detect specific strengths and weaknesses. Their most important use is to diagnose rather than to predict. Prediction at best is precarious because one cannot know all the factors involved or foretell the forces that may be influencing the individual in the future. Diagnosis should lead directly to reinforcement of strengths and to remediation of weaknesses.

Research basic to the development of instructional materials

The third type of research leads even more directly from diagnosis to remediation through the development of practice material and reading methods. An example is the Frostig practice material to develop visual perception. Another example, on the beginning reading level, is the practice material developed by Rachel Burkholder (unpublished doctoral dissertation, University of Arizona) to improve certain psycholinguistic and more pervasive mental abilities underlying reading achievement. Each section of the practice material begins with concrete and simple tasks and leads up to the reading of words and sentences. The child with whom this practice material was used improved not only in the specific abilities practised but also in reading ability.

Analysis of mothers' and teachers' language and control patterns

A fourth kind of significant research was conducted by Robert Hess at the University of Chicago. He asked mothers of preschool children to teach their child a simple task, such as putting together a puzzle, while he observed their behaviour and recorded their language. Thus he obtained data on the mothers' language and their control patterns. He found that the lower socioeconomic group used more restrictive language, e.g. simple commands rather than the more elaborated language including complex sentences implying causation and other cognitive relationships. This type of research brings together cognitive and affective elements.

One of my students at the university of Arizona, Wilma Miller, carried Dr Hess' design further by relating the mother's language and control patterns to the child's readiness for reading and his achievement at the end of the first grade. She found a positive relationship between aspects of reading readiness and reading achievement and the mother's language and behaviour patterns. A similar research design might be used to study the effect of teachers' language and relationship on children's cognitive and emotional development.

Research on pupil teacher relationship

A fifth kind of research is a unique experimental design showing the effect of teachers' expectations on children's achievement. When teachers were led to expect unusual progress on the part of certain average children this seemed to have a subtle influence, mostly non verbal, on these children's achievement. Such research would alert teachers to their unconscious influence on children's reading achievement.

Psychobiological research

A sixth type of research has received emphasis recently; it is psychobiological research on biological changes that occur under certain psychological conditions. One example is animal experiments conducted by Dr Kretch at the University of California at Berkeley. As a result of a rat head start programme, he obtained evidence of actual changes in the size of the brain, the quality of neurons, and the adequacy of blood vessels supplying the brain.

Along the same line is recent evidence of the effect on the development of the brain of malnutrition, especially deprivation of protein, during the first year of life. The results are of concern to teachers inasmuch as they affect the learning capacity of school children.

Research on an integrated approach to reading programmes

A seventh kind of study is quite different; it is concerned with integrating or closely relating different aspects of the total reading programme. This might be called a global instead of a separatist approach.

Not only should the teaching of listening, speaking, writing, spelling, and reading be integrated, but three main aspects of curriculum development should be geared into one another. These are (1) to state definitely the goals and specific behavioural objectives in the sequential development of reading skills and appreciations; (2) to analyze each of these tasks from the standpoint of the learning process; (3) to describe the teaching procedures that would facilitate their accomplishment.

Many committees of teachers have set up goals, usually quite general goals rather than specific behavioural objectives that can be observed or measured. Such goals are necessary to show both pupils and teachers individuals' progress in the language arts. Rarely have these goals been analyzed into specific steps in the learning process from the most concrete and simple to the more abstract and complex. This analysis in turn should lead to development of teaching procedures and materials that would facilitate children's learning.

In using the results of research, the teacher directs his attention first to the child—to his abilities, attitudes, interests, and background. He attempts to match the learning situation to the abilities of the child at the moment the child responds. The teacher reinforces the desired response with recognition or approval. If the teacher has analyzed the task skilfully and has made a good match between the reading task and the child's capacity, the child will get satisfaction from his success; he will not need extrinsic reinforcement or rewards. He will be eager for the next reading experience.

By bridging the existing gap between practice and psychological theory and research, teachers may prevent much childhood failure and discouragement.

248